A

GUIDE TO INVESTMENT STRATEGY

OTHER ECONOMIST BOOKS

GUIDE TO INVESTMENT STRATEGY

How to understand markets, risk, rewards and behaviour

Fourth edition

Peter Stanyer and Stephen Satchell

PUBLICAFFAIRS

New York

PublicAffairs
Hachette Book Group
1290 Avenue of the Americas, New York, NY 10104
www.publicaffairsbooks.com
@Public_Affairs

The Economist in Association with Profile Books Ltd. and PublicAffairs

Printed in the United States of America

Originally published in 2018 by Profile Books Ltd. in Great Britain.
First US Edition: May 2018

Published by PublicAffairs, an imprint of Perseus Books, LLC, a subsidiary of Hachette Book Group, Inc. The PublicAffairs name and logo is a trademark of the Hachette Book Group.

Print book interior Typeset in Milo by sue@labledesign.demon.co.uk

Library of Congress Cataloging-in-Publication Data has been applied for.

ISBNs: 978-1-61039-979-1 (paperback), 978-1-61039-987-6 (ebook)

LSC-C

10 9 8 7 6 5 4 3 2 1

Contents

Figures

Tables

Acknowledgements

WE OWE A DEBT OF GRATITUDE to many individuals who helped with this book. First and foremost to our wives, Alex and Ana, for their continued support and patience through this edition's labour.

Very notably, Grant Wilder provided invaluable research assistance with this new edition.

Generous and insightful contributions on particular issues or chapters were provided by Elroy Dimson, Stephen Collins, Harold Evensky, Hugh Ferry, Masood Javaid, Tim Lund, Moira O'Shaughnessy, Steve Piercy, Mark Ralphs, Adrian Howe, Rory Percival, Jay Tallis and Richard Williams. We are most grateful to each of them, but any mistakes are our own.

We are also indebted to those firms whose data we have used in the numerous tables and charts. Without their support the book could not be published in this form. We would also like to thank Ed Lake at Profile Books for his encouragement, suggestions and support. Our thanks are also due to Penny Williams, who edited the previous editions, and Catherine Garson, who edited this latest edition – both were skilful and patient.

This book aims to help inform the process of seeking and giving professional advice, but it cannot be a substitute for that advice. Nothing should be interpreted as a recommendation to do or not to do anything in particular. It draws on and summarises research and investor perspectives on a wide range of issues, but it is not punctuated with footnotes citing sources for facts or opinions. Although important areas of debate are flagged with references to leading researchers, in other areas ideas which are more commonly expressed are presented but not attributed. Sources which were particularly important for each chapter are listed in Appendix 2.

Please note that the views expressed in this book are our own and may not coincide with the views of the investment funds or other bodies on whose boards or committees we are honoured to serve and advise.

Introduction: Back to basics, again

THE FINANCIAL CRISIS OF 2007–09 has had enormous consequences, but it has not led to major changes in the investment policies followed by institutional and private investors. One trend that has been accelerated by the crisis, and its aftermath of ultra-low interest rates, is the rapid move in various countries towards complete closure of company-sponsored salary-related pension schemes. Millions are now confronted with the challenge of building up their own pension pot to fund their retirement. Many of these, who, it is reasonable to suppose, have no particular interest in investment markets, need to be conscious of whether their savings are sufficient and "on track", and sensibly invested. This new edition is deliberately tilted to address these kinds of concerns of the private investor (see Chapter 3 on personal pensions, in particular).

Many of these concerns parallel those facing institutional funds. Since the crisis, earlier investment trends have been extended, rather than new trends emerging. There has been a growing recognition by all types of investors of the importance of globally diversified equity portfolios (Chapter 8), and although investment management fees have been squeezed by the rapid rise of inexpensive market-matching passive equity and bond funds, investment managers have been kept in the lifestyle to which they have been accustomed by continued growing allocations to high-fee "alternative" investments, such as hedge funds (Chapters 5 and 10).

Twenty-five years ago, both authors would have been confident that investment manager fees would have been under relentless pressure in the decades ahead. Time has so far shown such a prediction to have been only half-right. However, even the most modest investor can now find easy access to reputable low-fee strategies of equity and bond investments that might suit their needs and which are comparable to those discussed in the first part of the book. Norway's oil fund (formally known as the Government Pension Fund (Global)), which is reported to be the largest fund in the world, has essentially followed such a strategy, since 1997. Warren Buffet, who has a reputation as one of the most successful professional investors, suggested in 2017 that American investors who are saving for retirement should "consistently buy an S&P500 low-cost index fund... I think it's the thing that makes the most sense practically all of the time."

As very low interest rates have persisted, stockmarkets have seemingly become more expensive. Bond markets automatically translate low interest rates, which are expected to persist, into much higher bond prices and it is widely believed that this helps to explain the buoyancy of prices for a wide range of collectibles, from works of art to classic cars (see Chapter 11). There is though, no agreement on whether the same process has left stockmarkets dangerously overvalued, or simply as having adjusted to a new reality of prolonged low interest rates. Most investors have responded as if they are not sure how to read signs that markets may be expensive (see Chapter 5).

The stockmarket will always be intrinsically volatile, but at the time of writing, stockmarket volatility was as low as it has been in recent decades. Chapter 9 explores the close relationship between the higher yield offered on corporate bonds compared to that on government bonds (the spread). In late 2017 this spread was as low as it has been since 2007. This seems to be explained in part by (what were at the time) tranquil stockmarkets. The message is to expect bond yields to adjust if and when stockmarket volatility increases.

The suggestion that markets might be expensive sounds like a good reason to delay investing. The difficult subject of market timing when markets seem expensive or cheap is discussed in Chapters 5 and 6. When markets seem expensive, and also when they are volatile, the best strategy is normally to continue with a long-term strategy of making regular contributions to a pension savings accounts or to maintain balance in whatever strategy is being followed. Chapter 6 (Are you in it for the long term?) emphasises that some declines in prices are good news for investors. If bond prices (or the stockmarket) do decline from their current levels, that is unambiguously positive news for anyone saving for a pension, as they can now buy more pension with each monthly contribution. For those enrolled in company-sponsored DC pension plans, inertia is most likely (as in 2008) to keep regular contributions flowing unimpeded by all the noise and commentary from TV pundits. Those who already have a fund of investments, the best protection against ill-considered responses to news is a diversified investment strategy whose rationale has been thought through and agreed in advance with an adviser.

As with the previous editions of this book, the first part of the book describes the design of such "keep-it-simple" strategies of stocks, bonds and cash. Chapter 1 starts with the distinction between risk (which can reasonably be measured) and uncertainty (which cannot reasonably be measured and so is not captured by risk models, but is still important). It emphasises the importance of thinking how vulnerable our investments and savings are to bad times (because they do happen every now and again, and most probably will arise at some stage during your retirement).

The book is divided into two sections: Part 1 provides a framework for thinking about the different aspects of risk and how savings and investments might be allocated to meet investors' reasonable expectations. While keep-it-simple is a theme of this book, Part 2 provides more detail on equity and bond markets, giving an introduction to more complicated hedge fund and private equity investments, and more widely held real estate investments, including housing (Chapter 10), and ending with a focus on collections (however modest) of art and other investments of passion (Chapter 11).

The authors would welcome any feedback and can be contacted at the following email addresses:

Peter Stanyer: peter@peterstanyer.com
Stephen Satchell: ses999@yahoo.co.uk

Peter Stanyer
Stephen Satchell
December 2017

PART 1

The big picture

Setting the scene: What is risk for a personal investor?

Think about risk before it hits you

Risk is about bad outcomes, and a bad outcome that might arrive at a bad time is especially damaging and requires particularly attractive rewards to compensate for facing that risk. Investors and their advisers have typically judged the riskiness of an investment by its volatility, but in the words of Antti Ilmanen, author of *Expected Returns: An Investor's Guide to Harvesting Market Rewards*, not all volatilities are equal, and the timing of bad outcomes matters for risk as much as the scale of those bad outcomes. A theme throughout this book is that investors should think about how investments might perform in bad times as the key to understanding how much risk they are taking. There is little discussion of what constitutes a bad time, which will vary from investor to investor, but it is best captured by Ilmanen, who defines it as a time when an extra dollar of ready cash feels especially valuable.

What constitutes a bad outcome is far from simple. It is typically specific to each investor. Thus, a bad outcome can vary from one investor to another and from investment to investment. If an investor is saving for a pension, or to pay off a mortgage, or to fund a child's education, the bad outcome that matters is the risk of a shortfall from the investment objective. This is different from the risk of a negative return. In Chapter 6, the distinction is drawn between threats to future income (which is of concern to a pensioner) and threats to the value of investments (which matter to a cautious short-term investor). This indicates that the short-term risk of losing money is inadequate as a general measure of risk.

As mentioned earlier, there is a temporal dimension to risk. In practical terms, this means that a multi-period strategy gives multiple opportunities to review the strategy as time passes. Thus risk is also about the chance of anything happening before the investment matures, which undermines an investor's confidence in the future objective of the investment being met.

To complicate matters, there is a distinction between risk and uncertainty. Gambling on tossing a fair coin constitutes risk as the outcomes and their probabilities are fully known, even though the actual result of the coin toss is not. Being hit by meteorites, abducted by aliens, and other such phenomena, while tossing the coin, brings a different dimension to the situation as we cannot fully describe the outcomes or their probabilities. The latter concept is referred to as uncertainty.

Financial decisions are a mix of risk and uncertainty. In 2017, we were in a world of low financial risk and high political uncertainty. It is clear that this uncertainty will also vary among individuals. Since those working in the investment business are uncertain about market relationships, it is reasonable for investors to be at least as uncertain. It is also reasonable for their confidence to be shaken by disappointing developments along the way, even if those developments are not surprising to a quantitative analyst.

Investors' expectations are naturally updated as time evolves and as their own experience (and everyone else's) grows. As far as the investor is concerned, the perceived risk of a bad outcome will be increased by disappointments before the target date is reached, undermining confidence in the investment strategy.

The pattern of investment returns along the way matters to investors, not just the final return at some target date in the future. This focus on the risk of suffering unacceptable losses at any stage before an investor's target date has highlighted the dangers of mismeasuring risk. An investor might accept some low probability of a particular bad outcome occurring after, say, three years. However, the likelihood of that poor threshold being breached at some stage before the end of the three years will be much higher than the investor might expect. The danger is that the investor's attention and judgment are initially drawn only to the complete three-year period. As the period is extended, the risk of experiencing particularly poor interim results, at some time, can increase dramatically.

The insights from behavioural finance (see Chapter 2) on investor loss aversion are particularly important here. Disappointing performance disproportionately undermines investor confidence. The risk of this, and its repercussions for the likelihood of achieving longer-term objectives, represents issues that investors need to discuss regularly with their advisers, especially when they are considering moving to a higher-risk strategy.

Research findings from behavioural finance emphasise that investors often attach different importance to achieving different goals. The risk of bad outcomes should be reduced, as far as possible, for objectives that the investor regards as most critical to achieve, and, ideally, any high risk of missing objectives should be focused on the nice-to-have but dispensable targets. Investors may then be less likely to react adversely to the disappointments that inevitably accompany risk-based strategies. They will know that such targets are less critical objectives.

Risk is about the chance of disappointing outcomes. Risk can be managed, but disappointing outcomes cannot, and surprising things sometimes do happen. However, measuring the volatility of investment performance, as a check on what the statistical models say is likely, can be helpful in coming to an independent assessment of risk. But it will always be based on a small sample of data. Thus we can attempt to measure the risks we perceive. Uncertainties that exist but that we neither have the imagination nor the data to measure will always escape our metrics. There are no easy solutions to the problem of measuring uncertainty. This led Glynn Holton to write in the Financial Analysts Journal in 2004: "It is meaningless to ask if a risk metric captures risk. Instead, ask if it is useful." It is worth commenting that the availability of more and better data, which is a strong feature of modern finance, does mean that some of yesterday's uncertainties may become tomorrow's risks.

More often than not, the real problem is that unusual risk-taking is rewarded rather than penalised. There are numerous investment strategies with names like Low Volatility, or Low Beta, that appear to have lower-than-market risk but higher-than-market returns (see Chapter 7). Two points can be made about this. First, we may not be measuring risk correctly. Second, we need to avoid drawing the wrong conclusions about the good times as well as the bad times. This theme is captured by a photograph at the front of Frank Sortino and Stephen Satchell's book Managing Downside Risk in Financial Markets. It shows Karen Sortino on safari in Africa, petting an intimidating rhino. The caption underneath reads: "Just because you got away with it, doesn't mean you didn't take any risk."

Fraud and betrayal

If risk is about bad outcomes, to be a victim of fraud is a particularly bad outcome. Yet when we look after our own savings and investments we are often our own worst enemies. Many people expect savings and investments, in which they have no particular fascination, to be a difficult subject that they do not expect to understand. Any opportunity that presents itself to take a short cut and, in the words of Daniel Kahneman, a Nobel laureate in economics, and Eugene Higgins, emeritus professor of psychology at Princeton University, to "think fast", which easily leads to avoidable mistakes, rather than "thinking slow", which requires some concentration and effort, will be tempting. Our lazy inclination to "think fast" (see Chapter 2) is readily exploited by fraudsters who are attracted to our money and our behavioural weaknesses like bees to a honey pot. The enormous Madoff fraud that unravelled in December 2008 provides salutary lessons for us all. It is a mistake to think "it couldn't happen to me". It could, and do-it-yourself investors are probably particularly vulnerable. Fraud in financial markets is depressingly common.

At the end of November 2008, the accounts of the clients of Bernard L. Madoff Investment Securities LLC, an investment adviser registered by the US Securities and Exchange Commission (SEC), had a supposed aggregate value of $64.8 billion invested in the supposedly sophisticated investment strategy run by Bernie Madoff. His firm had been in operation since the 1960s and it is thought that his fraud started sometime in the 1970s. It lasted until the 11th December 2008 when he was arrested and his business was exposed as a huge scam, probably the largest securities fraud the world has ever known.

The amounts that Madoff's investors thought they owned had been inflated by fictitious investment performance ever since they had first invested, and the amount that Madoff actually controlled was further reduced because early investors, who then withdrew money, were paid their inflated investment values with billions of dollars provided by later investors. The court-appointed liquidator has estimated the actual losses to investors of money they originally invested to be around $17.5 billion. Nevertheless, at one stage investors believed that they had assets – which, unknown to them, were mostly fictitious – worth $65 billion invested with Madoff. By October 2017, the liquidators had recovered or entered into agreements to recover, often from early beneficiaries of the fraud, $12.7 billion or 73% of the estimated losses of amounts invested with the firm, and actual distributions to investors totalled $9.5 billion. Although, it is likely that the trustee for the liquidation, Irving S. Picard, will succeed in recovering much more than was initially feared of the amounts originally invested, actual distributions to investors represent just 15% of the aggregate inflated value reported by Madoff just before his scam unravelled in December 2008. His investors have been left nursing huge losses from what they had believed was their wealth. Unless they remain alert, others are in danger of repeating the mistakes that led so many to lose so much. So how can investors protect themselves?

Madoff's investment strategy seemingly offered the attractive combination of a long-run performance comparable to the stockmarket but, supposedly thanks to the clever use of derivatives, with little volatility.

Marketing material from fund distributors presented the track record of Madoff's fraud in the way shown in Figure 1.1 for Fairfield Sentry, a so-called feeder fund, which was entirely invested in Madoff's scam. It showed the seductive combination of apparently low risk and high, but perhaps not outrageous, returns. But an experienced adviser or investor should immediately recognise that the track record shown for Fairfield Sentry looks odd. It is always safe to assume that no investment strategy can deliver such smooth returns well in excess of the guaranteed rate on Treasury bills, and that there are no low-risk routes to returns well above the return on cash.

Madoff's strategy was a simple Ponzi scheme, whereby a fraudulent rate of return is promised, seemingly verified in this case by the experience of those early investors who had been able to withdraw

FIGURE 1.1 **If it looks too good to be true, it probably is:** Madoff's Fairfield Sentry fund's fictitious cumulative performance compared with market indices, Dec 1990–Dec 2007, Dec 1990 = 1

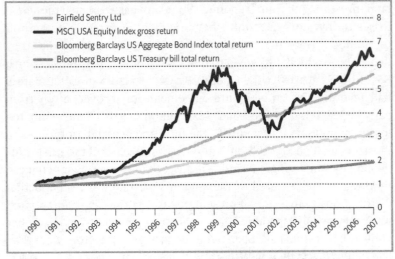

Sources: Bloomberg LP, Fairfield Sentry client reports

inflated amounts. So long as only a few investors demand their money back, they can be paid what they have been told their investment is now worth. But what they had been told was a lie, and the inflated returns were delivered to a few by redirecting cash from the most recent investors. As with any Ponzi scheme, Madoff relied on robbing Peter to pay Paul.

Ponzi schemes are named after an American fraudster of the 1920s, and they are usually built around a plausible-sounding investment story. However, these scams always collapse as soon as the demands of investors who want to sell their investments outweigh the cash provided by new investors. The Madoff fraud grew so large because it survived many years. Its undoing was the credit squeeze of 2008 when too many investors, who were presumably happy with Madoff's reported investment performance, had to withdraw funds to meet losses elsewhere. This caused the Madoff house of cards to collapse.

The victims were mostly based in the United States, but there were also many from around the world. They included wealthy individuals, charities and a number of wealth managers, but relatively few institutional investors. Many were introduced to Madoff through personal recommendations, which would have stressed his respectable community and business pedigree as a former chairman of the NASDAQ stock exchange and philanthropist.

A large part of the problem is that so many people can be seduced by the belief that they have found a low-risk way of performing surprisingly well. And yet, surprisingly, good investment performance always involves risk.

Madoff was not an isolated instance of large-scale fraud or suspected fraud, even though the scale was unprecedented. These episodes provide important lessons for investors and for their advisers. Some of Madoff's investors were following the recommendations of investment advisers, who appeared to take pride in their professional diligence in identifying good managers. The advisers could often point to the name of one of the leading accountancy firms as the auditor of the third-party so-called feeder fund that was the conduit to Madoff Investment Securities, but this provided no protection for investors.

How was someone who had followed the recommendation of an adviser or a friend supposed to identify the risks? Ten old lessons re-emerge:

1. The old and seemingly trivial saying that "if it looks too good to be true, it probably is" remains one of the most valuable pieces of investment advice anyone can give.

2. Returns in excess of the return offered by the government can be achieved only by taking risk.

3. Risk is most obvious when an investment is volatile and is least obvious when a risky investment has not yet shown much volatility. This is rarely mentioned in books on investment.

4. Investors should be particularly questioning when an adviser recommends a low-volatility investment that offers superior returns.

5. Do not invest in something you do not understand simply because a group of your peers is doing so. A desire to conform can explain many decisions that we would otherwise not take.

6. Whatever your adviser says, make sure that your investments are well diversified. But keep in mind that diversification is most difficult to assess when risky investments are not obviously volatile.

7. Pay particular attention if an adviser gives you inconvenient cautious advice (such as a recommendation to avoid something that you would like to invest in or advice to sell a hitherto well-performing investment).

8. Social status may not be a good indicator of honesty.

9. Do not assume that because an investment firm is regulated by the authorities they have been able to check that everything is all right.

10. The ability to rely on good due diligence on investment managers is the key to minimising exposure to risk of fraud. An authoritative post-mortem report on the Madoff affair is called "Madoff: a riot of red flags". Most private investors would not spot these red flags, but it was not by chance that few institutional investors lost money with Madoff. A challenge for private investors is to ensure that they also have access to good-quality manager due diligence.

Betrayal aversion

The Madoff fraud puts a spotlight on the relationship between advisers and clients. Investors are at their most vulnerable in their dealings with advisers, and yet establishing a bond of trust with one or more advisers is probably the most important ingredient for the successful management of wealth. Iris Bohnet and Richard Zeckhauser, respectively professor of public policy and Ramsey professor of political economy at Harvard University's Kennedy School of Government, have found that individuals systematically require a premium return to compensate for the risk that they might be betrayed by an agent who is supposed to be working for them. This premium is greater than the premium that would be asked to accept the same probability of a poor outcome where there is no likelihood of betrayal. As Bohnet has written:

> People care not only about outcomes, but about how outcomes came to be ... that doesn't strike anyone but an economist – like me – as a surprise.

This highlights the importance of trust in the adviser-client relationship, and the psychological gains that flow where it is present and the psychological and possibly financial damage that results when it is not.

How much risk can you tolerate?

The assessment of investor risk tolerance is a fundamental step in designing any investment strategy, but advisers and academics approach it in different ways. Academic economists use mathematical assumptions to model risk aversion. These assumptions are attractive to them in part because they can be used in models (and also because they can be tested empirically). Meanwhile, behavioural finance stresses the importance of loss aversion rather than risk aversion, and the asymmetry of response between gains and losses, which is revealed in behaviourist studies (see Chapter 2).

Wealth managers have for a long time used questionnaires to categorise their clients by their attitudes to risk-taking. These questionnaires may cover investors' circumstances (age, family, income, wealth, expenditure plans, and so on) as well as their attitude to risk. One problem is that questions posed by wealth managers about risk may use language and concepts that are unfamiliar to non-experts. Anecdotal evidence suggests that people who are not familiar with investments often expect a risk questionnaire to be difficult to complete. They may therefore ask their advisers to help them answer the questions. This introduces errors and also seems to introduce systematic bias, as investment advisers appear to be more tolerant of risk than their clients. For these reasons, conventional risk questionnaires may fail standard criteria for assessing people's attitudes.

In recent years a number of psychometric profiling services have developed, typically in liaison with academic researchers. Making use of focus groups to ensure that their questions are easily understood, they are widely used by wealth managers to address these concerns. This improvement in the rigour of profiling clients has been accelerated by the rise of online investment services provided by web-based automated advisers or so-called robo-advisers, who need to assess the suitability of their clients for different investment products, with little or no direct interaction with those clients before the adviser recommends an investment. The robo-adviser needs to be satisfied that suitable investment advice is being given to the investor. For the robo-adviser an inconvenience can be that clients often give inconsistent answers to related but different questions, which may call for human intervention (rather than a machine-driven response) to iron out apparent discrepancies.

A long-established example of a psychometric risk profiling service is that provided by Finametrica, an Australian consultancy. It has built up a database of over one million responses from around the world to its questionnaire, which itself grew out of research by psychology academics in the United States. These responses reveal some interesting patterns. For example, Finametrica reports that the pattern of responses does not vary much by country; individuals' tolerance for risk is, on average, fairly stable over time; women tend to be more cautious than men (which is important for investing family wealth); and investment professionals tend to be more tolerant of risk than their clients (who in turn tend to be marginally more tolerant of risk than the population as a whole). The database also shows quite a wide variation of responses for individuals around these average characteristics.

The finding (which is repeatedly confirmed) that investment advisers are on average more tolerant of risk than their clients may help to explain instances of investors saying to their advisers: "I didn't realise we were taking that much risk." This greater tolerance of risk might be interpreted as reflecting advisers' greater understanding of investment risk than that of their clients. Separate survey findings (also from Australia) suggest that investor education (for example, through attendance at seminars) has little impact on the risk tolerance of investors, even though it can be effective in persuading employees to save more for retirement. This suggests that investment advisers may think it reasonable to take more risk than most people would wish, not because they have a better understanding of investment risk, but because their nature is to enjoy the proximity to volatile markets. It seems that cautious people probably cannot be educated out of their disposition to be cautious, and it also seems likely that well-designed psychometric testing may help to categorise the risk appetite of investors better than ad hoc questionnaires.

However, a single score on a risk-tolerance questionnaire, even a well-designed one, will not be an adequate guide to an investor's willingness or capacity to take risk. Advisers sometimes talk of an investor's apparent need to take a particular level of risk in order to meet their objectives and this is sometimes contrasted with their appetite and capacity to take risk.

An investor is likely to have different financial accounts for different purposes: one or more may be critical to achieve and another purely aspirational; one may be for a short-term objective and another for a long-term one (such as pension saving). A well-designed risk score might provide a starting point for discussing risk-taking, but it will not give the differentiated answers that are probably needed, nor will it cope with the different ways that investors respond to the experience or threat of losses, sometimes by increasing risk-taking (see Chapter 2).

Attitudes to risk and the financial crisis

A suggestion that investors became much more risk averse during the financial crisis of 2008 would be accepted as self-evident by many economists. Risk asset prices declined because investors were no longer as comfortable holding them; in other words, they became more risk averse. An alternative explanation is that prices fell because earnings expectations declined, justifying lower stock prices (and also wider spreads between the rates at which companies and creditworthy governments borrow). But the spike in the VIX index of stockmarket volatility in 2008 (see Figure 5.1) indicates that the stockmarket became more risky, and so investors with a given degree of risk aversion might reasonably feel uncomfortable with their existing allocations to risk assets unless they had a strong view that the increase in risk was a temporary phenomenon. These alternative perspectives are important for investors, and those who have benchmark allocations to risky and cautious assets will typically find themselves underweight risk assets after a decline in equity markets. These investors may then rebalance back to benchmark weights, but if they do this they will be taking on more risk when others wish to take less (see Chapter 5).

These considerations contrast with the data that emerge from psychometric tests, which suggest that investors' tolerance for risk was, on average, surprisingly stable during the financial crisis, although there are indications that their assessment of stockmarket risk was increased (see Fig 1.2). In other words, they might have been equally willing to tolerate risk, but less willing to tolerate stockmarket risk, because it had increased.

As with much in finance, the relationship between assessments of risk tolerance, risk aversion and loss aversion (see Chapter 2) remains an unresolved issue.

Know your niche

The style of involvement in decision-making is one of the most important things that investors need to decide. How hands-on or hands-off do they wish to be, and what are their preferences and special areas of investment expertise? This is a natural starting point for discussions between any investor and a new investment adviser.

FIGURE 1.2 **Risk tolerance scores and equity market returns**
2002–2017

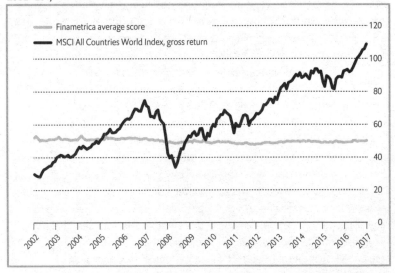

Sources: Finametrica Pty Ltd, Bloomberg LP

Some investors like to devote much time and personal effort to their investments. Others prefer to delegate as much as possible to someone they trust. Neither policy is inherently superior, so long as keen investors have grounds for believing that their interventions are likely to add value (or to save value), and disinterested investors are sure that their advisers properly understand their investment objectives and that a reliable process of review has been established.

Successful entrepreneurs often have specialist skills that put them in a privileged position in the assessment of new business opportunities in their specialist areas. This role as potential informed investors is likely to open doors to investment opportunities that are not available to others. But it will be unclear how these investments should fit into an overall investment strategy and how the entrepreneur should weigh the risks.

Such investors need to consider whether and how far to diversify away from their niche area to provide a downside layer of protection (see Chapter 2), or a safety net for at least part of their wealth. How much should be allocated to such rainy-day investments depends on personal circumstances, preferences and willingness to tolerate extreme disappointment. For example, there is great scope for disappointment from individual venture capital investments, even when skilfully selected. For successful venture capitalists, it is likely that the risk of an individual investment failing is greater than the likelihood of that investment being a runaway success. But one runaway success will more than pay for several failures. One temptation for specialist investors will be to try to diversify into related areas. In these cases, a quiet review of the behavioural biases that commonly affect decision-making could prove invaluable (see Chapter 2). Investors should ask themselves the following questions:

- Am I moving away from my natural habitat where I am confident of my "edge"?
- Do my skills and specific expertise translate to this new market?
- Will I have the same degree of control?
- Do I have the same degree of confidence in my access to information and in my feel for these new businesses?

If an investor cannot be confident of replicating the ingredients of success that were successfully used in the original niche, there will be no basis for expecting the extra performance needed to justify the risk that goes with this pattern of concentrated private investments. In any event, an investor should ask whether this new venture provides the diversification of risk that is being sought. It may be better to seek a professionally managed approach to financial investments for part of the overall wealth. If all goes well, it is most likely that the "natural habitat" investments will perform better than the diversified investments. But this simply reflects the old saying that to become wealthy, it is necessary to concentrate expertise, but that to conserve wealth, it is necessary to diversify. However, risk concentration where there is no information advantage is a recipe for ruin.

Wealthy individuals are often entrepreneurs, and their own businesses will often represent the bulk of their wealth. Although the risks and opportunities of each business will vary considerably, when considering overall investment risk, it is usually appropriate to treat the business, which will typically be a private company, as if it represents a concentrated exposure to equity market risk. A mistake that is often made is to allow familiarity with a business to cloud perceptions of that business's intrinsic risk. Just because it is not possible to observe the volatility of the stock price of a private company does not mean that its value is not highly volatile. Whether a company is quoted or unquoted, an investor's familiarity with it – even the knowledge that the company is well managed – is no guide to its lack of volatility or risk as an investment.

Successful entrepreneurs often have such investments dominating their risk profile. Allowance needs to be made for this when setting investment policy for financial investments that are held separately from the business. Typically, and depending upon financial needs, this will result in cautious recommendations for such investments, even if the investor is tolerant of financial uncertainty. Not surprisingly, most investors are concerned to conserve as well as to accumulate, to have a layer of downside protection as well as upside potential.

War chests and umbrellas

Where financial investments are being managed alongside business investments, they may constitute a liquid war chest to help fund future new opportunities, which may arise at short notice. In this case, the time horizon is likely to be short, with a premium put on liquidity and the stability of capital values, no matter how tolerant of risk the investor might be in other contexts.

Alternatively, a family with a volatile business may wish to build up a rainy-day umbrella fund, either to help the business through tough times which the family expects to be short-lived, or to provide an alternative source of income should the business fail. Many family-business investors have learned not to trust the umbrella of loan facilities willingly extended by banks during good times to be available when it starts raining seriously and have therefore arranged financial "umbrellas" from their own resources. In such cases, a low-risk umbrella investment strategy would be expected to include a significant allocation to investment grade bonds.

Base currency

Most investors have no difficulty defining their base currency. This is the currency of their home country: the currency in which they measure their wealth and in which they formulate their expenditure plans. Anything outside this base represents foreign currency and entails a risk of adverse fluctuations against the base currency.

The position is more ambiguous for many investors. Most private investors in Latin America, the Middle East, Africa and parts of East Asia seem to continue to use the US dollar as the accounting currency for their investments. But a convenient accounting currency is not necessarily a base currency. For many of these investors, the role of the US dollar will be different from the role it plays for a purely domestic US investor. Meanwhile, consultancy Finaccord has estimated that globally there are now around 500,000 expatriate international executives, many of whom have earnings and residency in one currency and nationality and perhaps also retirement plans in another. This ambiguity alters the benchmark for measuring success or disappointment from investment returns. It is also particularly important in constructing appropriate investment strategies to meet particular commitments in different currencies. Consider, for example, a European working in New York, subject to severe earnings volatility and with alimony payments in euros, or a financially constrained foundation with commitments to support projects in more than one country. In both cases, the concepts of base currency and currency risk management need thoughtful reflection.

Discussions with international investors whose investments are typically accounted for in US dollars suggest that this currency ambiguity is rarely considered an important issue in Latin America or Africa, but it is recognised as a potential issue in the Middle East and is regarded as a material concern by many investors in Asia. Asian investors may have their investments reported and measured in US dollars, but they are concerned by any marked depreciation of the US dollar against the yen, the won or other Asian currencies. One practical and easy way to address this is to diversify holdings of cash across currencies in a way that approximately meets their particular needs. International families may feel more comfortable with their safe-harbour investments, especially cash, spread among currencies in which the family has obligations, rather than exclusively in the US dollar. These families are acknowledging that there is no one investment which is free of risk.

2

Understand your behaviour: "Hope for riches and protect yourself from poverty"

Insights from behavioural finance

The opportunity to hold wide-ranging investment seminars with wealthy families or institutional investors is one of the privileges that can go with the role of an investment strategy adviser. They are invaluable opportunities to listen and to learn from investors about their goals, experiences and preferences. But sometimes it is possible to hear something and still not understand. A good illustration of this sits on the wall of one of the authors. It is a framed 500,000 Reichsmark note, which had been issued by the German central bank in 1923 during the period of hyperinflation that destroyed much of the private wealth of German families. It was a gift from an investor whose family decided to implement an equity-oriented strategy for their new foundation, going against the strong advice that it should have a significant anchor of fixed income. The adviser was told: "You simply do not understand the perils of inflation."

In this case, the family's deep concern about inflation, and their clear preference to avoid long-term inflation risk had been heard but was not taken on board in the investment recommendation. The adviser thought he knew better. Since then, the development of markets in inflation-linked government bonds has made the direct hedging of inflation risk easier. However, advances in behavioural finance also provide a framework that enables us to better explore and understand investor preferences, and to delve into the biases that affect how we take decisions, how advisers give advice, and how these together may cause us to deviate from the textbook assumptions of how rational investors ought to behave. An appreciation of these influences is a prerequisite for ensuring that appropriate investment strategies are recommended to investors.

During the past 30 years research by experimental psychologists and advances in behavioural finance have enormously enriched economists' understanding of how we take decisions. These insights have differed markedly from the assumptions that underlay the traditional models of economists and finance academics. They matter for a range of reasons, of which the most important for this book is the prediction that in many instances we are inclined to take worse decisions than the models of traditional finance would predict. An understanding of these weaknesses ought to help us to take better financial decisions.

Traditionally, economics and finance have focused on models that assume rationality. There is an old story about economists that highlights the difference between the two approaches:

> An economist [was] strolling down the street with a companion. They come upon a $100 bill lying on the ground, and as the companion reaches down to pick it up, the economist says: "Don't bother – if it were a genuine $100 bill, someone would have already picked it up."

The economist's theoretical prior belief tells him that the anomalous observation must be a data problem. The behaviourist, however, would want to examine the evidence, in other words to conduct an experiment before concluding that the bill was probably a fake, without any prior belief one way or the other. This is a profound difference in approach which has important implications for investment advice.

Traditional models in finance can be caricatured as follows: "If investors are rational, and if markets are efficient, then investors ought to be behaving as follows." Almost all investors have been shown these models, for example in the neat "risk" and "return" trade-offs of an "efficient frontier" analysis, which implicitly assume that markets are "well behaved" and "efficient", that taking more market risk reliably gets rewarded; that investors should prefer diversified to undiversified portfolios of risky investments, and that they should view the risk of losses consistently with their attitude to the opportunity for gains. Since the financial crisis of 2007–09 such models have been the subject of increased criticism, but they remain useful (and are used to provide illustrations of policy alternatives in Chapter 6). However, investors should have some understanding of their potential weaknesses. A simple illustration will suffice. Many people buy lottery tickets; they expect to lose money, but they hope to gain riches. Traditional finance implicitly finds this behaviour inefficient. Nevertheless, it can be rational as it provides the best legal way to have at least some chance (however remote) of securing riches in the short term. If you do not buy a lottery ticket, it is certain that you will not win. An understanding of our willingness to gamble in some predictable circumstances, to overpay for insurance in others, and to be reluctant to pay for insurance (such as a life annuity) even when self-insurance may be very risky, can help us to manage our finances better (see below).

Behavioural finance uses research from psychology that describes how individuals actually behave, and applies those insights to finance. This has led to two major streams of research. The first concerns how investor behaviour might not accord with the textbook concept of the efficient rational investor. The other is how less-than-fully-rational investors may cause market prices to deviate from their fundamental values. The first strand of work, how investors behave, is used to look at how investment strategy should accommodate what investors want. The second, how investors' behaviour may affect how markets function, is used in Chapter 7 to look at whether active investment managers are likely to find it easier to outperform (for which the short answer is "no").

Recognition of the contribution that behavioural analysis is making in financial economics was reflected in 2002 with the award of the Nobel Prize in Economics to a professor of psychology, Daniel Kahneman (who won it jointly with Vernon Smith). This work, much of it developed jointly with the late Amos Tversky, a cognitive and mathematical psychologist, has been summarised and updated in Kahneman's retrospective tour de force, *Thinking fast and slow*. It developed from a series of experiments that led to strong conclusions about the biases of intuition that affect how individuals take both instinctive and even thoughtful decisions and how they form preferences. A good understanding of investor preferences is critical in giving investment advice, and an understanding of investor biases is important in understanding how investors may respond to particular events or developments. If biases are weaknesses that could injure the interests of an investor, investment advisers should not pander to them. This indicates, for example, a need for investor education. But investors and their advisers should be aware of these biases since they will help determine reactions to a range of predictable market developments.

Investor biases

Psychologists have documented systematic patterns of bias in how people form views and take decisions, which Kahneman has described as "biases of intuition". Although the primary research did not usually involve investors or investment decisions, it is directly applicable to investments. These biases influence how we form investment opinions, and then how we take investment decisions. For example, the observation that most car drivers think that they are better-than-average drivers reflects a general characteristic of optimism and wishful thinking. It would be naive to think that this characteristic did not affect our investment views. Furthermore, people are systematically overconfident, tending to put too much faith in their own intuition. Overconfidence in turn is reflected in confirmation bias, whereby we show too ready a willingness to accept as proof any information that reinforces our existing views, and also in self-attribution, for example attributing to our own innate ability and unusual skill any success that we may enjoy. Individuals who are unusually well paid might interpret this as evidence of their own unusual ability, for instance.

Correspondingly, self-attribution leads to a natural tendency to attribute any disappointment to bad luck rather than a lack of skill. Investment examples of this would be provided by most accounts of investment manager underperformance that an investor might have heard: outperformance reflects skill, while underperformance reflects bad luck. This is also associated with hindsight bias, whereby individuals are sure, after the event, that they expected whatever happened to happen: "It was obvious it was going to happen, wasn't it?" Or, if the outcome was a bad outcome: "It was a disaster waiting to happen." Unfortunately, the future is rarely so clear.

A similar bias is representativeness, or stereotyping, whereby individuals are too quick to conclude that they understand developments on the basis of too little information. For example, in 100 years of stock and bond market performance history, five separate (non-overlapping) 20-year periods can be observed (which is a small sample). Subject to the periodicity of the data, any number of overlapping 20-year periods can also be constructed – for example, 20 years to last year, 20 years to the year before last, and so on. This will help to slice and dice the data more finely and enable more fancy statistical analysis. Despite this, the inescapable fact is that we do not have many 20-year observations of performance to conclude much (purely using performance numbers) about, for example, the likelihood of stocks outperforming bonds over 20-year periods.

There are more sophisticated techniques that can be used to get a handle on the same issue, but it remains common to draw strong conclusions from small data sets when that is the only evidence available. In such circumstances, it is safer to be circumspect about any conclusions drawn from limited data.

Another bias (probably just displayed) is conservatism, which arises when it is widely recognised that the available data are insufficient to support strong conclusions. In this case, it is a common error to place too little weight on the available evidence, or even to disregard it and to rely solely on prior expectations.

Yet another bias is "anchoring", whereby we gravitate towards a quantity that has been suggested before addressing the appropriate answer in our particular case. One common example would be the proportion of financial wealth that an investor ought to invest in the stockmarket; inevitably the answer will be strongly influenced by what the investor is told the norm is. This is understandable (though often not appropriate). Anchoring is a surprisingly widespread phenomenon, and it can easily lead to us being misled.

A further bias is belief perseverance, which concerns the evidence that people cling to prior opinions for too long when confronted with contrary evidence that would be sufficient to convince equally talented newcomers to the field. In this way, individuals demonstrate a reluctance to search for evidence that contradicts their previous views, because they are reluctant to write off past investments in their own human capital, despite it being clear that they are partly obsolescent.

Biases often represent mental shortcuts (called "heuristics" by academics), which we use to avoid having to process large quantities of information. These shortcuts may derive from an established opinion of how markets work. For example, many investors expect to be able to identify good managers who will outperform. Sceptics, however, are more likely to ascribe outperformance to transient luck, and may be puzzled by apparent evidence of good managers. These differences in "received wisdom" can lead to shortcuts which cause some to think that much more analysis is needed before a decision is taken and others to readily conclude that the appropriate course of action is self-evident. This type of shortcut will have led some to feel comfortable that they had found a good manager in fraudster Bernie Madoff.

Increasing complexity (for example of investment products) makes it more likely that decisions will rely on shortcuts because of the difficulty of processing all the available information. The practical alternative to using shortcuts may often appear to be indecision. But where a decision appears to have relied on such a shortcut and the decision goes wrong, hindsight can be embarrassing. An alternative, increasingly common among institutional investors, is the adoption of a set of "investment beliefs", widely supported by the fund's decision-makers, which summarises a coherent view of the opportunities offered by markets and whether the fund is well-placed to exploit them (see Chapter 5). This can facilitate considered and coherent decision-making. All investors, large and small, need to consider whether their own views of how markets function might lead to shortcuts and whether they might compromise or improve their own chances of investment success.

Even when investors are able to sit back and consider potential biases dispassionately, there is no escape from the danger of regret risk. Regret is the emotion individuals feel if they can easily imagine having acted in a way that would have led to a more favourable outcome. Early behavioural studies emphasised that regret from taking action that was subsequently unprofitable is usually felt more acutely than regret from decisions to take no action that were subsequently equally costly. A typical investment example would be the different reactions to a fall in the price of investments. If it is a recently acquired investment, there is generally more regret than if it is a long-standing investment. For investors, this leads to the common (almost universal) dilemma of how and when to implement new investment decisions, even if investment risk arguments point to the desirability of immediate implementation (see Chapter 6 for a discussion about the issues involved in implementing investment strategy changes).

A theme of some research is that regret about a disappointing outcome following a change in strategy may be reduced if the decision was justified. This may lead to a distinction between regret about bad decisions and regret about bad outcomes. These do not always go together: sometimes bad decisions do not lead to bad outcomes. Other research also indicates a tendency to move away from decisions that have recently had disappointing outcomes. Nevertheless, if an unprofitable investment decision was unjustified, the investor will blame himself (or the adviser). However, if an investment decision was justified, the investor may regret the decision or its timing but should at least understand why it was taken.

Thus, good process should not only lead to more considered (and, hopefully, better) decision-making, but also support stability and confidence in the existence of a "steady hand at the tiller". This should help control the potentially harmful effect of some of the biases that can influence investment decision-making. One of the best ways to manage the impact of these may be to draw attention to them and discuss their potential impact before important investment decisions are taken.

Investor preferences

This chapter started with an anecdote about an investor whose strong preference was that investment strategy should allow for the threat posed to private wealth by inflation. Preferences should be distinguished from biases. If investor biases should be managed, investor preferences should be respected and reflected in investment strategy, in so far as it is both feasible and sensible.

There are two particular areas of investor preference that have been highlighted by behavioural finance. The first (perhaps not surprisingly) is loss aversion, which Kahneman has described as "the most significant contribution of psychology to behavioural economics". In behavioural finance, loss aversion fills the role of risk aversion in traditional finance. The second is mental accounting, which reflects the way in which investors assign sums of money to different actual or notional accounts for different purposes with varying degrees of risk tolerance, depending on the importance of achieving the particular objective. For example, an individual's summer vacation money will be in a different mental account (and probably a different actual account) from pension savings.

Loss aversion

Traditional finance assumes that investors behave rationally and evaluate the risk and potential return of investment strategies in terms of their expected utility or satisfaction. There are different ways of calibrating utility, but they all have the characteristic that they represent assumptions about how investors should be expected to express preferences. They have the additional characteristic that they can be modelled mathematically, which is convenient for modellers. Much less convenient is the widespread evidence that these rational utility models do not reflect how people view the prospect of financial gains or losses.

This has been reflected in prospect theory, which is built upon a wide range of experiments showing that people will take quite large risks to have some chance of avoiding otherwise certain losses, but that they are quick to bank any winnings. Investment banks tap into this investor preference through sales of highly profitable principal-protected structured products, which provide downside protection with the prospect of some combination of leveraged positive returns. In other words, they offer a seductive combination of "little fear and much hope". This relationship between the disutility or dissatisfaction that comes from losses and the utility or satisfaction that comes from gains is captured in the so-called coefficient of loss aversion, which across a wide range of experiments has come out at a value of around two. This measures how much more highly investors weigh losses than they weigh gains. Loss aversion is most commonly expressed in terms of a comparison of absolute gains and losses, but it also applies to gains and losses relative to a benchmark.

These experiments have highlighted the importance of how a

question is framed or asked as a determinant of the reaction to it. The choice of a benchmark becomes of great importance by helping to "frame" expectations for performance and whether an investor should be pleased or disappointed with an investment result. An investor, for example, may be disappointed that a fund has lagged well behind the performance of the stockmarket, whereas the manager may try to persuade clients to be happy that the fund has shown some growth in value. How expectations are set at the outset for an investment can become as important as the subsequent performance in determining whether an investment is judged to be successful.

A related challenge arises from the inconsistency between the wish to have stable, or at least protected, investment values, and the desire to have a stable income that is financed by those investments (see Chapter 5). These wishes are incompatible, because only long-dated, high-quality government bonds, which are volatile, can guarantee a stable income over time. This highlights the need for investors to be educated as well as asked the relevant questions, framed in an appropriate way.

The "fourfold pattern" of attitudes to gains and losses

Kahneman and Tversky's prospect theory, which is based on experiments into how individuals choose among risky alternatives, is commonly represented by a quadrant, such as the one below.

One of the differences between this approach and conventional finance theory is that uncertain events are defined relative to the current position rather than in absolute terms. This is made clear in the quadrant below, where the investor's attitude differs depending on whether they are currently doing well or badly, which would not be the case in the conventional world of expected utility, where decisions are based on final wealth. While these differences may sound academic, prospect theory offers a rich set of explanations and is supported by surveys of investor behaviour.

	Big gains	Big losses
High probability	Sell winners to lock in substantial but smaller than expected gain	Reject opportunity to crystallise existing losses, run risk of even larger losses to have at least some chance of avoiding likely big loss
Low probability	Buy lottery ticket to have chance of big win	Buy insurance to avoid small chance of big loss

The top left quadrant indicates a preference to accept less than the expected value of a successful gamble to lock in a certain gain. In the investment world, this translates into selling winning investments after a run of good performance.

The bottom left quadrant is the temptation to buy lottery tickets, even though the most likely result by far is the loss of the cost of the ticket. In the investment world, this too translates into the surprisingly large demand for structured products that offer large payouts in the event of plausible but unlikely events.

The top right quadrant is the tendency to hold onto lossmaking investments to avoid the pain of realising losses. This offers some hope of recouping losses, at the risk of incurring even bigger ones. In Kahneman's words, when confronted with only bad options, "we were just as risk seeking in the domain of losses, as we were risk averse in the domain of gains".

The bottom right quadrant is where investors openly buy insurance, to avoid the small risk of some loss.

Mental accounting and behavioural portfolio theory

A division of investments between safety-first, cautious accounts to meet basic needs, and more aggressive "aspirational" accounts to meet less critical or simply more distant objectives is one of the predictions of the mental accounting framework of behavioural finance. This approach is not found anywhere in the traditional finance textbooks, but it is common (some would say common sense) in everyday experience, as the following examples illustrate.

The subsistence farmer

Subsistence farmers often grow two types of crops: food for the family and cash crops with volatile prices. Growing food represents the safety-first portfolio. The allocation of land to growing food is determined first by basic needs, such as family size. The remaining land is allocated to the cash crop, which is the more speculative opportunity to raise living standards – in other words, the aspirational portfolio.

The champion poker player

Greg "Fossilman" Raymer gave this account of how he and his wife kept their "aspirational account" separate from their essential "safety-first" cash when he started out on his successful career at the poker table:

> I started getting steady wins, but I was now married, and [my wife] was becoming increasingly concerned about the time I was spending on it. She'd also hear horror stories about players bankrupting their families. In the end we made a deal: I was allowed a $1,000 poker bankroll on condition it stayed separate from our savings. And if I lost it all, I'd never play again. It never got to that.

Investment strategy and behavioural finance

These examples show a natural process of segmentation of risk-taking, with separate allocations to different accounts, with distinctive risk tolerances and time horizons dictated by particular objectives. Above all, this segmentation provides an easy-to-monitor, keep-it-simple management information system for individuals and institutions.

This mental accounting also helps to discipline future behaviour by highlighting deviations from decisions that have already been taken. For example, in a family context, someone might say, "no, we will not use that money to buy a new car, it's our pension savings"; or, in an institution, "no, we can't use that cash to finance a private equity opportunity, it is our ready cash to pay pensions".

Traditional finance does not segment financial resources in this way. It treats all a family's financial resources or all a pension plan's resources as a unified whole and seeks a total wealth-efficient solution to considering risk, return and investment strategy. It also considers money to be fungible (cash in this account is the same as cash in another account if it is owned by the same person and has the same tax status). Furthermore, and this is of great importance, traditional finance takes into account the relationships, for example, correlations, that may exist between the investments and the objectives or obligations of the different accounts. Separate accounting, with separate strategies designed independently for each account, would ignore these relationships. This can be a major inefficiency in the widespread practice of mental accounting. Mental accounting helps financial resources to be targeted for different purposes. Each person will have a different risk tolerance for achieving different objectives. Some goals are critical, but others are just nice to have. Decisions will be influenced by regulations that impinge on taxed and tax-exempt accounts, current-generation resources and trust or other tax-efficient accounts for future generations, and philanthropic accounts.

A more general example of mental accounting is quoted by Meir Statman and Vincent Wood in *Investment Temperament*, when they describe the pattern of responses to the following question in the Fidelity Investments Asset Allocation Planner:

> *If you could increase your chances of improving your returns by taking more risk would you:*
>
> 1. *Be willing to take a lot more risk with all of your money?*
> 2. *Be willing to take a lot more risk with some of your money?*
> 3. *Be willing to take a little more risk with all of your money?*
> 4. *Be willing to take a little more risk with some of your money?*

Overwhelmingly, the respondents indicated a willingness to take either a lot or a little more risk with some of their money. This indicates a preference to segment or layer risk-taking, which is generally considered to be at odds with the traditional risk–return trade-off commonly presented to investors. This addresses the performance and risk of the total portfolio, which would presume taking either a little or a lot more risk with all of the money. However, if a traditional efficient portfolio comprises a mixture of a holding of risk-free assets and an allocation to market risk, these responses would make sense in terms of being willing to shift some resources out of a safe-haven investment and into a market risk portfolio (see Chapter 5). In other words, the responses could be consistent with traditional finance as well as behavioural portfolio theory.

Parameter uncertainty and behavioural finance

Investors often like to test the reasonableness of major decisions from different perspectives before committing themselves. This is a rational way to proceed with decision-making when faced with uncertainty about the reliability of models or approaches. One of the themes that pervades this book is that the parameters used in financial models are subject to marked degrees of uncertainty, with some elements more uncertain than others. There is nothing new about this.

Even in the traditional model of rational markets and rational investors, investors have not generally faced a unique solution to their investment problems, although that may be what they were offered. Quantitative analysis may provide supposedly unique answers to asset allocation problems, but the investment markets have rarely (see Chapter 4) provided such clear answers. Instead, our understanding of the uncertain relationships between markets has always involved a trade-off between broadly appropriate alternative investment strategies which appear to lie within the range of what is best described as the "fuzzy frontier".

This means that in any particular situation there will always be strategies that are demonstrably inefficient or that involve a clearly inappropriate risk profile. There will also be a range of strategies that are each broadly appropriate, given our current state of knowledge of markets and investors' attitude to risk. This can give a surprisingly wide scope for the investment preferences of principals or fiduciaries to be reflected in investment strategy, while still staying consistent with the overriding desire to adhere to their goals and objectives. It also makes it more likely that investors will find that independent ways of presenting strategy, such as the behaviourist-layered pyramid approach, provide intuitively attractive cross-checks on the traditional quantitative approach.

The idea of a fuzzy frontier can be traced back to work on uncertainty in scientific measurement dating from the 1960s. Much of the uncertainty in measurement that we know exists cannot be adequately captured by statistics. This has potential applications in many different fields. One of its starting points is that we often do not know precisely how to categorise items that are being analysed. This was reflected in a debate over 25 years ago about whether US-quoted multinational corporations with US boards of directors but extensive overseas operations were really US companies. This was captured in the title of a 1990 article in *Harvard Business Review*, "Who Is Us?", by Robert Reich, a former US labour secretary. In reality, this is an issue that the staff of any investment firm wrestle with every day. Mechanical rules have to be applied, but rules differ from one investing institution to another, often in ways that purists would dispute, resulting in apparent arbitrary differences in investment allocations. Leading index providers have disagreed about whether South Korea is an emerging or a developed market. Investors buy UK stocks to gain exposure to a developed market, but is an African or Chilean mining company listed in London a UK exposure, or is an Israeli technology company listed on NASDAQ a US exposure? In high-level summaries of portfolio allocations, should a convertible bond be classified as debt or as equity? In finance, these classification issues are routinely put to one side in investment analysis, and yet they undermine the precision with which policy conclusions can be drawn.

Traditional finance, behavioural finance and evolution

In recent years steps have been taken towards synthesising traditional finance with the insights from behavioural finance, but there is much further to go before an integrated approach is agreed which combines both the rigour and comprehensiveness of "traditional" finance and evidence-based assumptions about investor behaviour from behavioural finance.

Some things are already clear. First, it is important for investors and their advisers to benefit from the insights of behavioural finance to understand better the influences on their own decision-making and preferences. Advice and strategy can then be adapted to accommodate that. This does not provide an excuse for ignoring the fundamental principles of diversification, correlations between different investments or the need to tailor policies to the time horizon of investment objectives. Equally, it would be arrogant to suggest that it is always poor practice for individuals to purchase the investment equivalent of lottery tickets, as this may be an efficient way of maximising the chances of acquiring riches. Furthermore, behavioural finance helps advisers gain a better understanding of how investors take decisions, why investors' portfolios are structured as they are, how investors are likely to respond to any instance of disappointing performance and the nature of their strong preferences.

As Statman writes in *Behavioral Portfolios: Hope for Riches and Protection from Poverty*:

> *We might lament the fact that people are attracted to lotteries, or we might accept it, and help people strike a balance between hope for riches and protection from poverty.*

Andrew Lo, Harris & Harris Group professor of finance and director of the Laboratory for Financial Engineering at MIT, puts it more starkly when he writes in *The Adaptive Markets Hypothesis* that "for all financial market participants, survival is the only objective that matters".

Against this background, the most important first step may be to start discussions of investment strategy with an assessment of whether an investor has sufficient wealth to guarantee survival. In other words, does the investor have sufficient resources to hedge against the risk of shortfall from critical objectives by investing in liability- or objective-matching high-quality government bonds? In the years after 2008, the era of ultra-low interest rates meant that the answer for many was "no". Survival, in terms of meeting what previously seemed reasonable expectations (for example, in terms of retirement income or retirement date), cannot be guaranteed and risk-taking, and the danger of worsening shortfalls, cannot be avoided. In the language of some advisers, a conflict may emerge between an investor's risk tolerance, their capacity to take risk (before threatening achievement of critical objectives) and their need to take risk in order to achieve those objectives. More traditional advisers would say that in such a case their role is to help the investor to adjust expectations to what they can realistically or prudently afford. The next chapter discusses these challenges in more detail.

3

The personal pension challenge

THE DECADE AFTER the onset of the global financial crisis in 2007 saw an increased focus on the challenge of providing private pensions. Surveys of Fortune 500 largest US companies show that until the end of the last century most offered new employees salary-related defined-benefit pensions on retirement. By 2015, over 80% of these companies offered pay-as-you-go defined-contribution pension arrangements, where the onus is placed on the employee to take responsibility for the adequacy of the investment fund which accumulates over their working life to finance their retirement. A similar pattern of moving away from salary-related pensions outside the government sector is found in the UK and other countries.

The features of individual pension provision are now subject to the personal decisions of millions in a way that was largely unknown in earlier generations. The advisory and computational challenges of assessing the adequacy of an individual's accumulation of savings from work to support their particular circumstances in old age has been described by Nobel laureate Professor William Sharpe as "the nastiest, hardest problem" he has ever come across in finance. When an individual is not a member of an employer's pension arrangement, their first task (and perhaps the most important) is to choose a trusted adviser, but often it is far from clear how best to do this (see Chapter 5). Millions are in good company in finding this all very difficult.

Typically, sponsoring companies mitigate some of this personal responsibility by suggesting "set and forget" model strategies into which employee contributions are commonly paid (as the default option) and then left to accumulate. If they are lucky, such default contributors will from the outset opt to have their pension savings kept as a fixed proportion of their pay, thereby benefiting from any pay increases over time.

Recent developments in pension arrangements leave them exposed to the impact of the characteristic personal biases discussed in Chapter 2, as well as individuals' incomplete understandings of risk. More positively, they also enable savers (should they so wish) to let their own preferences and circumstances influence the tailoring of their pension arrangements.

This individual decision-making covers the adequacy of pension-saving, the appropriate ways to invest those savings, and then when retirement beckons, whether to buy a regular annuity income from an insurance company or, if not, the appropriate rate at which to draw from that accumulated pot of retirement savings, or some combination of the two. For many, their financial needs in retirement do not follow a stable path. One consequence of increasing life expectancy is that increasing numbers of younger pensioners (or, those who might wish to retire or scale back paid work) can find themselves sandwiched between commitments to their much older parents and supporting their children. In many families, this will also include the need to make financial provision for a dependant with special needs. At the same time, those on the cusp of drawing their pension need to have a focus on the possibility of living into great old age and also of being among the significant minority who incur substantial and prolonged care costs in their last years.

This difficulty with organising one's own pension income reflects the need to juggle, judge and model an impressive range of variables and uncertainties. The list of unknowns and variables includes:

1. Their pension savings rate

2. Their existing fund of pension and other savings and investments

3. Their earnings and how it may evolve

4. Any continuing financial responsibilities to their family

5. Their customary standard of living

6. Their retirement date

7. The equity in their home

8. Whether they continue to work part-time while drawing a pension
9. The plausible range of the individual's life expectancy
10. The risk of incurring uninsured, substantial nursing or care home costs in old age
11. Their current and likely tax status
12. The rate of interest and how that is expected to evolve over time
13. The probable ranges of inflation over the decades ahead
14. How to invest and the range of returns expected from their accumulated savings
15. Their appetite and ability to tolerate risk and uncertainty
16. The fees and taxes to be paid on accumulated savings
17. Whether and how each of these risks, opportunities and preferences are shared with a spouse or partner
18. How these different uncertainties might diversify and counterbalance or offset each other

This range of uncertainties and needed decisions suggests a need for holistic advice covering a wide range of topics, including drawing tax-efficient income from a range of different sources. The personal pension challenge is not primarily an investment issue. Furthermore, the investment aspects of the challenge need to be met by considering together the non-pension savings and other resources (especially housing) of the retiree. Pensioners of all income levels often have savings in non-pension accounts which are comparable to their accumulated pension accounts. At the same time, the equity stake in their homes is for many their second most valuable asset after their accumulated savings. Downsizing to a less expensive home, where this is a realistic option, provides one efficient way of improving diversification (by lessening the stake in one particular house) and in freeing up liquidity to meet financial needs. (Reverse mortgages, whereby the elderly can borrow against the security of their home and the accumulated interest due is rolled up with the loan and paid when the pensioner moves house or dies, is another way of raising cash to meet the expenses of old age. Whereas an annuity shifts longevity risk to an insurance company, a reverse mortgage places longevity risk onto the pensioner's estate, leaving beneficiaries with much less if the home owner lives to a great old age.) Financial markets can provide insurance against some of the risks listed above. Judging which risks to insure and to what extent and how to avoid overspending on insurance is an important element in the challenge. Confronted with so much information to process and so many different decisions to take, the natural instinct is to take readily available mental shortcuts (see the discussion of investor biases in Chapter 2). These shortcuts will inevitably reflect a range of prior beliefs, which are unlikely to capture efficiently the trade-offs that preferably should be made when designing a suitable financial plan for retirement.

Retirement date uncertainty

Some of the uncertainties can be valuable sources of flexibility. Date of retirement is one, as can part-time work after leaving mainstream work. The ability to continue working and to delay drawing a pension for those who can, and especially if both can in a two-income home, is the easiest way for many to enhance their retirement income and represents an enormously valuable option for those with borderline sufficient retirement savings who are able to exploit such opportunities. Likewise, many continue working part-time to supplement their pension income.

For others though, these options are not available and anyone's prospective retirement date should be seen as a further source of uncertainty, which may not be a matter of individual choice. A 2014 report from Merrill Lynch and the consultancy Age Wave found that 55% of American pensioners surveyed retired earlier than planned. Three-quarters of these early retirements were involuntary, explained by personal health problems, unemployment or the need to care for a family member. This shows that we may target a particular retirement date, but it is unclear whether it is ours to choose. But for those who can, the ability to defer (or voluntarily to bring forward) retirement is a valuable option.

Life expectancy

Individuals commonly underestimate the length of their retirement and for how many years they should provide. Often, they are pessimistic about their own life chances and underestimate the likelihood of living to great old age. In the early stages of the transformations in life expectancy (as measured from birth, as is frequently the case) in the twentieth century, the major gains were in reducing infant and child mortality, with little impact on the time spent in retirement by those lucky enough to reach that stage. By contrast, in recent decades, reductions in mortality among those at the later stages of life explain the increases in life expectancy.

Over the last quarter of a century this has been reflected in a doubling of the proportion of the elderly who live into their late eighties, or beyond (see Table 3.1), as the time spent in retirement has increased. Often, this phenomenon is summarised by single numbers to denote the increase in life expectancy, which can then be broken down by gender (women typically live for a couple of years longer than men), or by lifestyle (smokers, heavy drinkers and the obese tend to die earlier than others) or a range of other characteristics. However, the most important message for planning retirement is that a single number for life expectancy is never sufficient to suggest how long a retirement plan needs to provide for. Life expectancy is no more than today's best estimate for the mid-point of a wide range of possible dates.

Table 3.2 gives some broad measures, based on US and UK data for how long retirements starting at age 65 may now be expected to last. It suggests that half of American women will live at least 22 years beyond their 65th birthday, and that one in ten American women will live at least 31 years beyond their 65th birthday, that is to age 96, while in the UK it suggests that at least one in ten women will live to age 100. There are numerous websites which fine-tune the national data to take account of self-reported personal characteristics of current age, lifestyle, health, gender, ethnicity and others. However, from a financial planning perspective, the key message is the great uncertainty of the period for which the pension will be needed. Table 3.2 also suggests that half of American men aged 65 will die before reaching age 85, but at the same time there is a 10% chance that a joint pension intended

TABLE 3.1 **Twice as many elderly now live beyond age 84 as a generation ago**
Percentage of all deaths by age in 1979 and 2015

Ages (years)	Women		Men	
	1979	2015	1979	2015
USA				
Before 65	26%	21%	40%	32%
65 to 84	50%	39%	49%	44%
85+	24%	40%	11%	23%
England and Wales				
	1979	2014	1979	2014
Before 65	17%	13%	29%	20%
65 to 84	59%	41%	61%	51%
85+	24%	47%	10%	29%

Sources: UK: Office for National Statistics (England and Wales); US: National Center for Health Statistics (USA)

TABLE 3.2 **How long might my retirement last?**
In years, assuming retirement from age 65 for both men and women in around 2017

UK data	50%	25%	10%
Men	21	29	34
Women	24	31	35
US data	50%	25%	10%
Men	19	23	28
Women	22	26	31
Couple (both 65)	24	28	32

Sources: UK: Office for National Statistics (England and Wales); US: National Center for Health Statistics (USA)

to provide for a couple, both aged 65, will be needed to pay out regular income until at least age 97.

So it is clear that a significant minority of pensioners will need to stretch their pension savings over more than 30 years. For the wealthy this may not be a problem. But for most pensioners, it is a tall order for life savings accumulated over working careers of 45 years, if that long. Providing cover against this "longevity risk" for pensioners is a natural role for insurance company annuity policies, and, where available, may be an attractive option, even if the pensioner is wealthy (see below).

It is normally dumb to self-insure big risks

Extreme weather conditions generate news stories of the financial misfortune of individuals who either choose to decline or cannot obtain insurance for their homes. It is almost never sensible for an individual deliberately to save on paying a modest annual premium (if it is) and forgoing the assurance of being made good in the event of an unlikely but catastrophic financial loss.

Aspects of the retirement challenge are in essence a choice between self-insurance and paying insurance companies to insure your risks. Table 3.2 gives an indication of the uncertainty surrounding the length of an individual's or a couple's retirement. The risk of financial ruin (that is of outlasting one's savings) by self-insuring this uncertainty for a 75 year-old who continues (as most do) to rely on drawing down regular instalments from their pension savings has been compared to a volatile strategy of investing 100% of their retirement savings in the equity market. This cost of unusually long retirements makes this a natural marketplace for insurance companies, which routinely insure this risk by selling life annuities which guarantee an income for life. Typically this will be a fixed, regular amount, but it can be linked to inflation or increase at a pre-set rate to offset gradual erosion by inflation. Many will pass up this opportunity because they are pessimistic about their own life chances and so they expect that a life annuity would be "a waste of money". However, enhanced annuities for those with poor life chances may be available.

Unless they have substantial retirement savings, rejecting the option to buy an annuity, with at least part of pension savings, risks burdening a pensioner's loved ones if they do reach great old age. Others who are wealthy might reach the same conclusion because they assess that they have enough to pay for an extended retirement. In the next breath they might say that they intend to leave the residue of their estate to their loved ones and or to good causes. In effect, they are asking their estate to underwrite their own mortality risk.

It is no surprise that financial economists are particularly attracted by insurance policies which take at least part of this longevity risk away from the individual. Self-insurance ties up personal resources in excessive precautionary saving and reduces potential spending (and standard of living) in retirement. The ideal policy for many economists is a deferred inflation-linked annuity, which protects the individual against the twin financial risks of a very lengthy retirement and cumulative inflation.

In practice, in what may appear to some to be modest individual amounts, this is already widely available. Mitigation of personal longevity and inflation risk can be provided by taking advantage of options to defer, and so increase from a later start date, entitlements to regular, inflation-linked payments of social security in the US and state old-age pensions in the UK. For many, this will provide the best way to reduce, to a degree, uncertainty of their standard of living in great old age and of the estates that they can bequeath. In the US, insurance companies offer deferred annuities which start making payouts at a specified date in the future, and these can be available with various options, including joint life policies for couples.

A range of studies from different countries has found that the finances of retirees are typically characterised by a higher level of expenditure in the earlier years of retirement and also by the persistence of savings patterns by those of pensionable age of all income groups and all age groups. While this pattern of saving by the elderly is consistent with risk aversion increasing with age, academics disagree about whether attitudes to risk do materially change with age.

For many, saving in old age will include precautionary saving, or self-insurance, to meet the potential burden of end-of-life care expenses. For this, the elderly are presumably not concerned with being able to meet average health and care costs of old age (about which they will likely have little knowledge), but rather with the risk of incurring much larger costs which are sometimes incurred (and on which they are likely to be quite well informed from the anecdotal evidence of friends and family). A 2017 report based on 18 years of detailed data on nursing home use in the US and associated out-of-pocket expenses for

TABLE 3.3 **Lifetime nursing home use in USA from age 57**

Percentile	Months' stay
10	0
25	0
50	0.3
75	7.9
90	32.9
95	49.2

Source: Hurd, Michael D.; Michaud, Pierre-Carl; Rohwedder, Susann; Rand Corporation and Network for Studies on Pension, Aging and Retirement, Tilburg University, 2017

TABLE 3.4 **Lifetime out-of-pocket nursing home costs in US$***
in the USA from age 57

Percentile	Costs $
10	–
25	–
50	–
75	1,072
90	19,647
95	46,660

* spending expressed in 2013 dollars as a present value at age 57

Source: Hurd, Michael D.; Michaud, Pierre-Carl; Rohwedder, Susann; Rand Corporation and Network for Studies on Pension, Aging and Retirement, Tilburg University, 2017

families, weighted so as to represent the US population over the age of 50, found that one in twenty elderly Americans spend more than four years in a nursing home while half of elderly Americans spend a total of ten days or less during their lifetimes (for example, in rehabilitative care following a stay in hospital). From the perspective of managing personal retirement savings, the range of costs of nursing-home care incurred by the elderly (after allowing for diminution of other expenses) is at least as important as the average cost. Most of the elderly avoid the cost of long-term care, but for a significant proportion long-term care represents a major financial burden. The risk of this will be a worry for any elderly individual and this will affect their spending and savings behaviour in retirement, unless they have been able to arrange insurance against this risk.

Income uncertainty

Over an average working life, which often spans four or more decades, income uncertainty from year to year is a given. Earnings and careers progress, or suffer greater or lesser setbacks so there is no certainty from one year to the next. Old-style-final salary company (or government sector) pensions, where employers assumed responsibility for paying their former employees contractual pensions for the remainder of their lives did offer the prospect of such certainty. Income certainty comes at a heavy price, and those pensioners who pay an insurer in exchange for receiving a regular annuity for the rest of their lives, sometimes approaching the length of time they were at work, pay dearly for this assurance. Insuring against mortality risk in the early years of retirement can hinder flexibility and be wasteful. Those who choose instead to rely on regular payments drawn from their own pension savings should consider which risks they particularly need to insure against and which they do not. Inflation is one of the principal sources of risk, even in an era of seemingly very low inflation.

How much income can I draw?

An indication of how much regular income one might receive in retirement is provided by the easy-to-find online annuity calculators. In late 2017, these indicated that a 65-year-old in the US might get from an insurance company an annual fixed income of around $65,000 in exchange for a one-off payment of US $1,000,000; whereas in the UK in exchange for £1,000,000 an insurance company might provide a pension of just over £52,000. The higher proportionate pay-out in the US than the UK takes no account of personal circumstances and instead will reflect the higher interest rates, slightly shorter life expectancy and market differences.

These seemingly attractive level incomes will erode over time with inflation. Monetary policy in developed countries commonly targets price stability, which is defined as 2% per year by the Federal Reserve. If you or your partner do live for 35 years after first drawing a level life pension, the value of that pension would have halved if the Fed meets its "price stability" objective (see Table 3.5). If it fails, and inflation is on average higher, the pension could be worth very much less, even though the average inflation rate could still be judged quite low. The income from a fixed annuity should be seen as including an element of compensation for the erosion of their capital by inflation. Inflation risk, like longevity, can be hedged. The most cautious of investors can (though few seem to do so) purchase a lifetime annuity whose income is indexed to the rate of inflation. In the US in late 2017, online calculators suggest that an annual cost-of-living-adjusted pension of around $40,000 might have been bought (by a single male, aged 65) with $1,000,000 and in the UK the corresponding inflation-linked pension would have been around £30,000 per £1,000,000.

TABLE 3.5 **The corrosive impact of modest inflation on fixed pensions**
Purchasing power of $50,000 over time with different average inflation rates

	10 years	20 years	30 years	35 years
1%	$45,264	$40,977	$37,096	$35,296
2%	$41,017	$33,649	$27,604	$25,001
3%	$37,205	$27,684	$20,599	$17,769
4%	$33,778	$22,819	$15,416	$12,671

Source: Authors' calculations

It is rare for a pensioner to choose to exchange all (or any) their accumulated pension savings for a lifetime annuity which is indexed to inflation. Nevertheless, the annual monetary payment from an inflation-linked annuity and also from a level fixed annuity provide invaluable benchmarks (the first free from both longevity and inflation risk, the other free only of longevity risk) against which to assess any financial plan prepared by an adviser or financial planner.

Financial advisers commonly back-test model asset allocations from stocks and bonds to show an approximate "safe" withdrawal rate, which could, with hindsight, have provided a sustainable level of income, growing through time to match inflation. An early influential example of this was an article from 1994 by William Bengen, a former US financial planner, whose research led to what became known as the "4% rule". Based on then available US historical market returns, Bengen calculated that a pensioner aged 65 should be able to withdraw an amount equivalent to 4% of their initial pension savings (assumed to be invested equally in stocks and government bonds), and that this amount in dollars could then be indexed to inflation, and drawn down over a retirement of 30 years. For the period he considered, Bengen found resilience for back-tested inflation-linked drawdowns which start at 4% of the initial portfolio, and are subsequently indexed to inflation.

Bengen's model has been tested and reappraised extensively since then, making use of a longer data set, and greater availability of international data. However, William Sharpe, emeritus professor of finance, Stanford University - Graduate School of Business, and his colleagues Jason Scott and John Watson, in a 2009 article "The 4% rule – at what price?" noted that Bengen was proposing "to finance a constant, non-volatile spending plan using a risky, volatile investment strategy". Bengen had used the longest run of data on US market returns then available to him, from 1926 to 1992, 66 years in total. Despite being able to construct a reasonable number of overlapping 30-year periods (his principal chosen length of retirement), in reality he only had two distinct 30-year periods, which is not a big dataset. The 4% inflation-linked drawdown "rule" has played a powerful role in anchoring (see Chapter 2) expectations ever since. Economists have since pointed out that at times, for some pensioners, a higher inflation-protected drawdown of more than 4% could have been assured through insurance policies. These could not only have offered inflation linking, but also removed the risk that the pensioner might face financial ruin by living for more than 30 years into retirement. Even if an investor is willing to pass up the risk management benefits of committing at least part of their assets to buy a fixed lifetime annuity, there are still issues with Bengen's recommendations and further refinements are still needed to derive a corresponding "rule-of-thumb" withdrawal rate. One is the need to include an appropriate allowance for adviser and fund manager fees (Bengen did not allow for these). Another is to allow for the extent to which the historical record may be a misleading guide to the future. The starting point is now historically low interest rates, which have raised returns from stocks, bonds and almost all other assets in recent decades. The reasonable starting point is that prospective returns have been reduced and that past performance of balanced holdings of equities and especially bonds are a really poor guide to future returns (see Chapters 4 and 5). Personal pensions cannot appeal to historical market experience to suggest that, going forward, risk-taking is less than it demonstrably is.

Running throughout this book is the theme that the risk of failing to meet reasonable future spending needs is best measured by the extent to which those future needs have been hedged, for example by government bonds or insurance policies, rather than supported by risky or mismatched investments. Those future needs can most obviously be hedged by inflation-linked annuities, but government bonds, both fixed and inflation-linked can hedge near-term liabilities. Chapter 5 includes a discussion of the late James Tobin's portfolio separation theorem, which looks at strategy and risk-taking as if investments are split between two investments: government bonds and a basket of risky investments. It also includes an explanation of how government bond ladders can help to secure pension income.

The attention of advisers and investors is often focused on attempting to manage the consequences of using risk assets to provide a stable flow of income. This includes the damaging impact on sustainable living standards of selling investments to pay pensions when the prices are lower than was assumed when a financial plan was put in place. Equally, there is a beneficial impact on solvency when investments are sold at higher prices than assumed in the plan. Planners often call this "sequence risk", and generally emphasise the importance of regular reassessment of the financial plan and, if necessary, the pension payment, as time passes. In addition, advisers commonly recommend building a buffer of liquidity to ensure that projected drawdowns over a specified number of years can be met from expected investment income and cash holdings. The idea is that this reduces the need to sell assets at depressed prices in "bad times". To many financial economists, this comes close to a naive policy of reliance on a short-term bounce in markets to restore the solvency of a financial plan which was agreed in better times. However, the undoubted advantages of such a buffer of liquidity to meet near-term needs, whatever happens in markets, is that it facilitates "hand-holding" by advisers and allows for time to reflect and consider different options. It also improves the likelihood that a temporary spike of illiquidity, which raises trading costs, will correct itself. Of course, depressed market valuations might also recover in time to help a plan.

This emphasises that the starting point for any pension plan should be a comparison with the income offered by lifetime annuities from highly rated insurance companies. Ideally, these would be uprated in line with inflation, in conjunction with the potential for deferred social security or state pension benefits. Investors can then decide how far to move away from the typically expensive and illiquid (a decision to buy a simple life annuity cannot be reversed) insurance route. The extent to which they decide to move away from the insurance route enables investors to retain a greater degree of control and flexibility over their wealth while giving options to respond to changing needs. This opens up exposure to increased opportunities from managed investments, but comes with accepting the risk of an unanticipated depletion of resources and even the possibility of money running out. How investment risk-taking from managed investments might best be structured when seeking to secure retirement income is discussed in the following chapters. No one needs to allocate all their financial savings to a life annuity, but retirees ought to consider how they can help manage longevity and investment market risk.

4

Investment returns

THE FINANCIAL MARKETS should be seen as a place to protect and grow wealth, not as a place to grow wealthy. This chapter looks at expectations and uncertainties for future equity- and government-bond market returns. An important message is that the start of this century, with two of the worst equity bear markets in history, has set the tone for less favourable equity returns than those enjoyed in the 20th century, and for very modest returns to be earned from creditworthy government bonds, which offered unprecedentedly low yields in the second decade of the century. But the main qualification remains that even over long periods of time, we are unclear about how markets are going to behave.

Traditionally, domestic Treasury bonds and bills have been considered free from credit risk and safe havens for investors. This has been a cornerstone of much modern portfolio theory and practice, but it has been shaken by the government debt crises that flowed from the credit crunch of 2007–08. Despite this, appropriately interpreted, it is a foundation that remains largely intact (see Are government bonds risk-free? below).

Inflation-linked government bonds are an innovation that can provide an important degree of security for cautious long-term investors. But the extraordinary monetary easing after early 2009 led to negligible rates of interest being paid on all types of creditworthy government bonds. This has posed severe challenges for cautious investors, for whom the cost of security has often been too high. An unwelcome degree of risk-taking and standard-of-living uncertainty became unavoidable as the security of income from government bonds became too expensive for many.

Sources of investment performance

In a country with a creditworthy government, investment performance can be described as coming from six sources:

1. **Treasury bill yield.** The short-term (less than one year, and typically 1–6 months) risk-free rate of interest.

2. **Inflation-indexed government bond yield.** The long-term inflation-risk-free rate of interest. It is unclear whether these inflation-indexed bonds need to offer a premium return over Treasury bills.

3. **Conventional Treasury bond yield.** The long-term nominal risk-free rate of interest. This rate of interest is subject to the risk of unexpectedly high inflation. It should include a premium over inflation-linked bonds to compensate for expected inflation, and probably also a margin above this for the uncertainty of that inflation (but see below).

4. **Market risk premium.** The compensation that any rational saver should seek in return for putting money or future income at risk of loss. This specifically refers to the equity market, which can be conveniently thought of as a portfolio of individual stocks. The market provides this reward for bearing "market risk". This is reflected in the equity risk premium (the amount by which equities are expected to outperform bonds or cash) and the credit risk premium (the extra yield paid on corporate bonds to compensate for the risk that a company might default – see Chapter 9). Less obviously, market risk premiums seem to be offered in return for accepting various types of insurance risk and also for different types of equity risk (for example, small-company risk separately from equity market risk). These are discussed in Chapter 8 (equity investing), and Chapter 10 (alternative investments, which includes hedge funds and real estate).

5. **Investment manager skill.** Manager skill is believed to generate investment performance, or alpha, that is separate from the performance of the market, or beta. Frequently, investment performance that managers attribute to their skill (which is an

expensive, scarce commodity) gets confused with aspects of market performance (which can be accessed inexpensively).

6. **Noise.** Introduced to investment performance by unskilful managers of investors' portfolios. Noise is often (erroneously) described as "alpha" when it is positive. (Sceptics have described alpha as "the average error term".) Distinguishing noise from skill is one of the most difficult tasks for investors. There are always likely to be more unskilled "noise" managers with marketable track records than skilled managers who, in addition to being skilled, also have a marketable record at any point in time. Noise will normally bring some extra volatility; it will also incur fees and distract investors, thus wasting their valuable time and possibly their money.

This summary simplifies matters considerably, by ignoring cross-border investment in government bonds and by assuming that all investors have an unambiguous base currency, which, as discussed in Chapter 1, is not the case. Nevertheless, this provides a useful introduction to the building blocks of investment performance. The first three sources can be accessed easily and inexpensively by anyone, through direct holdings of government securities (or through funds, including exchange traded funds, which hold only government securities). Equity market risk can also be accessed inexpensively through index funds or exchange traded funds. Some investment markets and some aspects of market risk premiums (for example, private equity – see Chapter 10) can be accessed only if the investor is willing to take a view on investment manager skill.

The pattern of returns available from exposure to market risk can also be re-engineered through "structured products" which contain combinations of embedded options with exposure to particular markets. These do not generate performance, but they can provide insurance (which must be paid for) against the risk of disappointing outcomes in ways that may suit investors.

Are government bonds risk-free?

The idea that government bonds are free of credit risk is routinely used as a building block in designing investment strategies, but it seems to be at odds with ample evidence to the contrary. The highest rating assigned by the credit-rating agencies (see Chapter 9) is AAA, which denotes a debt of the highest creditworthiness, when in the words of Standard & Poor's, the issuer is "judged to be of the highest quality, subject to the lowest level of credit risk". Nevertheless, credit-rating agencies frequently assign ratings to sovereign and other central-government debt, which imply some degree of risk that the government's obligations will not be honoured. In recent years, one or more of the three leading rating agencies has rated the domestic central-government debt of the United States, Japan, France, the UK, Italy, Spain and Ireland below AAA. Furthermore, modern credit markets enable investors (or speculators) to buy or sell insurance contracts, called credit default swaps, which can give a market assessment of the likelihood of a government defaulting on its debt, and can track fluctuations in market assessments of a government's creditworthiness (although the credit crisis highlighted counterparty issues with these contracts). Most obviously, there is a history of governments defaulting on their international and (but less frequently) domestic debt.

The importance of these ratings depends upon how default is defined. For example, a default can be defined as a late payment or non-payment of the bond coupon and so a rating gives us an implicit measure of the probability of such an event. But a country with its own central bank, such as the UK, can always create money to pay such a coupon, while a country such as Greece, being part of the euro zone, would not be able to do so. These structural features are not always reflected in the ratings awarded.

Surveys of the historical experience of defaults by governments (see Appendix 2) have sometimes misinterpreted market refinancing of sovereign debt – when a government exploits a contractual opportunity to redeem a loan and refinance it at a lower interest cost – as a *de jure* default, which it is not. Between 1952 and 2008 there seems to have been no instance of the central government of a developed country failing to honour the nominal face value of its marketable debts, although there have been examples from emerging markets (most notably Russia in 1998–99, and the forcible termination of US dollar or inflation indexation of debt in a number of Latin American countries in the 1980s), as well as Greece in 2012.

Debasement of government debt through inflation has been a characteristic behaviour of over-indebted sovereign governments since time immemorial, and it is a risk faced by holders of the debt of any government. But it is also clear that developed-market (and many emerging-market) sovereign governments can be counted on to take honouring the face value of their marketable debt extremely seriously and, at least in respect of their unindexed domestic obligations, they should always have the means to ensure that they can meet those obligations.

Not surprisingly, when governments do default, there seems to be a hierarchy of risk exposures, with foreign-currency-denominated or linked and inflation-indexed obligations more vulnerable than unindexed domestic debt. For this reason, the proportion of sovereign debt that is denominated in foreign currency or which is indexed is a useful credit risk indicator.

Sovereign risk and "a country called Europe"

An important financial difference between a sovereign and a local government is that, if it needs to, a sovereign government can debase its currency to meet its obligations, which are fixed in its own currency, but a local government does not enjoy this degree of freedom. This means that an over-indebted sovereign government has the scope to try to devalue its way out of a domestic debt crisis but an over-indebted local government does not.

This is not a new insight, and for some European countries, the opportunity to replace the discredited temptation to devalue and to accommodate fast inflation, and the high interest rates which came with that freedom, with a new regime with the discipline of a fixed exchange rate, apparently tight fiscal-policy guidelines, and a tie-in to low rates of inflation and interest, was seen as a major attraction of European currency union ahead of its introduction in 1999. This involved some voluntary yielding of financial sovereignty, and the credibility of monetary union depended on an expectation that this was irreversible.

For government bond investors this meant (though scant attention was paid to it at the time) the substitution of inflation risk with the credit risk that a national government might be unable to honour its obligations. In the euro zone, member countries have their own government bond markets, and efforts are made to co-ordinate fiscal policy between member countries, but there is no dominant euro zone fiscal policy or the issue of collective euro zone government debt, underwritten by the euro zone taxpayer – although there have been steps towards this with financing arrangements put in place after 2009. For euro-based investors, it follows that the choice of a safe-harbour government bond is more judgmental and nuanced than for investors from other countries. But this has parallels with US investors, who must weigh the tax and creditworthy status of different municipal bonds, which form core long-term "safety-first" holdings in many personal portfolios (see Chapter 6).

Safe havens that provide different kinds of shelter

If investors take no risk, they should not expect to receive a premium return. But one investor's safe haven may be a risky investment for another:

■ For a short-term investor, domestic Treasury bills represent the minimum-risk investment that provides capital protection over the short term.

■ For an individual, a bank or an insurance company wanting to secure an income, domestic Treasury bonds give that security for the lifetime of the bond. Treasury bills that mature every three or six months are risky for this purpose as they are immediately vulnerable to cuts in interest rates which a Treasury bond, if held to maturity, is not. The risk from these bonds is that inflation may pick up (and, separately, that interest income may have to be reinvested at lower yields). Figures 4.1, 4.2 and 4.3 show how the pre-tax income yield on offer for ten years to buy-and-hold investors in ten-year Treasury bonds has compared with the yield on offer for the next three months for holders of Treasury bills for the United States, the UK and the euro zone.

■ An individual who wants a secure income that is also protected against inflation can use inflation-linked Treasury bonds. These provide the low-risk investment, insuring against adverse inflation and adverse real interest-rate surprises, but the illiquidity of inflation-linked markets is a concern.

Each of these investors has a different safe-haven investment: Treasury bills for the short-term investor; conventional fixed-income Treasury bonds for the investor who is not concerned about inflation

FIGURE 4.1 **Income yield from 10-year US Treasury notes and 3-month Treasury bills** % per year, 2004–2017

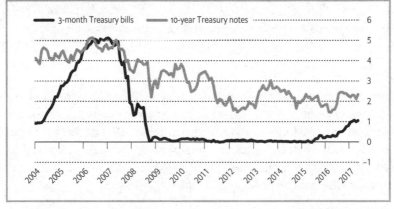

Source: www.ustreas.gov

FIGURE 4.2 **Income yield from 10-year UK gilts and 6-month Treasury bills** % per year, 2004–2017

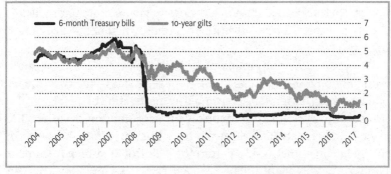

Source: www.bankofengland.co.uk

FIGURE 4.3 **Income yield from 10-year Euro Treasury bonds and 3-month Treasury bills** % per year, 2004–2017

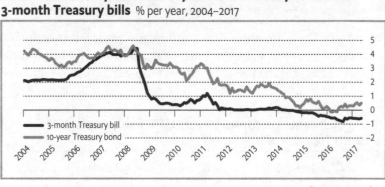

(most commonly an insurance company with contracts to pay fixed monetary amounts); and inflation-linked government bonds for the prospective pensioner who is concerned about inflation. Each investor takes a risk when they venture outside their own safe haven. Often they will feel they have little choice, but they need to consider how and whether they will be rewarded for taking that risk.

Which government bonds will perform best?

In the examples above, the insurance company does not need to be paid a premium yield by the taxpayer to be persuaded to hold Treasury bonds, nor does the pensioner to hold inflation-linked government bonds. This means that it is unclear how much premium return, if any, should be expected from government bonds, whether indexed or not, over cash.

However, different groups of investors have their own separate natural or preferred habitats in different segments of the government bond market. This is often determined by the duration of their liabilities if institutions and their preferences for consumption over their life cycle if individuals. From time to time this can affect the shape of the yield curve (that is, the pattern of yields offered on government bonds of varying maturities – see Figures 4.4, 4.5 and 4.6). This can sometimes make it hard to rationalise the differences in interest rates

FIGURE 4.4 **US Treasury conventional and real yield curves**
% per year, October 1, 2017

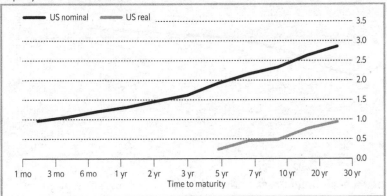

Source: www.ustreas.gov

FIGURE 4.5 **UK Treasury conventional and real yield curves**
% per year, October 1, 2017

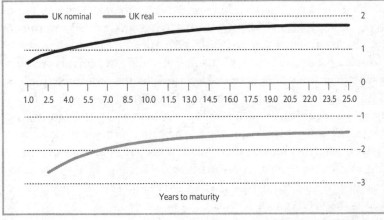

Source: www.bankofengland.co.uk

FIGURE 4.6 **Euro-zone AAA rated Treasury, conventional yield curve**
% per year, October 1, 2017

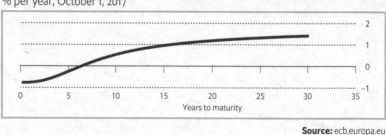

Source: ecb.europa.eu

that a government pays to different groups of investors. The barriers that can limit attempts to arbitrage away apparent pricing anomalies are looked at in Chapter 7.

The normal shape of the yield curve has been an area of extensive, and often inconclusive, research in macroeconomics. The historical pattern is clear on two things. First, there has normally been an upward-sloping yield curve – in other words, longer-dated Treasury bonds have offered higher yields and returns than shorter-dated government bonds, in particular Treasury bills. (See Appendix 1 for definitions of Treasury bonds and Treasury bills.) Second, the extent of this premium varies over time. This is often described as the term premium that short-term investors need to be offered to tempt them to buy longer-dated bonds (because such bonds are subject to price volatility). But insurance companies do not need to be paid a term premium because longer maturities provide their "natural habitat", and investors may in any event wish to hold government bonds because they are, or at any rate have been (see Chapter 5), the best and most liquid diversifier of equity market risk.

Since the introduction of the markets in inflation-linked government bonds (see below), there has been growing emphasis on the premium in conventional government bond yields as an inflation risk premium. Pensioners should not normally buy conventional bonds unless they offer compensation not only for the expected rate of inflation, but also for the risk that the actual rate of inflation might be higher than the rate that is expected. This is the inflation risk premium.

(This ignores taxation issues, which are important in deciding between different types of government bonds.) Long-term investors who are primarily concerned with securing a stable standard of living will feel more comfortable holding conventional government bonds when they have greatest confidence in inflation being kept within the target set by the central bank. If not, they will need to believe that there is sufficient premium in the yield on conventional government bonds to compensate for the threat to their standard of living posed by an uncertain inflation rate.

A market expectation for inflation can be deduced from the difference between yields on conventional government bonds and the yields on these indexed bonds. This is the so-called "break-even" inflation rate. (If inflation turns out at this rate, an investor will get approximately the same return from holding indexed government bonds as from conventional treasuries of the same maturity.) But whether the break-even rate really is a market forecast for inflation is controversial.

Is the break-even inflation rate the market's forecast?

Inflation-indexed government bonds are now available in each major financial market. They were introduced in the UK in 1981 and since then they have been made available in Australia (1985), Canada (1991), Sweden (1994), the United States (1997) and Japan (2004), with government issues in the euro zone from France (1998), Italy and Greece (2003), Germany (2006) and Spain (2014). A number of emerging markets, including India, Brazil, Israel, South Africa and Russia, have also made use of inflation-linked bonds. They now represent an instrument whose characteristics investors in each country should understand. In the United States, these bonds are known as Treasury Inflation Protected Securities or TIPS, and that acronym is used here to refer to any inflation-linked government bond, not just those issued by the US government. The pattern of 20-year inflation-linked and conventional US and also UK Treasury bond yields and the implied 20-year break-even rates of inflation are shown in Figures 4.7–4.10.

FIGURE 4.7 **US 20-year yields** % per year, 2004–2017

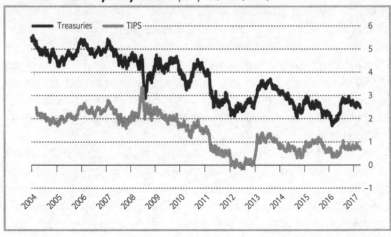

FIGURE 4.8 **US 20-year "break-even" inflation (difference between 20-year Treasury and TIPS yields)** % per year, 2004–2017

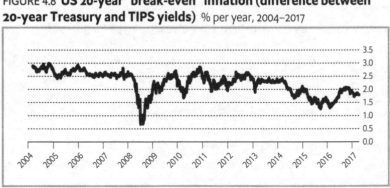

Those unfamiliar with inflation-indexed bonds are advised to check the difference in yields from conventional and index-linked issues of government bonds. Break-even inflation rates can be deduced from any table of government bond prices and yields (and are regularly published on official websites). The break-even rate of inflation is affected by a number of technical factors, which

FIGURE 4.9 **UK 20-year yields** % per year, 2004–2017

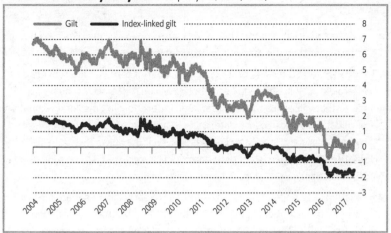

Source: www.bankofengland.co.uk

FIGURE 4.10 **UK 20-year "break-even" inflation** % per year, 2004–2017

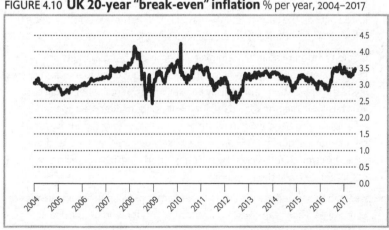

Source: www.bankofengland.co.uk

may mean that it is not a true market forecast for inflation. These include the following:

- An inflation risk premium. This would cause, if it exists, the break-even rate to be higher than the market's forecast for inflation.

- In the United States and other countries, but not the UK, TIPS provide an insurance against deflation as the bonds will be redeemed at the higher of par or that value plus their accumulated indexation. In times of low inflation or deflation, this can cause differences in break-even inflation rates implied by new issues and long-standing bonds even if they have the same maturity date. (In the UK, persistent deflation could cause an issue to be redeemed at less than par.)

- Taxation differences. These can distort the relationship between inflation-linked and conventional government bonds. Tax treatment of inflation-linked bonds differs among countries. In the United States, for example, taxable investors must pay tax on both the real yield and the inflation accrual. So when inflation (or expected inflation) increases, a fall in TIPS' prices is needed to keep the after-tax real yield unchanged, and vice versa for reductions in inflation expectations. By contrast, in the UK income tax is levied only on the coupon of inflation-linked government bonds, not on the inflation compensation on the outstanding principal.

- Liquidity differences. Inflation-linked government bond markets are generally less liquid than conventional government bond markets. Investors value the option to be able to buy and sell investments at negligible cost, which is available from liquid government bond markets, and so the inflation-linked bond yield may contain a premium to compensate for its comparative illiquidity. This premium is likely to vary over time, and may at times be strongly influenced by the demand of long-term investors, who do not intend to trade their holdings.

- Regulation and valuation rules for tax-exempt pension funds and insurance companies. These can cause concentrations of demand for particular segments of the conventional and inflation-linked markets, leading to valuation anomalies which require particularly long time horizons to arbitrage. This can be reflected in differences in break-even inflation rates over different maturities (and can represent investment opportunities for long-term investors who are guided by their own financial needs rather than arbitrary rules or benchmarks).

■ Biases in the measure of inflation used to index indexed bonds. Such biases are reflected in the break-even rate of inflation. For example, in the UK index-linked gilts are compensated for changes in the retail price index (RPI), and a combination of a different index weighting methodology and different coverage causes the RPI to increase by around 1% per year on average faster than the internationally comparable consumer prices index, although the difference is quite volatile. A consultation with interested parties (largely investors) to gauge support for a move towards international standards of measuring inflation found, not surprisingly, little support for change, which would have led to a fall in investment values. As a result, in the UK government bond market real interest rates are materially higher, and the break-even rates of inflation materially lower, than they appear to be.

These factors can cause the break-even rate to differ from an inflation forecast and these differences vary between countries, over time and even between maturities of bonds. The break-even rate is a readily available, crude "rule of thumb" for a market forecast of inflation, but these other factors need weighing up before taking an investment decision. If a long-term investor has strong views that differ from the apparent market rate of inflation, these views can influence how the investor moves away from the safety of inflation-linked government bonds in implementing strategy. Investors whose safe-harbour investment is an inflation-linked government bond should have a strategic position in conventional government bonds if they expect conventional bonds to provide an adequate reward for expected inflation, including a margin for uncertainty.

What premium return should bond investors expect?

It is rarely in doubt that creditworthy governments will make the payments that are due on their debt, but how these payments on different types of government debt relate to each other is still unclear.

We know from the international comparison of 23 markets undertaken by Elroy Dimson, professor of finance at Cambridge Judge Business School and emeritus professor of finance at London Business School, Paul Marsh, also an emeritus professor of finance at London

Business School, and Mike Staunton, director of the London Share Price Database at London Business School, that from 1900 to 2016 US long-dated bonds delivered a premium (geometric) return over Treasury bills of 1.1% per year and that the premium for the index for 22 countries outside the United States since 1900 was 0.7% per year. However, it is unclear how much premium, if any, should be expected from inflation-linked government bonds over Treasury bills. The experience to date is strongly influenced by the monetary policy background and the tax regime in the countries concerned and is too short to be conclusive.

John Campbell, Morton L. and Carole S. Olshan professor of economics at Harvard University; Robert Shiller, Arthur M. Okun professor of economics at Yale University; and Luis Viceira, George E. Bates professor at Harvard Business School, in their 2009 study "Understanding Inflation-Indexed Bond markets" highlight a number of different factors influencing the relationship between conventional and inflation-linked government bonds. Although there are good reasons to expect conventional government bonds to outperform index-linked over long periods, there are contrary influences that could cause them to underperform. Campbell, Shiller and Viceira conclude that the experience of recent years of marked short-term volatility and very low yields for inflation-linked government bonds does "not invalidate the basic case for these bonds, that they provide a safe asset for long-term investors".

The place of safe-harbour government bonds in strategy

The conclusions in deriving assumptions for modelling investment strategy (developed further in Chapter 6) can be summarised as follows:

■ Inflation-linked bonds should provide a benchmark for long-term investors just as Treasury bills provide a benchmark for short-term investors.

■ It is reasonable to assume that they will provide no premium return over Treasury bills in the medium term.

In the absence of inflation surprises, conventional bonds are likely to provide some inflation risk premium over inflation-linked bonds, but this may average no more than 0.25% per year. However, there may be an illiquidity premium in yields on inflation-linked bonds which offsets this. In the UK, biases in the official measure of inflation mean that UK real interest rates appear unusually low in comparison with other countries, but, despite this, conventional gilts (UK government bonds) may outperform inflation-linked gilts by only a small margin in the future.

The most cautious long-term investors may have an anchor holding of inflation-linked bonds, but at times of lesser inflation uncertainty (or greater confidence in the monetary authorities' ability to restrict the range of future inflation), high-quality conventional bonds are likely to replace inflation-linked bonds as the core holdings of many long-term investors. This reflects both their greater liquidity (and so lower transaction costs and flexibility), a possible inflation risk premium and the convenience of their greater regular income distribution.

The equity risk premium

Triumph of the Optimists is the title that Dimson, Marsh and Staunton gave the first edition, published in 2002, of their path-breaking review of returns since 1900 from stocks, bonds and cash in 17 countries (which has since been extended to 23 countries). Their message was that equity investors had done better than they should reasonably have hoped in the 20th century and that they should expect the 21st century to be less generous for long-term equity investors. As if on cue, the new century started terribly for equity investors, and despite a strong recovery after 2008, by December 2016 the total return on world equities in US dollars, after allowing for inflation, was just 1.9% ahead of the end-1999 level, and for probably most investors, after allowing for fees, trading costs and, for many, taxation, would have been behind. According to the Dimson, Marsh and Staunton data, 2008's total return, before fees and expenses, of -37% for US equities was the second-worst calendar-year performance ever recorded for the United States; and for the world, excluding the United States, 2008's performance of -43% was the worst on record. (Rolling 12-month data for the 1930s indicate much worse experiences in 1932.) For the ten years to December 2008 the return, again before expenses and also before allowing for inflation, for the

US market was -0.6% a year, the first negative ten-year return since the 1930s; it was not until 2010 that the ten-year return was positive again.

So what performance should equity investors expect and how does it relate to the performance from bonds and cash? This is an area of great controversy and therefore uncertainty. This uncertainty matters and needs to be reflected in the design of investment strategy.

The starting point is history. In recent years much academic research into historical market performance has been published. The original pioneers in this were Roger Ibbotson, a professor in the practice of finance at Yale School of Management, and Rex Sinquefield, co-founder of money managers Dimensional Fund Advisors, who in 1976 jointly published long-run databases of carefully constructed returns data for the United States back to 1926. Shiller has extended this back to 1871. In the past few years this US work has been substantially extended, most notably by the Dimson, Marsh and Staunton international research.

FIGURE 4.11 **US cash, government bonds and stockmarket cumulative performance*** in pounds sterling, after inflation, 1900–2016, Dec 1899 = 1.0

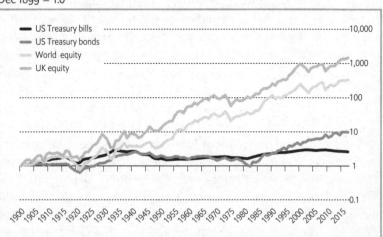

* Performance before all costs, fees and taxes.
Source: Dimson, E., Marsh, P. and Staunton, M., 2017

FIGURE 4.12 **UK cash, government bonds and stockmarket cumulative performance*** in pounds sterling, after inflation, 1900–2016, Dec 1899 = 1.0

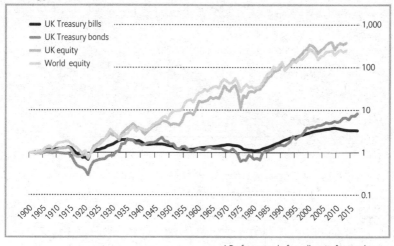

* Performance before all costs, fees and taxes.
Source: Dimson, E., Marsh, P. and Staunton, M., 2017

TABLE 4.1 **Long-run market performance and risk**
After inflation but before all fees and expenses, 1900-2016

	Performance % pa*			Volatility % pa			Minimum annual return		
	World **	US	UK	World**	US	UK	World**	US	UK
Treasury bills	..	0.8	1.0	..	4.6	6.3	..	−15.1	−15.7
Bonds	1.8	2.0	1.8	11.2	10.4	13.7	−32.0	−18.4	−30.7
Equities	5.1	6.4	5.5	17.4	20.0	19.6	−41.4	−38.4	−57.1

* Geometric annualised returns including impact of inflation on volatility of returns.
** World bond index is weighted by GDP; world equity index is weighted by capitalisation; world index returns and volatility are shown in dollars.

Source: Dimson, E., Marsh, P. and Staunton, M., 2002 and 2017

FIGURE 4.13 **Cumulative performance of equities relative to long-dated government bonds** 1899–2016, Dec 1899 = 1

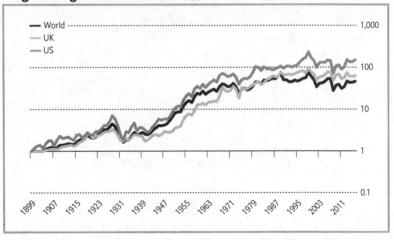

Sources: Dimson E., Marsh P. and Staunton M., 2002 and 2017

The data conclusively show that, apart from two notable exceptions, in all countries covered by Dimson, Marsh and Staunton's work equities have, over the longest periods measured, outperformed both government bonds and Treasury bills and so risk-taking has eventually been rewarded. The two exceptions are Russia, where investors in stocks and bonds effectively lost everything in 1917, and mainland China, where investors lost almost everything in 1949. The more general and familiar pattern is highlighted in Figures 4.11 and 4.12, which show historical investment market performance from the perspective of investors with the US dollar or the UK pound as their base currency. Table 4.1 gives a summary of the performance and risk as revealed by the Dimson, Marsh and Staunton annual data for 23 countries from 1900 to 2016, showing results for the world (as measured by these 23 countries) and the United States and the UK, the two most important national markets over the past century. In Table 4.1 the data incorporate the impact of the losses in Russia and China (Russia represented around 6% of world equity market capitalisation in 1899, while China was much smaller).

Recent experience and a close examination of the data reveal that this pattern of equity outperformance has sometimes taken a long

FIGURE 4.14 **20-year equity risk premium over Treasury bills**
% per annum, 1919–2016

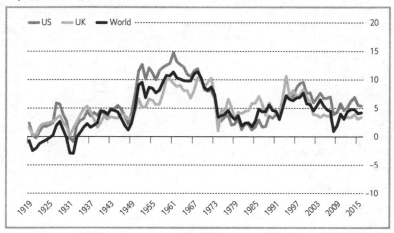

Source: Dimson E., Marsh P. and Staunton M., 2002 and 2017

FIGURE 4.15 **20-year equity risk premium over government bonds**
% per annum, 1919–2016

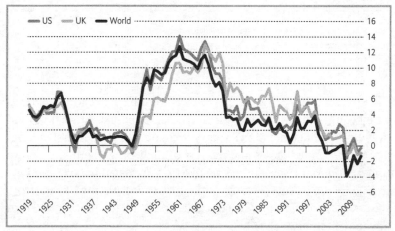

Source: Dimson E., Marsh P. and Staunton M., 2002 and 2017

TABLE 4.2 **Longest periods ending December 2016 of equities underperforming long-dated government bonds***

	Geometric return, % per year, after inflation	Excess over cash, % per year
USA: Dec 1980–Dec 2012		
Cash	1.6	
Treasury bonds	7.2	5.4
Equities	7.1	5.3
UK Dec 1986–Dec 2015		
Cash	2.7	
Treasury bonds	6.2	3.4
Equities	6.2	3.4
World Dec 1968–Dec 2012		
Cash	0.9	
Treasury bonds	4.9	4.0
Equities	4.6	3.6

* Data shown is after inflation and before fees, transaction costs and taxes.

Source: Dimson, E., Marsh, P. and Staunton, M., 2002 and 2017

time to assert itself. Figure 4.13 shows there have been long periods when equities have not outperformed cash or bonds. This applies not only to individual small markets, which are not well diversified, but also to the United States and the rest of the world. Figure 4.13 shows underperformance by equities relative to long-dated bonds from 1980 to 2012 for the US equity market, from 1986 to 2012 for the UK, and from 1968 to 2012 for the world in aggregate. These are long-term periods in anyone's lifetime.

Figures 4.14 and 4.15 show the 20-year excess returns from equities over cash (Treasury bills) and long-dated Treasury bonds from the United States, the UK and the world, as measured by the 23 countries covered by the Dimson, Marsh and Staunton research. The figures indicate that the long-term underperformance by equities relative to government bonds in recent years had parallels in the 1930s and 1940s.

Table 4.2 shows performance of equities, government bonds and cash separately for the longest periods to 2016 over which equities have underperformed government bonds. These show that these instances reflect not the weakness of equity market performance but the unusual, and surely unrepeatable, performance of government bond markets. Equity market performance over these periods has not been unusual relative to cash nor in absolute terms (after inflation). A repeat of such performance over similar numbers of years by government bonds from the low level of bond yields in late 2017 is almost inconceivable, and although the returns from equity markets shown in Table 4.2 are mostly higher than would on average be expected, they are comfortably within the range of likely outcomes.

So much for history: what matters for setting strategy is what we expect for the future. The majority view is that the 20th century was kinder to equity investors than they should reasonably have expected, and that the 21st century is likely to be pay-back time (because a margin of last century's performance was brought forward or "borrowed" from the future). The broad story is that a significant part of the outperformance by stockmarkets in the 20th century was because they started cheap and ended expensive, and that the process of becoming more expensive explains a significant part of their historical outperformance of both cash and bonds. Translating this into expectations for the future is impeded as there is disagreement about the normal level of the market, for example in relation to company earnings.

Academic economists often use the equity risk premium in theoretical models of asset pricing, one famous example being the capital asset pricing model (see Chapter 8). However, there are few simple well-known models that tell us what the equity risk premium is and how it might change if economic conditions change. For example, changes that might be pertinent could include whether the number of retail investors changed; or if the total amount of wealth in the stockmarket changed; or if there were technological changes.

We have noted that theory fails to explain what the equity risk premium should be. It also fails to explain how it might change in time. This is referred to as the dynamics of the stockmarket. One version of this, discussed elsewhere, is that prices follow a random walk so that returns are random. High returns could be followed by high or low returns without any predictability. An alternative view is the notion of mean reversion, by which we might look for valuations of the stockmarket to revert towards the average from the past (see Chapter 5). However, others suggest that we should expect the stockmarket to be priced more expensively than on average in the past because investors can now easily invest at less risk and less expensively because of the wider use of pooled funds, and especially index funds and well-diversified exchange traded funds. If investors can access the market less expensively, this raises the equity risk premium for those investors. There is apparent consensus that bond returns have in recent decades been unsustainable, as yields have been driven to historical low levels, and that going forward bond performance will be disappointing, either because bond yields will recover (as, to some extent, the markets are predicting) and so prices will tend to fall, or because yields will stay low for a long period and so provide a modest return. There is a range of views as to where government bond yields will stabilise. In the interim, for equities to be expected to perform poorly relative to bonds, they would need to be thought expensive in 2017.

At the start of the 21st century, finance experts differed on prospects for the superior return that should be earned from equity investing, and those differences show no sign of abating. There is increasing (but not consensus) agreement that medium-term prospects need to take some account of whether the market is cheap or expensive at the outset. A variation on this is that since market risk evidently fluctuates, investors should want and expect a higher risk premium when the market is more volatile. This may coincide with times that the market is less expensive, but it might not. Although this sounds like common sense, there is also agreement that it is difficult to exploit valuation indicators to earn higher returns (see Chapter 5), and there would be quite wide support for the idea that it is fruitless to adjust expectations used in long-term planning except when the stockmarket appears to be either unusually expensive or unusually cheap. Another complication is that the relevant equity risk premium will vary out from one investor to another. For example, if the margin over Treasury bills or bonds at which investors can borrow for a mortgage increases, they may find it more attractive to prepay their mortgage rather than invest in equities for their pension.

Lower estimates of future returns are produced by researchers who believe that the stockmarket is expensive. A survey of the future geometric average annual returns from equity investing (measured as a premium over the risk-free rate) in 2001 ranged from zero to 7%, with an average of just below 4%. There is increasing agreement that at some times the risk premium may be higher than at other times. A more recent range of projections would be similar, with the average close to 4%. But this is by no means universally agreed. In 2011, Rob Arnott, chairman of Research Affiliates, an investment manager, wrote:

This brief history lesson illuminates that the much-vaunted 4–5% risk premium for stocks is unreliable and a dangerous assumption on which to make our future plans. In our view, a more reasonable analysis would suggest 2–3%, which is the historic risk premium absent the rise in valuation multiples in the past 30 years.

Dimson, Marsh and Staunton, in their 2017 Credit Suisse Global Investment Returns Yearbook say, "we infer that investors expect an equity premium (relative to bills) of around 3–3½%" as a geometric average for world equities, and conclude that a reasonable premium for investing in long-dated government bonds is close to 1% per annum. This would mean that they infer that the expected equity premium return over fixed-income government bonds is a bit over 2–2½%.

Corporate finance asks a different but related question: what premium rate of return above the rate guaranteed by the government is required by businesses to tempt them to invest? Pablo Fernandez, together with Vitaly Pershin and Isabel Acin, all of IESE Business School at the University of Navarra in Barcelona, regularly publish the results of internet surveys of assessments of required rates of return from academics, investment analysts and business executives. Their 2017 survey produced over 4,000 responses from 68 countries, of which 64% were from seven countries: the United States, Spain, Germany, France, the UK, Italy and Canada. These show a noticeable pattern: the median responses from developed countries tend to be grouped between 5% and 7%, while for emerging markets they most commonly lie between 7% and 9%.

We have previously mentioned that there is a view that the pattern of stockmarket returns is essentially a random walk – that is, a matter of rolling the dice from one period to another. A view that reflects the random walk approach to the world can be found in the standard MBA corporate finance textbook, *Principles of Corporate Finance*, by Richard Brealey, Stewart Myers and Franklin Allen. As the authors point out:

> *Many financial managers and economists believe that long-run historical returns are the best measure available ... out of this debate only one firm conclusion emerges: Do not trust anyone who claims to know what returns investors expect.*

As mentioned above, there is though increasing support for the view that the level of the stockmarket (and the level of bond market prices) can tell us whether returns will be higher or lower in the period ahead. This is considered in more detail in the next chapter.

This debate has little effect on the likelihood of next year's equity market performance being disappointing. But it does have a large impact on the prospects for wealth accumulation from equities over long periods, particularly the potential for disappointing returns from equity markets over extended periods. The one thing any investor can do to raise their expected returns from equity investing is to be vigilant about the fees that they pay; this also has a large impact on wealth accumulation over extended periods of time.

Don't bank on time diversifying risk

The size of the equity risk premium would be of less concern if it was true that equities are "less risky" for long-term investors than for short-term investors. This is a separate area of debate with strong differences of opinion – and therefore much confusion – among investors. But what are the experts saying?

The longer the time horizon the more likely it is that stockmarket indices will outperform bonds or cash, simply because on average stocks are expected to perform better. Furthermore, the longer the period the more likely it is that this cumulative outperformance will translate into an increasingly large proportion of the initial investment. Long-term investors in equities should expect to do better on average than investors in bonds or cash, and the longer the period of time, the better in monetary terms they should expect, on average, to do. So long as equity investors are offered a positive risk premium, which more than outweighs the extra investment management fees they pay, this should be uncontroversial.

The real issue is the risk of disappointing results over longer periods of time and how this can compound into an increasingly large shortfall, and how strongly investors should be assumed to want to avoid the pain caused by such shortfalls. This has always been a central focus of finance, and it has been brought into even sharper focus through the work on loss aversion in behavioural finance. The experimental work on loss aversion discussed in Chapter 2 suggests that investors are probably twice as sensitive to the prospect of losses as they are to gains.

For long periods (up to twenty years or so), the risks of equities underperforming long-term bonds and cash are not negligible, even though equities are, on average, expected to outperform bonds and cash by a wide cumulative margin. Table 4.2 shows that it is possible to find long periods when equities underperformed long-dated government bonds. This is thirty-two years in the case of the Dimson data for the US ending in December 2012, and even longer – 44 years – for global data. These are very long periods, though as Table 4.2 also shows, stockmarket performance itself was not disappointing. These examples are, for many people, more persuasive than the health warnings produced by a quantitative model whose assumptions will always be subject to debate, and therefore doubt.

Table 4.3 shows the results of just such a modelling exercise in which 2,000 possible outcomes for equity markets have been simulated by replicating the summary characteristics of how the US markets have behaved since 1900. Of course, actual experience is only one of many possible outcomes. The table shows a range of outcomes for stockmarket performance, from the disappointing 5th percentile, through the median or 50th percentile outcome to the favourable 95th percentile outcome, and it shows these simulated results over 5, 10 and 20 years. It also shows that in at least half of the modelled scenarios, equities far outperform the expected performance of bonds and cash, with the potential in strongly favourable markets for substantial

TABLE 4.3 **Does time diversify away risk of disappointing equity market performance?**

	100% Treasury bills as low-risk strategy			100% Treasury bonds as low-risk strategy		
	5 years	10 years	20 years	5 years	10 years	20 years
$100 in low-risk strategy "becomes", after inflation *:	105	110	121	111	123	152
$100 in all equity strategy "becomes" :						
95th percentile	263	482	1,305	263	482	1,305
50th percentile	135	182	331	135	182	331
5th percentile	69	69	84	69	69	84

* 50th percentile outcomes for bonds and Treasury bills shown.
Source: Authors' calculations based on historical risks and returns using Dimson, Marsh and Staunton data for returns, after inflation, for US stocks, bonds and cash 1900–2012.

outperformance. Nevertheless, the 5th percentile unfavourable outcome for equities is shown lagging behind cash and bonds over each period.

In recent years, there has been growing agreement that the standard statistical assumptions underlying Table 4.3 understate short-term risk (crashes happen more often than the models assume) and might overstate long-term equity risk. This is because a body of academic research supports the widely held view that, to some extent, markets "overreact" (in relation to the standard assumptions underlying the table). If this is true, then if investment returns have been above average, they are likely subsequently to come down, and if they have been below average, they are likely to increase. This process of overreaction, where good market performance is expected to be followed by poorer performance, is called "mean reversion". A result of this is that equity markets would vary less over time than traditional models would suggest. If this is true, stockmarket volatility measured over, say, decades or 20-year periods would be "less" than would be expected if we were simply to extrapolate short-term volatility. However, the degree to which it is the case, and its explanations, are controversial, particularly among academic researchers.

The simple, easy-to-use modelling that underlies Table 4.3 (and many savings planning exercises) has been widely criticised. But these approaches continue to be used, partly because there is no agreement on how to replace them. However, the weakness of these models needs to be reflected in how wealth planning is presented. An expectation that a risk-based strategy is likely, but not certain, to achieve an objective is often reassuring enough. If investors want more certainty (for their "safety-first" portfolio – see Chapter 2), the underlying investment strategy needs to be based on hedging using tailored inflation-linked or conventional government bonds. Often the honest message is that the price of such insurance is too high, and many investors have little choice but to live with a significant degree of uncertainty.

At present, the best guide to the risk of equities underperforming cash or bonds is given by examining the historical data. As discussed above, the prevailing view of finance academics is that the 21st century is likely to be less favourable to equity markets than the 20th century was. Furthermore, allowance needs to be made for the drag of investment fees and transaction costs and, where relevant, for tax. So a reasonable assumption would be that the incidence of disappointing equity markets will be higher in the 21st century than it was in the 20th. The first decade was certainly consistent with this. As recent experience shows, the risk of equity strategies underperforming safe-haven investment strategies over long periods needs to be taken seriously. These are not remote events to be dismissed as exceptional bad luck: these things happen.

Finally, we should mention that the notion that the equity risk premium is a constant, whether it is 3% or 6%, is open to question. As discussed earlier in this chapter, yields for different bonds will vary with their time to maturity; the usual situation being that as time to maturity increases, yields increase. Likewise, the presence of mean reversion in the equity market would suggest that expected market returns can vary with the holding period measured in per–year terms. Consequently, the risk premium itself is likely to vary.

Manager performance

The choice of investment manager may seem critical to both retail and institutional investors. There are, however, some circumstances where the variation in manager performance may be small. Indeed, there are some circumstances where one may not wish to choose an active manager, but rather to invest in index funds or exchange traded funds, both of which typically have low costs. This situation will arise when the market is efficient and there are few opportunities for active management. Recent research based on hundreds of US institutional accounts monitored by eVestment LLC, a database provider to institutional investors and fund managers, shows how managers' ability to outperform seems to vary from one market to another. (See "Information ratios and the distribution of skill" by Hall, Satchell and Spence. (2017))

This research found that active equity accounts in US large capitalisation stocks have tended to underperform the index while charging active fees, while in other markets active management can be attractive. For example, the research shows that emerging market equity funds have often outperformed their appropriate index. However, in the world of retail funds, changes in assets under management (AUM) are strongly correlated with the last few months of fund returns. If funds have done well recently, retail investors will place their money in these funds. Regulators always advise against this, but this advice is routinely ignored.

The evidence appears to be that this pattern of recent good performance attracts new inflows which then leads to future poor performance. Intuitively, this seems to be due to the diseconomies of scale associated with investment processes. This means that a particular strategy will have some optimal size beyond which the returns per dollar invested will start to decrease. Given this, the criteria for manager selection assumes importance. Instead of recent performance, more appropriate criteria for selection include:

1. Long-term performance
2. Investment style
3. Risk-adjusted performance

4. Forecasting ability
5. Ratings

Long-term performance is usually based on three or more years of past returns. Funds that fail to have this are often excluded by consultants as potential investment choices. Investment houses sometimes run what are called *incubator funds*. These run for say, three years, and the ones that have done badly are withdrawn from consideration. The ones that have done well are then presented to the investors. If we were to take a thousand funds, randomly constructed, which on average have a return of zero, then we might expect 500 to have returns above zero, and 500 to have returns below zero and 125 to have outperformed by chance in each of three successive years.

Investment style describes ways in which active funds communicate to the investor their particular mode of investment. Typical examples might be value or growth funds; the former describes a strategy of buying stocks that are currently cheap, the latter describes a strategy of buying stocks whose dividends/earnings are expected to grow in the future (see Chapter 6). These funds can charge extra fees relative to index funds and this gives fund managers the incentive potentially to misrepresent their activities. Such miscreance is referred to as "closet indexing". Broadly speaking, value funds and growth funds can be distinguished from an index fund, but blended funds, which are sold as mixtures of value and growth, can look remarkably like index funds.

Risk-adjusted performance. Although investors are often happy to get higher returns, however they are gained, more financially literate investors would want to know how much risk the fund has taken with their money. They would calculate the risk premium of the fund divided by the risk of the fund (often measured as a standard deviation). Such a ratio – which has many names including the Sharpe ratio, the Information ratio, and the Sortino ratio – can be a sensible way to consider risk-adjusted performance (so long as the underlying investments are liquid) and has the added benefit that we need only know the return histories of the fund and the benchmark to calculate these quantities.

Forecasting ability. Active managers and analysts are often seen as forecasters of future returns of assets that they invest in or advise on. One metric of active manager performance is called the information coefficient, which looks at the correlation between the forecasts made by the manager and the actual outcomes. The difficulty with this measure is that this information is usually not made available by the active manager. In addition, analysts are notoriously unhappy about having their recommendations investigated rigorously. Thus, the advice that one should buy an asset is based on the idea that it will reach or exceed some target price at some unspecified time in the future. Generally, attempts to investigate their performance are hampered by the imprecision of the advice offered.

Fund ratings. The global financial crisis and the collapse in value of many financial instruments with very high ratings led to a reputational loss for the rating companies. This is unfortunate in that many of these companies had teams of highly experienced, professional employees who had spent many years looking at retail investment products. The ratings that they give have been highly informative about the overall management structure of the fund. Some empirical findings by Louth, Satchell and Wongwachara (2014) suggest that higher rated mutual funds have better returns and suffer less from client outflows when the market is falling, although their returns tend to be lower than low-rated funds when the market is rising. If a smooth return to investments is better than a volatile return, then high rated funds may be preferred.

Investment manager selection is one aspect of investing wealth. It is not the most important. There are further considerations which fall into a broader concept, which is termed "wealth management". This would include wealth management for families. Manager selection in this context means finding someone who will appreciate saving and spending decisions through time, possibly across individuals, and even generations. This now becomes very specialised and the exercise is one of matching the highly idiosyncratic needs of private investors with the skills of the potential managers. Although many wealth management firms claim to possess the entire gamut of skills, in reality this is unlikely and simple mechanisms that match clients and managers are desirable. One such mechanism is to set up wealth funds based on profession, which will automatically create a great deal of homogeneity and can allow managers to improve their skills without having to consider numerous extraneous and irrelevant issues.

5

Advice and investment strategy

Choosing an adviser

Choosing a financial adviser or financial planner is the most important investment decision that investors make and is likely to influence strongly the investment strategy they adopt, and how their wealth and the income it generates evolve over time. Good financial planning advice is extremely valuable, so investors must be willing to pay for it. Giving good advice will involve teasing out from investors their objectives and their motivations as well as their aversion to incurring losses or failing to meet objectives. Such discussions can be intensely personal, and for the relationship to be successful, the investor needs to be frank with an adviser. For this, there needs to be respect between the investor and the adviser. A successful advisory relationship is rarely restricted to investment advice. If self-advised investors or investors who are advised by pure investment advisers fail to account for the full range of financial planning issues (including, for example, tax and generational planning), they may not know if they are meeting their objectives, or if they are doing so efficiently.

An often overlooked feature of investment advice is the extent to which it is influenced by the particular views of the investment adviser: how the adviser thinks that investments should best be managed. For a successful relationship to develop, an adviser's principles and opinions about wealth and investment management need to be well aligned with the objectives and preferences of the investor.

Investment beliefs

Different advisers embrace different approaches to investment, which often reflect deeply held beliefs about how best to invest. For example, some advisers will look at the roller-coaster journey of equity markets in the years after 2000 and conclude that investors have to try to time markets, to avoid the "bad times" and to pay quite high fees to invest in funds which try to do this. Others will be more sceptical, and suggest that this is unlikely to be rewarding, and will more naturally stick to a pre-agreed strategy, perhaps anchored in the security of government bonds. A third group will from time to time suggest revisions to the strategy if they are convinced that one or other market is markedly overpriced or underpriced. These three options represent important differences of approach, which will be reflected in different levels of activity in a portfolio, and potentially quite different investment outcomes. These are areas of debate on which advisers may have strong views, which would be reflected in their investment advice. Another major area of difference is whether an adviser expects to identify skilled managers who can, net of fees, with some consistency outperform in particular markets (see the previous chapter). Related to both these is the issue of whether to invest in high-cost investment vehicles, such as private equity or hedge funds.

These differences of opinion are reflected in debates about how the largest and also the most modest investors should invest. Institutional investors often describe their views on these debates as their "investment beliefs". Many institutional investors take time to record their beliefs, and publish them, as a form of public accountability. These are tailored to their understanding of the opportunities presented by markets and their own particular circumstances, and they reflect (or should reflect) the way they invest.

Investment beliefs are implicit in how an investor invests. The same applies to the varying recommendations that different advisers make to investors. These will reflect differences of opinion – for example, on the costs and benefits of paying high or low fees, or accepting illiquidity, and on the ability to time markets – and, more generally, differences in style of investing. An important part of building trust in a relationship with an adviser is for investors to have an understanding of their adviser's investment beliefs, and to find them both credible and appropriate for their particular circumstances.

One risk for self-advised investors is that they may not have properly thought through their attitudes to investment markets. This can be particularly dangerous if they fail to account sufficiently for the likelihood of "bad times" in how they design their strategy. Furthermore, in bad times, having a trusted adviser to consult, and to remind them why the strategy is designed as it is, can be of great value. A poorly self-designed strategy that, for example, generates income in good times only by incurring risks of loss of capital and income in bad times can easily prove to be an irreversible mistake.

Conflicts of interest

Regulation in a number of countries is pushing advice towards explicit advisory fees and away from transaction commissions. This is helpful for encouraging an advice-driven rather than a sales-driven culture in the management of wealth. However, both good and poor advice can come from either approach to remunerating advisers.

The potential for conflicts of interest between investors and their advisers is often known as the principal–agent problem, or more loosely as "agency issues". These arise because the principal (the investor) has inferior access to information than the agent (the investment adviser) does. This can encourage advisers to use superior information in a way that serves their own interest rather than the best interest of the investor. Although institutional investors typically have structures that can mitigate this, such conflicts are common. One way investors can reduce their exposure to these conflicts is to distance themselves from much of the detailed investment decision-making, and employ discretionary investment managers whose remuneration is transparent and who are (depending on the jurisdiction) under an obligation to provide best execution to their clients. However, this can easily lead to advice which is less well tailored to the circumstances of an investor, and some investments, which best suit particular investors, may be available only on an advisory basis.

Many private clients prefer an advisory relationship where they retain control over each investment decision. The danger is that this can also lead to the accumulation of a portfolio of ad hoc investments, each of which "seemed a good idea at the time". However, with good advice this can be avoided, and effective management of overall risk and balance in a strategy maintained. The danger, though, is that investors will be sold what an adviser wishes to sell rather than deciding to buy what they need for their investment strategy. The best safeguard is for investors to satisfy themselves that their interests and those of their advisers are appropriately aligned, and that conflicts of interest are in the open. In practice, reassurance on this will depend more on the characters of the individuals concerned than the institutional arrangements within which they work.

Ultimately, no advisory business model will be successful if it fails to put the establishment and nurturing of trust between clients and their advisers first. However, investors must always be aware that conflicts of interest are endemic in the financial services industry. The key to unlocking the problem of these conflicts is to have transparency of fee arrangements and then to decide, on a case-by-case basis, how to proceed. The general message is "buyer, beware". For some categories of investor (or investor account) in some jurisdictions, regulators insist on disclosure of all sources of investment management or private bank remuneration from a client account. Clients should request information on the adviser's (or the bank's) financial interest in a proposed transaction.

Lastly, remember that good advice is valuable, and when the going gets tough, simple handholding by an adviser which prevents short-term mistakes may be the most valuable service that the adviser provides. Superficially it will come for free – but there is a relationship that provides fee income for the adviser and access to advice for the investor. The self-advised investor misses out on this. Know what you are paying, and review but don't quibble over each item. Make sure that you are comfortable with the overall level of fees, and do, from time to time, ask your advisers whether they would make a recommended investment on their own account. Low fees do not ensure that good advice is being offered, or that an investment strategy is sensible or that risk-taking is appropriate, but over periods of years, differences in fee levels do make a significant difference to wealth accumulation.

How should investor strategies evolve?

Model investment strategies

The debate discussed in the previous chapter about the returns to be expected from the stockmarket is partly a debate between those who think that stockmarket performance over time can best be explained as a statistical "random walk", where forecasting is pointless but on average risk-taking gets rewarded – and those who think that market returns are mean reverting, with higher than average returns being followed by periods of disappointing returns and vice versa. This debate has important implications for the design of investment strategy and the role of long-term model allocations between stocks, bonds, cash and other asset classes. These are sometimes called "strategic asset allocations" or "policy portfolios". The role of such models, and how they help to differentiate between investors with different appetites for taking risk, is discussed in Chapter 6, but an important feature is that they anchor actual investments around the model allocations, no matter what is happening in markets.

In 2003 the late Peter Bernstein wrote an article in the Economics and Portfolio Strategy newsletter titled "Are policy portfolios obsolete?" This question has probably become more relevant with the passing of time. In the first decade of this century, adherence to fixed long-term asset allocation models led many investors to experience declines in investment values that exceeded their worst-case expectations, first after the bursting of the technology and telecom stockmarket boom in 2000, and then as the banking crisis unfolded in 2008–09. As the previous chapter showed, over time periods that matter to investors, a fixed approach to risk-taking cannot be fully relied on to be profitable. In 2017, Andrew Lo wrote that "risk isn't necessarily always rewarded – it depends on the environment". Likewise, in 2003 Bernstein wrote: "Investment policy in today's environment should be opportunistic, to be played more by ear than by rigid policy allocations." He went on to quote Keynes, who wrote in 1924:

> [The] long run is a misleading guide to current affairs. In the long run we are all dead. Economists set themselves too easy, too useless a task if in the tempestuous seasons they can only tell us that when the storm is long past the ocean will be flat.

Even long-term investment funds such as university endowments or sovereign wealth funds, which may be confident of enduring from generation to generation, may find it difficult to act as truly long-term investors. The mundane necessity of needing to maintain the confidence of a long-term fund's stakeholders matters throughout the investment journey. Investment policies, which are prospectively rewarding but in recent years underperforming, may easily lead to a reversal in policy, which with hindsight might be judged ill-timed. To paraphrase an aphorism attributed to Keynes, markets can stay irrational longer than stakeholders will tolerate an underperforming investment committee.

Underlying the criticism of fixed long-term investment strategies is a belief that analysis can tell us whether markets are cheap or expensive, and that when a market is expensive the risk of losing money is increased. Few claim to be able to predict when a market will correct, but they do not doubt that markets do eventually correct, or that they revert to their average relationships. A similar but slightly different criticism of long-term strategy models is that markets experience different regimes or environments and that investment policy ought to respond to the different market conditions that they represent.

The notion of different market climates can best be illustrated by looking at how stockmarket volatility has fluctuated over the years, and of how the pricing of the stockmarket has evolved. Figure 5.1 shows the leading indicator and measure of stockmarket volatility, VIX, from 1990 to 2017. It highlights both the extraordinary increase in stockmarket volatility in 2007–09 and also how benign the market environment appears to have between 2003 and 2007 and in 2016–17. Since VIX reflects option pricing, it indicates fluctuations in the cost of insuring against a stockmarket crash, this being low when VIX is low and high when VIX is high. Figure 5.1 also shows what would be described as regime changes. Almost any investment strategy had a much higher risk of exceeding some threshold tolerance for negative returns in the more volatile environment of 2008–09 than when it was more moderate. This suggests that investors who are particularly sensitive to the risk of losing money should attempt to return towards their safe haven of government bonds or cash when market volatility increases. One practical issue with this is that a sudden increase in

FIGURE 5.1 **VIX indicator of US stockmarket volatility** Jan 1990–Sep 2017

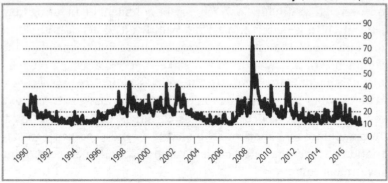

Source: www.cboe.com

market volatility is likely to have been caused by a sudden fall in prices, making such a response a reaction to recent losses.

The argument that markets overreact and then revert towards trend or even overshoot in the opposite direction is closely related to the arguments in favour of a value style of equity investing (see Chapter 8) and the search for "inexpensive" equities and the desire to avoid those that are thought to be overpriced. Corresponding arguments also apply to the level of the stockmarket. Figure 5.2 shows Robert Shiller's cyclically adjusted price/earnings ratio, also known as CAPE, or the "Shiller PE". The Shiller PE is the ratio of the inflation-adjusted level of the S&P composite stock price index to the inflation-adjusted ten-year moving average of the reported earnings of the companies in the index. Shiller made considerable use of this indicator of stockmarket value in his book Irrational Exuberance, the publication of which in early 2000 coincided with the peak overvaluation, as indicated in Figure 5.2, since stockmarket records began. The Shiller PE focuses on the valuation that the stockmarket places on the historical stream of corporate earnings, and shows a pattern of stockmarket overreaction and reversion to the mean. Shiller includes a chart relating the value of the cyclically-adjusted PE ratio to the subsequent ten-year performance of the stockmarket: for well over 100 years. High levels of the Shiller PE have tended to be followed by relatively poor stockmarket performance, and low levels of the Shiller PE by better-than-average performance.

FIGURE 5.2 **S&P 500 "Shiller" price/earnings ratio** 1880–2017

Source: Shiller, R., *Irrational Exuberance*, as updated, www.econ.yale.edu

FIGURE 5.3 **Spread between single A credit indices and highest-rated government bond indices** % per year, 2000–2017

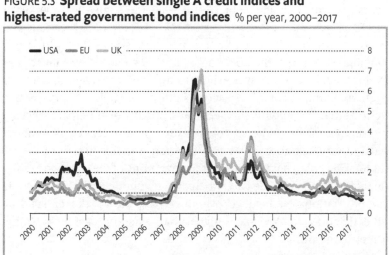

Source: Bloomberg LP, using Bloomberg Barclays indices

With hindsight, few would dispute the importance of the message this gives at extremes of valuation, and this emphasises the benefits of being able to adjust strategy. The equity market is not alone in appearing to show valuations revert towards trend. Figure 5.3 shows for the United States, the UK and the euro zone the difference between the yields on single A-rated investment grade debt indices (see Chapter 8) and indices of government debt (Germany in the case of the euro zone).

Differences between the indices mean that the comparisons in Figure 5.3 are indicative rather than exact measures, but corporate bond yields provide another indicator of value that seems to range between periods of offering too little reward for risk-taking (as immediately before the credit crunch) and periods of offering the prospect of generous risk-adjusted returns. This is discussed further in Chapter 9.

Figures 5.1, 5.2 and 5.3 reflect the incidence of booms and busts in risk asset markets. Advice to avoid speculative excess is easier to give than to implement successfully. In practice, success does not come easily to professional investment managers who seek to time markets, and some consultants have at times given up trying to identify managers who can add value in this way. The equity bear market of 2008–09 was much more severe than that of 2000–02, which followed a boom in technology, media and telecoms stocks. But with a few notable exceptions, the 2008–09 equity bear market was much less well anticipated in advance. The buoyant credit markets in 2005–07 were much more commonly seen as offering inadequate prospective returns than were equity markets. The difficulty of anticipating events presents a major challenge for investors, and it echoes a comment made in August 2002 by Alan Greenspan, then chairman of the US Federal Reserve. Looking back on the unwinding of the late 1990s equity market boom, which he had anticipated by publicly voicing concerns about "irrational exuberance" over three years prior to the market peak in early 2000, at a level 80% higher than when he gave his warning, Greenspan said:

> As events evolved, we recognised that, despite our suspicions, it was very difficult to definitively identify a bubble until after the fact – that is, when its bursting confirmed its existence.

Greenspan's comments should encourage people to be modest about their ability to call markets successfully. This sense of modesty encourages some to argue that long-term investors should stick close to their strategic asset allocations and buy-and-hold equities through thick and thin. The reasoning behind this recommendation is that market timing is hazardous and, for many advisers, equities are less risky for long-term investors. John Campbell and others agree that equities seem to be less risky over long time horizons than is suggested by their short-run volatility because equities "mean revert". If this is correct, Campbell argues that investors should overweight equities when they are expected to perform better than average and underweight them when they are expected to do worse than average. Many would say that this is "easier said than done, except after the event".

Following 2008, the more usual concern was the dilemma of how to react to unusually low government bond yields. "Quantitative easing" by central banks was initially designed to relieve financial market distress in 2008–09 and then evolved into supporting the economy (and, in the euro zone, of relieving the crisis in peripheral government bond markets). The US Federal Reserve and the Bank of England acquired in excess of one-quarter of the US and UK national debts respectively (while the European Central Bank and the Bank of Japan greatly facilitated their lending to banks). In the United States and the UK, these bond-buying programmes (including in the United States purchases of mortgages by the Federal Reserve) were intended to reduce the yields on low-risk assets and so lower the cost of borrowing, whether for mortgages or for business. In the process, existing holders of Treasury bonds were enticed to sell, and presumably to buy higher-risk assets instead. Quantitative easing was a policy intended to force cautious investors to take more risk than they would normally wish to, and in so doing Treasury bond prices were forced higher. Figure 5.4 shows ten-year US Treasury bond yields over the 55 years after 1962: between April 2012 and September 2017, these averaged 2.2%, compared with an average of 6.7% over the previous 50 years. Central bank purchasing of large segments of the Treasury market was an evident distortion that was to some degree responsible for these extraordinarily low bond yields. The challenge for investors was how to respond to this distortion, and to know how long it would take to unwind.

Set against this background, Bernstein's criticisms of buy-and-hold approaches to wealth management look even more relevant. The price of an investment should matter, and there is a price at which it makes sense to exchange the assurance of a high-quality government bond for a cheaper, less well-suited or less secure substitute. The first steps may

FIGURE 5.4 **US Treasury 10-year constant maturity yields**
% per year, Jan 1962–Sep 2017

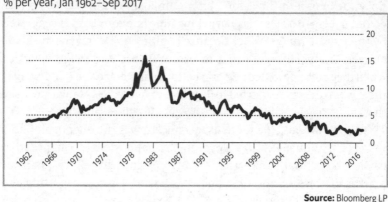

Source: Bloomberg LP

be the easiest, as portfolio rebalancing leads to sales of government bonds. However, many advisers will suggest going beyond this and scaling back considerably exposure to the security of government bonds. One of the biggest problems facing investors who accept this is that no one knows how much Treasury yields have been influenced by central bank purchases (though various estimates exist) or how much continuing influence on yields will be felt by the presence of the US Federal Reserve and Bank of England as long-term holders of Treasury bonds. In other words, no one really knows the "fair" price for a Treasury bond. This is a major difficulty for those investors who were persuaded to sell their core holdings of government bonds, because they were too expensive, but who need to decide when to return to the assurance of Treasury bonds.

The years since 2007 have radically altered the investment environment for any investor. Most notably, interest rates in the major financial markets have stayed much lower than previously, often at historical low levels (see Fig 5.5).

This has translated into higher bond prices and it should be expected that it also helps to explain higher share prices. Coincidentally, a number of recent studies has documented a noticeable decline in the share of wage or labour income in leading economies since 1970; the corollary of this has been an increase in the share of income accruing

FIGURE 5.5 **10-year real interest rates in Germany, UK and USA**
% per year, 2003–2017

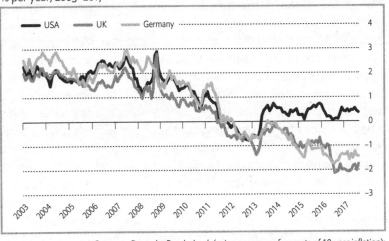

Sources: Deutsche Bundesbank (using consensus forecasts of 10-year inflation);
Bank of England; US Treasury

to profits and robust profit margins. Unusually low interest rates coupled with unusually high profit margins help to justify unusually high stockmarket valuations. This does not mean that either high stock prices nor the factors that appear to justify them will be sustained. But they might.

Bernstein's call for investment policy to be "opportunistic, to be played more by ear than by rigid policy allocations" surely applies to such a change in the investment landscape. In practice, the broad patterns of asset allocation have evolved but not changed markedly for different groups of investors in the years since 2007. The changes that are evident are often continuations of trends that were evident before the global financial crisis, rather than arising in response to it. Whether consciously or not, most investors have responded as if they are not sure how to interpret indications that markets in late 2017 were expensive.

Asset allocation models: an essential discipline

This chapter opened with a criticism by the late Peter Bernstein of policy portfolios, which others call strategic asset allocations or high-level benchmarks. He argued that the usefulness of such model allocations is undermined by fluctuating market volatility and changes in investment opportunities as market prices change. Despite this, many investors – including the largest sovereign wealth funds, university endowments and public pension funds, as well as large investment houses which advise a wide range of investors and many boutique investment firms – make use of formal or informal policy portfolios. These provide a framework against which the management of investments is anchored, often within pre-agreed limits. They help to express an attitude to risk-taking (even though it is known that market volatility fluctuates), and in particular an attitude to the division of investments between safe-harbour and risk assets. They also express an attitude to liquidity and provide a context for a review of investments and investment opportunities as well as performance.

The role of anchoring is particularly important: an investment adviser may think that safe-haven government bonds are undesirably expensive, and may recommend moving quite a long way from the allocation and duration of the benchmark allocation into other assets. These different investments will introduce new risks, but, if the adviser's forecast is correct, they should reduce the exposure of a capital loss being incurred on expensive bonds. The policy portfolio provides a benchmark against which to measure that decision. It also provides an anchor to drag investments back towards the model if the pricing "anomaly" subsequently corrects. Policy asset allocation models provide an important discipline for any investor to keep investments in line with a previously agreed approach, to judge moves away from that agreed approach and sometimes to anchor moves by investment managers from that policy in pursuit of tactical market opportunities.

One of the great insights of modern portfolio theory, which should be used in designing model portfolio strategies, is the portfolio separation theorem of the late James Tobin. Tobin suggested that the degree of investor risk aversion only influenced the allocation of an investment strategy between risky and cautious investments. As Willem Buiter, global chief economist at Citigroup, wrote in 2003 in an appreciation of Tobin's contribution to economics:

> This is an important and beautiful result, which is not done justice by Tobin's own summary: "Don't put all your eggs in one basket". Indeed, Tobin's remarkable result is better summarised as "regardless of your degree of risk aversion and caution, you will only need two baskets for all your eggs".

A great deal of damage has repeatedly been inflicted on investors' wealth because investment advisers repeatedly lose sight of this essential principle, partly because they think they have discovered new and improved ways of diversifying investment portfolios which falsely offer the benefits of security at higher rates of return. (See Appendix 2 for further comments on the portfolio separation theorem.) One dilemma facing investors in the first quarter of the 21st century is how to benefit from Tobin's insight while making some adjustments to allow for the historical low rates of interest paid on high-quality government debt. Cautious advisers choose to stay quite close to Tobin's insight.

This chapter and the next discuss investment strategy models for short-term and long-term investors with different tolerances for disappointment risk. In each of these models, government bonds or Treasury bills provide an anchor for the strategy. The weight given to them is driven by the appetite for risk of the investor. Risk assets are represented by allocations to equities. Whether equities alone represent the most efficient way of gaining access to premium returns needs to be assessed in the light of market valuations and expectations for performance, risk, and correlations from different asset classes at a particular point in time. It will be normal to invest in a range of risk assets including, for example, credit. These opportunities are discussed in Part 2. But no matter what an adviser believes about the predictability of market returns or which asset class is cheap or dear, a cautious investor will be keener on having safe-haven assets than an aggressive investor, and a cautious long-term investor will be more interested in government bonds than a short-term investor, who will want more cash.

When safe-haven investments are themselves expensive, cautious investors face a particular problem. They need to decide how much to pay for what is in effect insurance and how much risk to incur by moving away from the safe haven. For cautious long-term investors, bond ladders can be particularly useful in these circumstances (see Laddered government bonds below).

Risk-taking and portfolio rebalancing

At times of market turmoil, measures of volatility increase and the value of risk assets falls. Any investor who has benchmark allocations to risk assets and conservative assets will then be underweight risk assets but overweight safe assets. In these circumstances, investment advisers – who, as discussed in Chapter 1, may enjoy taking risk more than their clients do – often recommend rebalancing back towards the strategic allocations and, for example, taking profits on government bonds and reinvesting the proceeds in risk assets. At times of great stress in markets, opportunities to rebalance will be greatest. At such times, this counter-cyclical policy is not for the faint hearted. It provides liquidity to distressed sellers and increases risk-taking in "bad times" when risk premiums may be unusually high. If markets tend to overreact and "mean revert", this added risk-taking will be a source of added value

Automatic rebalancing is a natural role for a long-term investor, but it is a way of taking more risk when others wish to take less (or avoid taking more) as market volatility increases. It is a mechanism for selling government bonds (and liquidity) when their price is high and buying government bonds (and maintaining liquidity) when others are increasing their exposure to illiquid assets. It is also a way for investors to anchor policy to a previously agreed strategy that was justified with reference to past long-term averages for market risks, which are unlikely to reflect the circumstances at the time of the rebalancing.

Short-term investment strategies

For short-term investors, the safest strategy is to have 100% of their investments in Treasury bills, or highest-quality money-market funds. The "war chest" or "umbrella" fund might be considered a short-term portfolio (see Chapter 1). Short-term investors are absolute return investors. Their focus is immediate and they have no need to hedge against risks in the future. Although the textbook benchmark against which success should be judged is the performance of Treasury bills, the reality is that achieving a positive investment return provides a line in the sand that matters above all else to short-term investors.

Moving strategy away from the safe haven of cash (Treasury bills) brings both the hope of a better performance and the fear of a disappointing outcome. Initially, it is simplest to constrain investment choices to the traditional areas of stocks, bonds and cash.

How safe is cash?

The anchor investment for short-term investors is cash. Cautious investors who want more security should hold more of it. Investment books, such as this one, often proceed as if cash was always invested in Treasury bills. This is rarely the case. One of the most shocking features of the credit crunch's early stages in 2007–08 was the sudden erosion of confidence in cash investments held at banks and in money-market funds. This was coupled with uncertainty about the attitude of governments to bank failures and the extent of government deposit insurance. It was a ripe environment for crowd behaviour by savers as they responded to rumours of impending bank failures.

The first major collapse was that of a British retail bank, Northern Rock, in September 2007. Its online cash withdrawal service was overwhelmed and customers formed long lines in the street to remove their savings. It was the first run on a British retail bank since 1866. One year later, in September 2008, a $64 billion US money-market fund, the Reserve Primary Fund, "broke the buck" by marking down its unit price to 97 cents following losses caused by the failure of Lehman Brothers, a global financial services firm. As a result, within days investors withdrew over half the assets managed by the fund, and the US authorities moved to shore up confidence in money-market funds by providing a temporary guarantee to underpin their value. There were other signs of sudden loss of depositor confidence in banks. But concerns about the security of bank deposits were allayed by the clarification of deposit guarantee schemes, and in particular by the growing understanding shortly after September 2008 that deposits at major banks would be protected, not least by the steps taken to bolster bank capital. It remains the case that unguaranteed cash investments in banks need careful due diligence.

Do bonds provide insurance for short-term investors?

The answer is sometimes yes and sometimes no. The normal pattern is for equity markets and bond markets to be positively correlated with each other. When equities do well, bonds tend to do at least quite well. At times of crisis and flight to quality, however, the relationship has often broken down as investors flee to government bonds. During the stockmarket declines of 2008, the volatility of long-term government bonds provided an invaluable lever to offset the declines in equity markets. But the scale of the insurance "pay-out" depended critically on the size of the allocation to bonds and the duration of those government bonds. Cash, the safe haven for short-term investors, provided little help. This paralleled the experiences of the 2000–02 equity bear market. But at other times in the past, for example during the sustained increase in inflation expectations during the 1960s, equities did well while bonds were eroded by inflation and suffered a gradual increase in yields. There have been several years when fixed income suffered negative returns while equities performed strongly.

In times of crisis, bonds normally appreciate, but (even for longer maturities) not necessarily by much, and not by as much as equities fall. Aspects of the historical record since 1987 are summarised in Tables 5.1 and 5.2. It is evident from the experience of the months of October 2008 and February 2009 that equity market setbacks do not necessarily coincide precisely with strong performance by the US Treasury market (see Table 5.1). However, Table 5.2, which records the worst calendar-year experiences of US equities, shows that in those years the US Treasury market performed strongly with, as expected, long-dated bonds performing strongest.

Table 5.2 looks "quite good" for supporting the insurance role of bonds. However, the overall message regarding the insurance role for bonds is that it sometimes works but not always, and furthermore that US Treasury bonds provide better insurance than corporate bonds and

TABLE 5.1 **Bond diversification in months of equity market crisis**
Performance, total return in $

	MSCI US Index	MSCI World Index	Bloomberg, Barclays US Treasury Long-term Bond Index	Bloomberg, Barclays US Treasury Intermediate- term Bond Index	Bloomberg, Barclays US Aggregate Bond Index
Oct-87	−21.3	−19.6	7.3	3.0	3.6
Oct-08	−17.1	−16.3	−3.3	0.7	−2.4
Aug-98	−13.9	−13.8	4.5	2.0	1.6
Sep-02	−11.3	−11.0	4.2	1.9	1.6
Feb-09	−10.2	−8.9	−1.0	−0.4	−0.4

Data sorted by worst monthly performance of MSCI US Equity Index, Jan 1987–Sep 2017

Source: Bloomberg LP

TABLE 5.2 **Bond diversification in years of extreme equity market performance**
Performance, total return in $

	MSCI US Index	MSCI World Index	Bloomberg Barclays US Treasury Long-term Bond Index	Bloomberg Barclays US Treasury Intermediate- term Bond Index	Bloomberg Barclays US Aggregate Bond Index
2008	−37.1	−38.3	24.0	11.4	5.2
2002	−22.7	−23.8	16.8	9.3	10.3
2000	−12.5	−9.6	20.3	10.3	11.6
2013	32.6	29.6	−12.7	−1.3	−2.0
1997	34.1	22.9	15.1	7.8	9.7
1995	38.2	20.0	30.7	14.4	18.5

Note: Table 5.2 shows equity and bond market performance during the best and worst three years for the MSCI US Equity Index between 1987 and 2017.

Source: Bloomberg LP

other components of the Bloomberg Barclays Aggregate Index (see Chapter 9).

The other message is that the relationship between different maturities of bonds is generally predictable, with the longest-dated (and most volatile) US Treasury bonds appreciating most in periods of stockmarket crisis. But this does not always happen. When it does not, the shape of the bond yield curve can shift markedly, which argues for diversified exposure to bond maturities. Long-dated bonds are unquestionably much further away from a short-term investor's safety zone than short-term bonds and so are much more risky. But the pay-out of short-term bonds is much less when fixed-income markets are providing insurance.

So the process for short-term investors should be first to decide how much risk they want to take, and then to make sure that risk-taking is itself diversified across asset classes. Offset equity exposure with at least some fixed-income exposure, not in this case for income, but for insurance. But do so knowing that this is one of those insurance policies with loopholes in the small print.

How do investors invest?

Any investor likes to know how their investment strategy compares with others. This harks back to Chapter 2 and is a reminder that the role of anchoring is crucial in how we take decisions. Everyone's circumstances are different, but as a cross-check on how the discussion in this book of the place of different investments in strategy, Tables 5.3 and 5.4 provide dollar-weighted average data for the asset allocation of high net worth private investors, pension schemes from the major markets and also US endowments.

TABLE 5.3 **Indicators of global investable assets since 2002**
Total assets, $bn

	2002	2007	2012	2016
Global private clients	27,200	40,700	46,200	63,500
Global pension funds	14,259	24,680	27,779	33,427
US endowments	225	411	406	515
	2002	**2007**	**2012**	**2016**
Average US Treasury bill yield	1.6%	4.5%	0.1%	0.3%
Average yield on 20-year US Treasury bonds	5.4%	4.9%	2.5%	2.2%
Average yield on long-dated US TIPS	3.1%	2.3%	0.2%	0.7%

Sources:

Global high net worth financial investments: Capgemini and Merrill Lynch Wealth Management World Wealth Report 2003; Capgemini and RBC Wealth Management World Wealth Report 2013, Capgemini World Wealth Report 2017. "High net worth" refers to individuals with at least US $1 million financial wealth, excluding primary residence, collectibles, consumables and consumer durables.

Global pension funds: Towers Watson Global Pension Asset Study 2017. Asset allocation data refers to sub-sample of seven largest pension fund markets, Australia, Canada, Japan, Netherlands, Switzerland, UK, US.

US endowments: NACUBO-Commonfund Study of Endowments 2012, 2016.

Bond yields: US Treasury.

TABLE 5.4 **Pattern of asset allocation by global investors, 2002 and 2016**
% of total assets

Global high net worth financial investments

	Equities	Fixed income	Real estate*	Alternative investments	Cash and equivalents
2013 March	26	16	20	10	28
2017 March	31	18	14	10	27

Global pension funds *

	Equities	Bonds	Other	Cash
2002	50	38	9	3
2016	46	28	24	3

US endowments

	Listed equities	Fixed income	Alternatives	Cash and other
2002	50.2	23.4	24.3	2.2
2016	35.0	8.0	53.0	4.0

*Real estate excludes primary residences.
**Includes both defined-benefit and defined-contribution pension arrangements.

Sources: as for Table 5.3

6

Are you in it for the long term?

THE PURPOSE OF WEALTH, however large or small, is to fund expenditure in the future. This might be tomorrow or it might be in 20 years' time, but the time horizon for most investment objectives cannot be described as short term. For long-term investors who are concerned with targeting a minimum standard of living, or, for an endowment, a minimum level of disbursements, the strategy should not target a particular level of wealth. Wealth is a means to an end, but not the end in itself. The sufficiency of wealth is best examined from the perspective of the level of income or disbursements that the wealth can support.

The time horizon for private and institutional wealth

The income that a defined-benefit pension fund or an insurance company is obliged to disburse can be modelled by actuaries years in advance with a reasonable degree of accuracy. There are issues related to the uncertainty surrounding these projections and whether this has increased with regulatory and corporate changes and with greater life expectancy. But this is of a different order of magnitude compared to the uncertainty related to the spending of much private wealth.

The obligations of endowments and charities (and also sovereign wealth funds) are again different in nature. Their spending is constrained by what they have, by the bequests or inflows that they receive, and by the need to balance the interests of today's beneficiaries with those of tomorrow. This need to ensure equitable treatment in making allocations between different generations of beneficiaries is a particular concern for "perpetual" endowments, such as college foundations, and some sovereign wealth funds, whose investment strategy needs to assume that the foundation will last "forever".

The increase in wealth of tax-exempt endowments with both professional investment management and successful fund-raising offers the prospect of accumulation that is bounded only by their endowments' fund-raising capacity. David Swensen of Yale University gives a revealing account of the differing evolution of the Yale, Harvard and Carnegie Institution investment funds since the early 20th century. In 1911, Carnegie and Harvard had funds of around $23 million while Yale had around $12 million. By June 2016, the Carnegie Institution's investment portfolio, which devotes itself to supporting scientific research, had more than kept pace with inflation, with an endowment of $903 million. However, this was dwarfed by Harvard's $35.7 billion and Yale's $25.4 billion. The reason for this scale of difference is not superior investment management, but the much greater access of the university foundations to new bequests.

Private wealth is different. Families continue from generation to generation, but family wealth gets spent. There is little scope for the intergenerational exponential wealth accumulation that may be enjoyed by educational foundations. Private wealth is consumed, dissipated in fees, paid in taxes, or donated (as with the Carnegie and more recently, among others, Gates and Buffet family wealth) to charitable foundations. If this did not happen, the parsimonious among the wealthy could become stupendously wealthy. For example, in the 117 years to December 2016, the cumulative return from US equities after inflation, but before all costs, taxes and fees, was 6.4% a year. This implies that a very wealthy family with perhaps $20 million in 1900, equivalent to around $525 million in today's prices, could have an inherited fortune of over $700 billion if it had been invested in the diversified US stockmarket, and if that family had consumed nothing apart from what they earned independently of that wealth and had contrived to pay no taxes or investment management costs. Such a scale of inherited wealth does not seem to exist. So while private wealth is inherited, it is also spent or disbursed.

There is often little predictability in the spending plans of individual family members. This creates asset-planning issues that do not affect institutions. By contrast, the purpose and strategic direction of endowments and institutions are legally fixed by trust deeds or equivalent documents. With families, strategic objectives and actual disbursement of wealth can evolve at short notice, sometimes in surprising directions. This introduces uncertainty into the time horizon for the management of private wealth, which has few parallels for endowments or institutional investors. However, a change in regulations for pension funds and insurance companies (there have been many in the last few decades) can have a sudden impact on the time horizon of institutions. Regulated institutions that thought they could invest almost as if they had the time horizon of a permanent endowment can easily find that the investment journey matters much more than it once appeared to, and that the journey might be much shorter.

In setting strategy, the importance of different points on the time horizon for an investor needs to be clarified. For family wealth, the objective is not normally precisely defined. Sometimes there are clear dates associated with particular financial goals which can easily be benchmarked using government bonds; in other cases, wealth is explicitly needed for opportunities (or contingencies) which may arise in the short term. But usually this is not the case and plans often need to evolve as circumstances change and as more information becomes available. However, this should not be used as an excuse for assuming that such investors are, by default, short-term investors, as the adoption of a medium- or longer-term investment strategy could well help protect the purchasing power of their investments.

Long-term investors

Long-term investors have much greater flexibility than short-term investors to make adjustments to improve the likelihood of meeting financial objectives. Long-term investors are not just at the mercy of the investment markets and their initial choice of investment strategy. Depending on the investor's circumstances, financial disappointment "along the way" often leaves time to elicit a response, which provides extra degrees of freedom that reduce risk in the ability to meet objectives. For example, there may be time for a revision to the investment strategy, or for an individual to postpone retirement or to reduce current expenditure or current savings. For an endowment, there may be time for a drive to raise additional bequests, and for an individual, time to raise the level of regular pension contributions. These options provide flexibility for the long-term investor that is not available to the short-term investor. For any individual or foundation (or perhaps pension plan) that relies on a regular injection of savings or contributions to fund future financial needs, variations in these sources of income are often a much bigger source of risk and opportunity to meet expected commitments than are market conditions.

Financial planning and the time horizon

Short-term investors have a clear focus on total return as a measure of the success of their investment strategy. Long-term investors will often focus on the same measure. However, this is understandable but wrong. For example, it is common for individuals to have a target for accumulated savings before they feel able to retire. Over quite short time periods an amount that was broadly appropriate can become inadequate if long-term interest rates fall. The key is not the absolute amount of savings, but the ability of that amount, if appropriately invested, to support the intended level of retirement income. This leads to a focus on shortfall risk rather than the risk of generating a negative return. The benchmark for measuring shortfall is the performance of the appropriate "safety-first" strategy, and so shortfall risk is the risk of underperforming that strategy. A lifetime annuity provides this benchmark for a personal pension (see Chapter 3).

This focus of the security of income for long-term investors is well understood and reflected in financial advice and the "laddered" bond portfolios of many cautious private investors in North America. It is much less common, however, in the generic advice given to investors elsewhere. Internationally, it is common for private wealth holdings of bonds to be of short duration. Often this reflects concerns about the potential impact of inflation and a desire to avoid the risk of short-term negative returns from volatile assets, even if they are government bonds guaranteed to deliver a set amount at a given date in the future.

Outside the United States, it is widely believed that long-term bonds are inappropriate as investments for cautious private investors for whom the emphasis should, it is argued, be on controlling absolute volatility and short-term capital preservation. However, this is the appropriate focus only for cautious short-term investors. An error that often accompanies failure to design risk-taking strategies appropriate to an investor's time horizon is to confuse this time horizon with risk tolerance. The two should be treated separately. There are cautious long-term investors and there are aggressive short-term investors.

The danger of keeping things too simple

An overriding desire to "keep things simple" may encourage many to indicate that they are content to be considered as short-term investors, even though their objectives are longer term. This is the option to be treated as "absolute return" investors, for whom the safe-haven investment strategy is to be 100% invested in cash.

The danger is that these investors will miss two important differences between short-term and long-term investing. The first is the focus that long-term investors must have on the price level and inflation uncertainty. The second is that such investors will also fail to distinguish between a reduction in the price of future security (a fall in government bond prices) and a reduction in the market's assessment of an investment's quality.

Declines in prices are sometimes good for you

Sometimes you can be sure that a financial loss can be reversed. Pensioners living off the income generated from a well-constructed ladder of high-quality government bonds can respond to a fall in the market value of their investment portfolio following an increase in bond yields with composure. It should be of no concern. A creditworthy government issuer will keep them in the style to which they are accustomed. However, individuals who suffer a similar fall in investment value as a result of a downgrade in the creditworthiness of a corporate or even government bond, on which they are relying for pension income, might reasonably suffer sleepless nights, because there is less assurance that they will get paid.

For a short-term investor who wishes to realise objectives in the near term, either reversal should be viewed as if it might be a permanent loss which could need to be realised. For a long-term investor, only the credit downgrade should be of concern. It might be said that it is not the credit downgrade that should concern the pensioner, since it is only a default that leads to a loss of income. But this is a classic case of the dangers of mismeasuring risk. Investors lose sleep over their ability to support their future standard of living a long time before most downgraded corporate bonds default. A bond ladder comprising corporate debt that stretches many years into the future is more likely to suffer worrying credit downgrades at some stage than actual default.

Volatility, which is reflected in a reduction in government bond prices, reduces the cost of buying future income. This is unambiguously good news for anyone saving for a pension or a college education, for an endowment investing new money to meet future needs, or for a sovereign wealth fund trying to balance the interests of today's beneficiaries with those of tomorrow. For all these investors, higher real interest rates mean both lower bond prices and being able to meet more of tomorrow's needs with each new investment.

To achieve success as a long-term investor, this distinction between good and bad price declines should be accepted and reflected in how an investor responds to financial reverses. This is invaluable for private investors, who often regard any loss as if it is bad news, when it may represent an opportunity to lock in access to higher future income.

A lack of clarity about financial goals can encourage investors to focus on inappropriate time horizons. The one predictable consequence of this is inefficiency in the implementation of strategy. An example of this occurs if private investors, whose appropriate focus is on the long term, behave as short-term investors. They will fail to appreciate their vulnerability to changes in long-term interest rates and to the gradual erosion of inflation. Any change in long-term interest rates is likely to be misinterpreted, with positive performance arising from only partial exposure to falling interest rates being seen as "good performance" (it is not, it is poor, because it only partially hedged the fall in interest rates and should have been better), and negative performance owing to partial exposure to rising interest rates being seen as "poor", when underexposure to the safe haven of long-term bonds may (depending on the interest-rate sensitivity of existing investments) offer an opportunity to secure a higher future income with existing resources.

A financially disciplined endowment fund or institution managing cash flow obligations over a number of years is less likely to make these errors. The issue is that where the financial constraints are not naturally tight, market competition is not available to ensure that wealth is efficiently managed. Instead it requires deliberate decision-making and appropriate governance to make sure that a proper focus is maintained on the objectives that are suitable for the time scale of each investor.

Unexpected inflation: yet again the party pooper

The distinction between good and bad declines in prices is a useful device to help long-term investors understand the importance of the passage of time for the success of the investment strategy. It also helps differentiate between short-term and long-term investors. Strictly, so-called good declines in prices refer primarily to the prices of government inflation-linked bond yields, such as TIPS (Treasury Inflation Protected Securities). The reason is that a fall in conventional government bond prices which reflects an increase in inflation expectations (rather than an increase in real interest rates) is not good news for an investor, for it indicates an expected irrecoverable devaluation in the worth of all nominal bond investments. This is the process that explains why, in most countries for which there are data, bonds provided disappointing returns in the 20th century.

"Keep-it-simple" long-term asset allocation models

"Diversify, diversify" asset allocators often say. However, in designing low-risk strategies, which should always be the starting point for asset allocation, the first step should be to design the best hedge to neutralise risks of failing to meet objectives. For some investors, as was suggested in Tobin's portfolio separation theorem (see Chapter 5), it is conceivable that this could be achieved through a single holding in a particular government bond. An example would be the acquisition of a long-term inflation-linked government bond whose maturity date coincides with when a young child's university expenses are expected to be payable.

Diversification becomes an issue as an investor moves away from this "best hedge". Any such move needs to be made efficiently, which will call for diversification of avoidable risks.

So what does a long-term investment plan look like, and how should it be structured? It is not a wealth plan – it is a long-term income or spending power plan. An income plan needs to take account of your financial and other assets, your likely earnings, your financial obligations and your spending plans. As discussed in Chapter 3, the first step for those planning for retirement should be to use as a reference point the income that the retiree could buy from an insurance company either linked to inflation or as a fixed annual monetary amount. This will establish a base case to see if there is a minimum-risk approach to "hedge out" (if the inflation-linked option is followed) retirement plans, given current resources and current levels of interest rates. Often this will provide a point of departure to think about the different types of risk and uncertainty faced by pensioners (see Chapter 3). Table 6.1 gives a stylised indication of what a risk-based alternative to hedging uncertainty with an inflation-linked annuity might look like, for different levels of risk-taking.

The focus is on the risk of shortfalls from the fully hedged strategy instead of the risk of negative returns. So instead of showing the expected return and its trade-off with the volatility of that return, the focus is on the expected surplus or deficit in meeting objectives, compared with the minimum risk of a full hedging investment strategy. Note that Table 6.1 assumes that even a cautious managed long-term strategy is likely to involve a risk of falling short of financial objectives.

Should long-term investors hold more equities?

The discussion about stockmarket bubbles in Chapter 5 reintroduces the question of whether stockmarket risk is reduced with time. For if booms and busts in the stockmarket predictably follow each other, it may be possible to profit from this pattern. However, if we doubt our ability to time markets, even though we believe in market cycles, this predictable cyclical nature of equity returns will reinforce the case for a somewhat higher allocation to equities for long-term investors. To a degree this has been reflected in Table 6.1.

TABLE 6.1 **Stylised model long-term strategies, with only stocks, bonds and cash**

	Unaggressive ("income protection")	Moderate	Aggressive
Equities	25	60	80
Long-term conventional government bonds	50	40	20
Cash	0	0	0
Inflation-linked government bonds	25	0	0
Expected surplus (% per year)	1.3	2.2	2.6
Volatility of surplus	7.6	12.9	16.8

Source: Authors' calculations

A number of studies, notably by Jeremy Siegel in *Stocks for the Long Run*, have suggested that over long holding periods (for example, 30 years or more) an investor might be more sure, or at least less uncertain, of what after-inflation performance to expect from equities than from conventional government bonds. This builds on the experience of the 20th century, when the impact of unanticipated inflation made cash and bonds much riskier for holding wealth over long periods than shorter-term experience would suggest. The evidence that Siegel uses to support this comes primarily from the United States, but it also appears to be supported, almost without exception, by international data. Taken together, these would suggest skewing, at least to some extent, the investment strategy allocation for long-term investors towards equities and away from bonds for cautious as well as aggressive investors.

However, he makes clear that although this model does reflect the effect that unanticipated 20th century inflation had on the investments in conventional government bonds and cash of cautious investors, it does not incorporate the potential role of inflation-linked government bonds.

The introduction of inflation-linked government bonds has changed the ground rules for long-term investment strategy in the

21st century. Long-term investors may have medium-term as well as long-term objectives, and often, especially with private wealth, unexpected opportunities or requirements to draw down investments arise. Taken together with the insights of behavioural finance into loss aversion, this suggests that it is now neither necessary nor desirable to recommend high equity allocations for long-term cautious investors. However, if long-term cautious investors have confidence in the equity mean reversion story, especially if they have access to other sources of income, they might reasonably hold more equities than would be recommended for cautious investors with a short time horizon. (Such an adjustment has been made in Table 6.1, whose equity allocations can be compared with the lower allocations in Table 6.2.)

Inflation, again

There is no role for cash in the long-term models in Table 6.1. This is because cash is volatile relative to the safe haven (inflation-linked bonds) and it normally offers no performance advantage. At the same time, the future relationship between inflation-linked bonds and conventional government bonds is sensitive to views on inflation. It should be assumed that these inflation risks cannot be properly reflected in any set of modelling assumptions, and that it will be necessary to rely heavily on judgmental opinions. Furthermore, the judgments of "experts" should probably not count for more than the views and experiences of informed investors on issues such as inflation expectations. However, the apparent views of the financial markets on the break-even rate of inflation should always be used as a point of comparison (see Chapter 4).

Views on expected inflation and the margins of error in these opinions should be reviewed from time to time, as a minimum with the help of some simple "what-if" illustrations for the price level at different dates in the future. In the stylised model for long-term investors shown in Table 6.1, a key decision will be the extent to which the holdings of government bonds should be in the form of inflation-linked or conventional bonds.

US municipal bonds

The municipal bond market is attractive to US private investors to hold in taxable accounts because interest on municipal bonds is generally exempt from federal income tax and from state and local tax in the issuing state. (Interest on US Treasury and government agency bonds is subject to federal income tax but exempt from state income taxes.) This makes the municipal bond market a natural habitat for the taxable savings of US private investors. However, in the past two decades, the rise in popularity of tax-deferred retirement accounts (where municipal bonds are disadvantaged) has meant that fewer individual Americans hold municipal bonds, with ownership increasingly focused on the taxable investments of the most affluent.

At the end of June 2017, US state and local authorities had outstanding obligations in the form of different types of municipal bonds of $3.8 trillion, making the "muni" market approximately one-quarter of the size of the US Treasury market. The market is highly diverse and fragmented with, according to a 2012 Securities and Exchange Commission (SEC) report, close to 44,000 state and local issuers and over 1 million different municipal bonds outstanding in 2011. This heterogeneity contributes to illiquidity in the market (see below). According to the SEC, individuals owned around 75% of outstanding municipal bonds in 2011, with around 50% held directly and 25% held through mutual funds (or other investment vehicles, such as closed-end funds or exchange traded funds – ETFs).

There are the two main types of tax-exempt municipal bonds: general obligation bonds and revenue bonds. General obligation bonds are backed by the full faith and credit of the issuer and are usually supported by the issuer's tax-raising powers. By contrast, revenue bonds are serviced from specific projects or businesses that have been funded by the bonds. If the project fails to generate sufficient income to service the debt, the bondholders have no access to other sources of revenue of the issuing authority. Other highest-quality municipal bonds include those where the original issue is "refunded" or collateralised, for example with US Treasury securities.

Before the 2007–08 credit crisis, as well as having tax advantages, investment in municipal bonds was aided by the role of the insurance companies, with just under 60% of the value of new issues in 2004–07 being insured, according to the SEC. Following the credit crisis, insurance companies greatly reduced this service. This coincided with growing concerns about the credit quality of issuers, increasing both the burden of due diligence on investment advisers in recommending specific municipal bonds to investors and the attraction of investing in mutual funds managed by well-resourced teams of analysts. It also shifted perceptions of creditworthiness: revenue bonds which are secured by predictable high-quality projects or business activities have become relatively more attractive as the role of insurance has declined and doubts about the "full faith and credit" of some issuers backing general obligation bonds increased.

Laddered government bonds: a useful safety-first portfolio

A bond ladder is a portfolio of bonds with staggered maturity dates. It secures a stream of income for years ahead, and it reduces the risk of sudden changes in that income resulting from interest-rate changes. As each bond matures, it will need to be reinvested at prevailing interest rates (or reinvested elsewhere) and this exposes the income from the ladder to a margin of uncertainty. But this reinvestment risk applies only to an individual rung of the ladder as it matures. It can take judgment out of timing movements in long-term interest rates and reduce uncertainty in a pensioner's future income. Spreading maturities allows more reinvestment opportunities and less exposure to regret at the terms with which any particular bond was reinvested. A greater number of bond issues also enables effective management of different types of risk exposure (see below).

The danger of having to reinvest at lower interest rates than prevailed when the maturing bond was purchased could have been avoided if a life annuity had been purchased instead of a bond ladder (though complicated tax issues arise if the annuity is purchased with taxable savings). However, the laddered approach is more appealing to many investors than a life annuity as it retains greater flexibility and control over their wealth and avoids the need to lock in a single long-term rate of interest on the day they purchase the life annuity. Although a ladder does involve reinvestment risk, it also offers reinvestment opportunity, namely the chance to reinvest at more favourable interest rates at a later date.

This can provide an element of inflation protection to retirement income. If individuals decide to buy a fixed-income life annuity rather than invest in a bond ladder, they will be wholly exposed to any unexpected increase in inflation for the rest of their lives. However, if an increase in inflation is expected to persist, bond yields will be higher, and the rungs on a fixed-income bond ladder will be reinvested at the new higher rate of interest. If an investor expects interest rates to rise, but is not sure when they will, having to reinvest maturing bonds allows income to be "averaged up" if rates do rise over time. If the objective is to secure a steady income, this prospect of securing a higher income should matter more than the temporary dips in capital value of the existing bonds as rates rise ahead of maturity.

This degree of inflation compensation is incomplete and less effective than what could be offered by inflation-linked government bonds. Furthermore, reinvesting a conventional maturing bond will always, if there has been any inflation, support a lower standard of living than when the bond was first purchased. Nevertheless, this partial element of inflation compensation in a bond ladder, in conjunction with the flexibility and discretion that it leaves the investor, will be an appealing feature for many investors.

A bond ladder is designed to mitigate interest-rate risk and it should encourage a proper understanding of the distinction between good and bad declines in prices. This is because an investor will find it easier to respond to a fall in government bond prices as an opportunity to lock in higher income when the next rung on the ladder matures. However, if the cause of the decline in investment values was a downgrade in the credit quality of a component rung, the result is likely to be, at least, a worried investor until the bond matures.

For this reason, ladders should be constructed from government bonds. With good-quality longer-term corporate bonds there is always the risk of a deterioration in credit quality, and this risk obviously increases with longer-maturity bonds. When constructing a long-term bond ladder designed to provide dependable income, it is safest to assume that there is no such thing as a blue-chip, entirely reliable corporate credit risk. For example, a US dollar corporate bond ladder built up in the initial years after 2000 would probably have included large exposures to several then highly rated financial institutions, including banks as well as AIG, an insurance company which had to be rescued by the US government in 2008. (See Chapter 8 for how corporate credit risk evolves over time.) An investor who wishes to take advantage of the higher yields available from assuming credit risk should follow a professionally managed approach to investing in credit risk and forgo the concept of a bond ladder. Investors can see sample portfolios (for example, mutual fund portfolios) of the most highly respected fixed-income portfolio managers. These will show that credit risk is well diversified with modest exposures to individual institutions. A bond ladder gives much less opportunity for such diversification.

In practice, building a bond ladder of high-quality bonds to generate a secure flow of income stretching over a number of years has mostly been associated with the US municipal bond market, and so with taxable accounts rather than tax-deferred pension accounts. The municipal bond market introduces credit-quality issues. Building a bond ladder involves a series of choices (which may be more limited than would be wished) and usually trade-offs between what is desirable for a buy-and-hold approach to investing and what is available. Bond ladders need to be constructed with care, taking account of the tax status of different issues, credit risk, the existence of call options that enable the issuer to repay the bond early, and the costs that may be incurred if the investor decides to sell the bond before its final maturity date.

What's the catch in following a long-term strategy?

At the time of writing, the "worst" month for the US TIPS market was October 2008. In that month the yield, according to the US Treasury, on long-dated (ten-year-plus) TIPS increased by 0.6% to 3.4%, and the Bloomberg Barclays Capital index of this part of the market showed a monthly performance of −10.7%. For an investor funding a pension plan from regular cash contributions to invest in inflation-linked government bonds, increases in yield and reduction in price, if taken in isolation, are clearly good news as it enables each contribution at the lower price to purchase more pension entitlement. This is at the heart of the distinction between good and bad price declines. For cautious long-term pension investors who were continuing to contribute to their savings plan, the October 2008 increase in real yields and fall in bond prices should not have been a concern, even though with hindsight they may regret not postponing purchases until the higher yields were on offer. But it is normally wishful thinking to believe that they might have been able to succeed at such market timing.

However, the most important feature of short-term and long-term models is that there is a fundamental difference in strategy design for cautious long-term investors and cautious short-term investors. These are not small differences that can be ignored: there is an essential difference between stabilising the income that can be generated from an investor's wealth, the objective for a cautious long-term investor, and stabilising the value of that wealth, the objective for a cautious short-term investor.

Market timing: an unavoidable risk

Whatever strategy is being followed, from time to time it is likely that investors will be persuaded of the need to change investment direction. But the process of changing strategy is fraught with risk for investors. There is often little advice available on how to decide when to change strategy. For larger institutional investors, investment managers and consultants provide much advice on how to insure against bad outcomes and how to manage transactions costs once an investor has decided when to change strategy. However, there is little profit for an adviser in answering the key question: "When?" But for all investors this is a crucial issue in managing investments.

Implementing strategy change involves unavoidable market timing. You know you have to get from A to B, but how to get there, and particularly when to get there, requires judgments about market timing. These have to be balanced against the knowledge that your investment risk profile is not what you want it to be (which is why you want to change strategy).

A simple rule to follow is that if investors decide that their risk profile is too aggressive, they should move to the new, more cautious strategy promptly, perhaps allowing a small amount of time for trying to predict market movements, but with little confidence that this will add much value. Such investors should not let seeming confidence in short-term market forecasts extend the period during which their risk profile is inappropriate. This is easily stated and perhaps more easily applied in the case of an institution rather than an individual or a family. This is because discussions about risk tolerance are rarely separated from views on market prospects in discussions with families.

However, for all investors, within each four- or five-year period there is a significant chance that circumstances may force a change of direction. The obvious group of investors for whom this might not apply is well-resourced "perpetual" endowments (such as some sovereign wealth funds, university foundations and charitable endowments). Adjustments to strategy involve taking views on markets and, typically, a significant degree of regret risk.

The real issue is not that market timing cannot be undertaken skilfully or profitably: it can. There are some investment managers whose skill in market timing has manifested itself over time. But these track records are not built by one-off "bet the ranch" decisions on the timing of corrections to inappropriate risk profiles. They are carefully managed and, within limits, diversified. Changing strategy is different. There is normally no way to diversify the investment decision or to give meaningful time to profit from the correction of perceived market anomalies.

It is often suggested that phasing implementation of a change in investment strategy from one asset class to another is the best way to proceed if an investor has to change strategy. The investor is likely to feel more comfortable with this approach. But the strong argument in favour of immediate implementation of change is that if an investor has decided that the risk of the current investment strategy is excessive, any delay extends unnecessary risk-taking. When faced with the need to make such a decision, there are always reasons why now is not the best time to act.

Some "keep-it-simple" concluding messages

The model allocations described in this chapter are simplified and will often need tailoring to suit an individual investor's needs as well as to market circumstances. But they give a flavour of what strategy might look like if the available investments comprised only cash, domestic conventional government bonds, domestic inflation-linked government bonds and diversified equities. In many cases, appropriate "keep-it-simple" strategies, consisting only of these investment classes, can be constructed for the financial needs of investors. Actual investment holdings can then deviate from these to reflect, within agreed limits, views on the cheapness and dearness of markets.

In practice, most investors will spend much more time focusing on the detail of implementation, which involves departures from this keep-it-simple approach. How much should go in hedge funds? Isn't finding the right manager more important than the right hedge fund strategy? Surely value will outperform growth? Is high yield too risky? What about emerging markets? And so on.

Despite the time that most investors spend on these issues, the most important one is the extent to which obligations or spending plans are hedged and future income secured. The keep-it-simple framework is more than adequate to address these fundamental issues. What is often thought to be the more exciting material about the different asset classes is covered in the second part of this book. When reviewing these more exciting and sophisticated opportunities, a key question to keep asking is: how will this product perform in "bad times" when reliable diversification will be most important to me?

The chance of a bad outcome may be higher than you think

What is a "bad outcome" or "minimum acceptable return" (MAR) for short-term investors? A cautious short-term investor will be less tolerant of short-term losses than an aggressive investor. Some illustrative model investment allocations are shown in Table 6.2 .

For unaggressive short-term investors, it has been arbitrarily assumed that the measured risk of a negative return of worse than −5% in any particular year should be no greater than one in 20. This is the target MAR. For moderate-risk short-term investors, the MAR is assumed to be −10% and for aggressive short-term investors −15%. In principle, any figure can be selected, but whatever it is, the calculated probability of breaching may be only one in 20 in any particular calendar year; however, over five years, for example, the probability of breaching the guideline in at least one of these five years will be more than

TABLE 6.2 **Model short-term investment strategies, with only stocks, bonds and cash**

Asset allocation:	Unaggressive strategy	Moderate strategy	Aggressive strategy	US Treasury bills	US government bonds	US equities
Equities	20	50	75	0	0	100
Bonds*	20	50	25	0	100	0
Cash*	60	0	0	100	0	0
Performance Dec 1900 – 2016 % per year**	5.2	7.2	8.4	3.7	4.9	9.5
Historical volatility	4.8	11.1	15.2	2.9	9.0	19.8
"Value at risk" (apparent 1-in-20 chance of return of this, or worse, in any one calendar year)*						
	−2.7	−11.0	−16.5	0.0	−9.9	−23.0
Extreme results since 1991 using Bloomberg Barclays and MSCI monthly data						
Worst 12-month result	−7.5	−20.5	−32.5	0.1	−12.6	−43.1
Best 12-month result	16.9	34.6	42.7	6.5	31.9	53.4

*Indicative allocations between bonds and cash for short-term investors sensitive to duration of bond benchmark.
** Geometric averages, before inflation. (Geometric average inflation was 2.9% per year from 1900 to 2016.)
*** See text comments on risk of more frequent occurences of disappointing returns.
Sources: Underlying data sourced from Dimson, Marsh and Staunton, and Bloomberg LP.

one in five. If, as is most probable, the investor's portfolio is monitored more frequently than once a year, say at the end of each month, the probability of at least one breach, measured on the basis of rolling 12-month periods, will be closer to 50%. (Note that the MAR probability refers to the chance of an outcome worse than the specified parameter in a particular calendar year.) These things happen and are not surprising, even if you think that a one-in-20 risk is a remote risk. A real problem for advisers is that investors may think that such a poor outcome is unlikely to happen, which places a particular responsibility on investor education.

Having selected these tolerances for losses, in theory we can design model strategies that give the best prospect for wealth generation, given these guidelines. These would be the conventional efficient portfolios that are optimal for each indicated level of risk-taking by short-term investors. Efficient portfolios give the best possible trade-off of expected risk and expected return. For any given level of risk-taking there is, in theory, only one optimal portfolio. It would be impossible to achieve higher expected returns with no increase in risk and it would be inefficient to pursue the same returns, but at higher risk. In practice, the uncertainties discussed in Chapters 4 and 5 mean that this does not work since, as discussed in Chapter 1, we cannot model uncertainty. We may expect that a particular outcome is unlikely, but we generally do not know with any precision how unlikely that result is.

A consequence of this is that these indicated MAR risk figures can support a range of very different strategies, and the intention would often be to manage the strategy to a lower level of risk-taking than indicated by the MAR. Consider the three illustrative short-term strategies, using only stocks, bonds and cash, shown in Table 6.2, which have stylised allocations to stocks increasing from 20% to 50% and then to 75%. The allocation of non-equity investments is divided between over-ten-year US Treasury bonds and cash.

Table 6.2 shows the average return for each strategy based on the historical performance of market indices, before all fees and expenses, since 1900 using data from Dimson, Marsh and Staunton. It also shows, based on historical relationships, the sort of returns that might be expected in a disappointing year. For example, the moderate strategy indicates that a return of –8.4%, or worse, should be expected with no more than a one-in-20 chance in any particular year. The back-testing of results using monthly data since 1991 shows that much larger negative returns would have been recorded in the past with such a "moderate" strategy, with market indices pointing to a negative return of 20.5% in the 12 months to February 2009.

This illustrates that actual experience can from time to time be a lot worse than would be suggested by the past average statistics for overall returns and volatility. The more comforting figures are provided by routinely used modelling exercises. These suffer from severe averaging difficulties which suggest, for example, that stockmarket volatility stays at one average level. It does not, and, as 2008 demonstrated, the worst news arrives when this is least true. More particularly, the risk figures are undermined by the "surprising" frequency of extreme returns – by trending or momentum in markets, and by the fact that at times of stress, "normal" relationships between different markets may not hold. Frequently though, the mood music and psychology of markets are benign, returns are positive but not euphoric, and a comfortable air of complacency surrounds investors.

There is another more specific reason why seemingly low-risk, normally low-volatility strategies may fail to provide the expected degree of protection in "bad times". Many low- volatility investments indirectly offer insurance to someone else and are in effect option-writing strategies, which collect a steady premium most of the time, but then occasionally suffer large losses. This does not just affect some hedge fund strategies (see Chapter 10). Less obviously, corporate bonds also fall into this category.

In Chapter 9 it is explained that an individual corporate bond can be seen as a combination of a government bond and an option (for which a premium yield is received) provided by the bond investor to other creditors to reimburse them in the event of default. Providing this insurance becomes more of a liability to investors as equity volatility increases, we should not be surprised if corporate bonds, as a group, perform particularly poorly when stockmarket volatility increases. Cautious investment strategies, which reach beyond government bonds to the more attractive yields on offer from corporate bonds, normally perform as expected with a decent yield and low volatility. But in bad times, as was seen in the financial crisis, they can perform particularly poorly. Typically, no hint of this intrinsic risk exposure will be evident from marketing track records and risk statistics for such "cautious" strategies, if they only reflect performance during tranquil markets.

PART 2

Implementing more
complicated strategies

7

Setting the scene

A health warning: liquidity risk

The "keep-it-simple" strategies described in previous chapters should be liquid as well as simple. Almost always, when investment strategy gets more complicated it starts to embrace more liquidity risk. Liquidity is a dimension of risk which is not captured by the off-the-shelf risk models that are routinely used in managing investments. This is because it is difficult to model, not because it does not matter. Illiquidity has been described as "the most dangerous and least understood financial risk". Part of this understanding shortfall is a consequence of the difficulty in defining it. In the words of Charles Goodhart in early 2008, "The word liquidity has so many facets that it is often counter-productive to use it without further and closer definition." One definition might be the proportion of current asking price you might need to give up in order to sell the asset immediately. Another definition might be the time it takes to sell an asset without dropping its price. In addition to time and price, there is a third dimension to liquidity risk: quantity. Quantity comes into play when we consider answers to questions such as the impact on the share price of the sale of 10% of the company's shares. This last concept is referred to as price impact. Finance academics often talk in terms of liquidity as a risk factor and different assets have different exposures to this factor. The risk factor attracts a risk premium which reflects the rate of return needed to compensate an investor for being exposed to this factor.

Investing in illiquid markets

A common error is for an investor to expect an illiquid investment to offer a premium return just because it is illiquid. This can be an expensive mistake. From an investor's perspective, the appropriate way to look at an illiquid investment opportunity is to see if it offers the prospect of a premium return that is sufficient, given the investor's circumstances, to compensate adequately for giving up the flexibility offered by liquidity. Net of fees, and given the investor's circumstances, the illiquid investment opportunity may often not pass the test.

This gives rise to two related questions: How should investors judge their appetite for illiquidity? This will determine their own trade-off between the potential to earn excess returns in return for accepting the near certainty of added inflexibility that comes with increasing allocations to illiquid investments. And how should investors assess the returns to be expected from a particular illiquid investment?

A theme explored in this book is that investors should not assume that they will be able to earn a market return (whatever that might be) in illiquid markets unless they can convince themselves that they have an "edge" that will enable them to perform better than average. This applies to alternative assets (Chapter 10) and emotional assets such as art (Chapter 11) but also to less liquid credit (Chapter 9). Without such an edge, it is safest to assume that they will underperform. One hurdle to overcome is the high level of fees, which appears to be an almost universal characteristic of investing in illiquid markets. Another is the series of issues covered by the umbrella heading "agency issues", which refers to the informational and other disadvantages handicapping clients in their dealings with investment advisers in private markets.

Andrew Ang, formerly Ann F. Kaplan professor of business at Columbia Business School, has analysed these and other issues that arise in trying to determine an optimal allocation to private equity and other illiquid investments. An immediate problem he identifies is that traditional "mean variance" optimiser models used to derive recommended asset allocations for investors assume that investors can rebalance their portfolios at any time, which does not apply with illiquid investments. This inability to rebalance investment allocations imposes real opportunity costs on investors, and can result in unwanted risk-taking. A particular aspect of this, which is easy to overlook in the search for premium returns from illiquid investments, is that the ability to rebalance portfolios back to a long-term strategic allocation (see Chapter 5) is a means of seeking a liquidity premium from normally liquid securities markets by providing liquidity to risk asset markets at times of crisis when others are fleeing to safety. Investors who are heavily exposed to illiquid markets will be much less able to benefit from this liquidity premium. Ang concludes that long-horizon investors do have an advantage in investing in illiquid asset classes. However, this does not mean that it is optimal for each long-term investor to hold illiquid investments.

"Liquidity budgets"

One of the lessons to emerge from the credit crunch of 2007–09 is that investors need a policy on liquidity management. This became evident as investors scrambled to respond to a situation where formerly liquid markets became prohibitively expensive to trade in, and illiquid portfolios of alternative investments generated less cash and made calls on the commitments investors had already agreed. Against this background it became important that investors should have a good balance between liquid and illiquid assets, if only so that liquid investments could be sold to raise cash; it also became evident that when the dust settled investors ought to have an explicit policy on allocations to liquid and illiquid investments.

Illiquidity in normally liquid markets

Liquid markets give investors the option to buy or sell an investment at a modest transaction cost at a time they choose at prevailing market prices; illiquid markets do not give them this option. Like any option this is valuable, though some investors will value it more highly than others. Furthermore, the value that investors put on it varies substantially over time and between investors. Investors who particularly value liquidity will need to be offered a premium rate of return before investing in illiquid assets. Correspondingly, investors should always pay less for an illiquid investment than for an otherwise identical liquid investment.

Liquid investments should provide the natural habitat for short-term investors, even for aggressive short-term investors. This is because they may need to realise investments at short notice (which is why they are short-term investors). Long-term investors can more easily accommodate illiquidity and with skill (or luck) may profit from it.

The global financial crisis showed that some markets that are usually liquid can become illiquid surprisingly quickly. When investors want to sell, which is the same as saying when they want to demand or pay for liquidity, they may be forced to delay transacting and so accept risks that they would prefer to avoid, or they may be forced to concede damaging prices that they do not wish to accept. If the intentions of large investors seeking to unwind or establish substantial positions in a short period become known to others in the market, they will always become victims of predatory behaviour by other market participants. The market never behaves benevolently in these circumstances.

Variable liquidity is both a risk and an opportunity. An alternative definition of a short-term investor is an investor who may need to demand liquidity at short notice. Short-term investors should review and limit the allocation of their portfolio to markets that might be subject to marked fluctuations in liquidity because in these markets the price of liquidity can become prohibitively high in a very short period. This is a clear threat to the achievement of short-term financial goals. Long-term investors, however large or small, can profit from these swings in liquidity, so long as they are able to use skill in "selling" liquidity. However, if they have used their long time horizon to load up on illiquid assets, they will not be able to do this, and often the best outcome will be to ride out liquidity crises without having to accept penal terms for buying liquidity when it is most expensive.

Long-term managers with a clear sense of investment philosophy and discipline who, at the required time, have the asset allocation flexibility, will be able to exploit the occasional extreme price paid for liquidity. But for waverers, hesitation will always be reinforced by the certainty that there will be highly reputable commentators who argue that prospects have changed for the worse and that what appears inexpensive is at best fairly priced. For long-term investors for whom risk assets represent a "natural habitat", who have the good fortune (or foresight, or both) to have significant resources awaiting investment at the moment of crisis, these events can present a one-off opportunity to significantly improve their finances. But it will be a reward for taking risk when the majority wanted security.

Behavioural finance, market efficiency and arbitrage opportunities

Illiquidity indicates a breakdown of market efficiency in securities markets. Any discussion of market efficiency should start by addressing a widespread heresy, a variation of which Robert Shiller has described as "one of the most remarkable errors in the history of economic thought". This is the notion that the very existence of inefficiency in markets is a sufficient reason to expect outperformance from skilful managers. This notion is wrong. It does not follow that there must be easy rewards for skilled investors simply because markets are inefficient. The reason is that inefficiencies can be difficult to arbitrage. Correspondingly, if there seems to be no easy rewards for active managers, this is not necessarily evidence of markets being efficient. The rule of thumb is that if the existence of a market anomaly can easily be demonstrated, the safest conclusion is that there must be some difficulty in profiting from the anomaly. As Aswath Damodaran, professor of finance at Stern School of Business, New York University, writes in his book *Investment Fables*: "If you see easy money to be made in the stockmarket, you have not looked hard enough."

Barriers to arbitrage

Anomalies in the pricing of contracts that offer the same economic risks can persist even in markets which are the natural habitat of investment banks and hedge funds.

The key to the potential persistence of these "anomalies" lies in the impediments to arbitrage which can prevent instances of irrational pricing translating into easy profit opportunities. These barriers are generally considered to be of three types.

Fundamental risk and arbitrage

The first barrier is the common danger that fundamental risk may undermine any effort to arbitrage away an anomaly. An example would be where one company in an industry is thought to be expensive and a similar one to be more sensibly priced. A hedge fund manager might sell the former and buy the latter, but the size of these positions will be limited because the arbitrageur will know that unexpected events could cause the expensive stock to appreciate in price and the cheap stock to decline, causing losses to both sides of the "hedge".

Once in a while a graphic illustration of an apparently good hedge resulting in large losses for hedge funds is revealed. In May 2005 Kirk Kerkorian, an American billionaire investor, announced his intention to increase his holding in General Motors (GM) stock (which increased in price), and almost simultaneously Standard & Poor's (see Chapter 8) downgraded the debt of both GM and Ford from investment grade to sub-investment grade, which fell in price. The problem was that a number of hedge funds thought they were "hedging" GM equity (which they had sold) with GM debt (which they believed to be cheap, and so had bought). The result was substantial losses for a number of hedge funds on both sides of the hedge whose prices, unusually, moved in opposite directions.

This example illustrates a characteristic of a number of hedge fund strategies: that they often provide an attractive earnings stream, accompanied by the risk of occasional substantial losses (see Chapter 10). The simple lesson from this is to make sure that a hedge is a good hedge, and to be careful how much money is invested trying to exploit an apparent anomaly. The more substantive lesson is that even the best hedges may fail, and the risk of this happening puts a limit on the scale of the arbitrage position that will be applied to correct apparent market anomalies.

To risk money on an arbitrage position, an investor must consider the time horizon for the position. A hedge fund that correctly identified in the late 1990s that "new economy" (technology, media, telecommunications) sectors of the stockmarket were overpriced relative to so-called "old economy" sectors could easily have bankrupted itself before the validity of its analysis was demonstrated by the collapse of "new economy" stock prices. This illustrates that some types of market anomaly, whose identification will always be subject to margins of uncertainty, may require such long time horizons that the investors best suited to try to exploit them will be long-term investment funds, not hedge funds. Hedge funds are not ideally suited to correct all pricing anomalies.

Herd behaviour and arbitrage

Hedge funds may in fact exacerbate anomalies in the short run. The second barrier to arbitrage is that "noise trader risk" may undermine arbitrage efforts by making an apparent anomaly even more extreme. A trend-following hedge fund, or any other short-term "momentum" manager or speculator, understanding that investors may behave as if recent past performance will continue, is more likely to follow and reinforce the anomaly than to hold out against it (see Chapter 8 for a discussion of momentum strategies). There is widespread support for the idea that short-term trend following can be a profitable strategy. This can be seen as one application of the "greater fool" theory, namely a confidence that profits can be made out of "hot" overpriced investments by selling them at a higher price on a later date to a greater fool (though the trend follower will not be interested in whether the investment is overpriced, only the trend in its price). This type of trading by market insiders is probably as old as markets: academics have identified evidence of such profitable investment behaviour by market professionals during the South Sea bubble of 1720.

These patterns of investing will exacerbate irrational market trends. Success in this kind of anomaly exacerbating behaviour, like a policy of dancing by the doorway when you know the music hall may burn down, requires the ability to identify and respond more quickly than others to events that may burst a speculative bubble. On average for all investors this is a doomed strategy, but wishful thinking about their own nimbleness encourages many to stay on and enjoy the party while it lasts. A few always get out in time through a mixture of skill and luck. The random element of luck is normally downplayed, leading many to conclude that they may have the skill required to play the game next time. The one predictable result is that the market process of correcting anomalies is undermined and, for a while, made less effective.

In these circumstances it can be dangerous to bet against some apparent irregularities with more than a modest investment position. Anomalies can persist for a long time, reflecting the inability of short-term arbitrageurs (such as hedge funds) to remove the mispricing.

The role of crowd behaviour in driving investment prices away from their fundamental value requires a particular collective role for what are sometimes known as "noise traders". This needs a wide interpretation, because it does not just include the actions of uninformed investors. As well as professional investors who try to exploit momentum trends in crowds of uninformed investors, there are professional investors who feel forced to implement investment decisions that they view with deep scepticism. Such investments should be regarded as generating "noise", in the sense that there may be little fundamental investment justification for the decision. This may arise from selling pressure from funds in illiquid markets caused by end-investors who may need to raise liquidity or whose confidence in a strategy is undermined just when the investment case for it may appear to the investment manager to be greatest.

Occasionally, noise may result from spuriously precise definitions of "prudential" regulations. More common, though, may be the impact of peer-group pressure generating herding behaviour among investors. This may be purely informal commercial risk management, where a money-management firm determines that its biggest risk is to be different from other firms. Or it may be imposed by formal or informal rules which dictate the margin of difference from the market or from other investors (this is often called relative risk or tracking error) that an investment fund may run. Where funds or managers are assessed relative to an index or relative to competitors this pressure will be present.

The herd mentality is probably reinforced by the legal backing to the "prudent person" rule, which is the benchmark for the assessment of the reasonableness of the actions of fiduciaries in many countries. The 1974 Employee Retirement Income Security Act (ERISA) in the United States defines the obligations of a fiduciary as being to use:

the care, skill, prudence, and diligence, under the circumstances then prevailing, that a prudent man acting in a like capacity and familiar with such matters would use in the conduct of an enterprise of a like character and with like aims.

As Shiller points out, this definition tests the reasonableness of a fiduciary's decision against the standard of how a peer might behave. In other words:

The prudent person standard refers to someone who does what most of us think is sensible. Ultimately, it must refer to conventional wisdom.

It is not clear how this standard might be improved, but the inevitable consequence is that it validates the reasonableness of crowd behaviour. As a result, the impact of this standard of care is more likely to reinforce than to correct any tendency towards market mispricing. It will encourage trades that follow and support market trends as managers control their differences from the market or the peer group of other reasonable investors, who are behaving in exactly the same way. The behaviour of investment funds responding to this pressure has in the past been likened to a parade of circus elephants following each other round in a circle, joined from trunk to tail. The honest conclusion is that institutional investors never completely break from this circle. Their fiduciaries are, rightly, always looking over their shoulder and comparing themselves with comparable funds. For private wealth there is more flexibility, which brings both more opportunity and more danger, though private wealth managers will manage and monitor their own differences from their peers.

Implementation costs, market evolution and arbitrage

The third potential barrier to arbitrage activities is that "implementation costs" can be prohibitive.

In 2008, client selling, withdrawals of borrowing facilities and regulation changes (such as restrictions on short selling) probably conspired to exacerbate rather than correct market anomalies. In times of crisis liquidity pressures can force hedge funds prematurely to close positions, thereby exacerbating the very anomalies that they were trying to arbitrage. The 1998 Long-Term Capital Management crisis provided earlier vivid testimony to the reality that funds cannot always afford to maintain large positions that they may want to sustain for a long period. (Long-Term Capital Management was a large hedge fund that failed in 1998 as a result of the failure of arbitrage strategies of enormous size.)

These influences mean that there is no inevitable tendency for markets to become progressively more efficient. The cycles of market liquidity show that market efficiency is also cyclical. Nevertheless, the pressures to arbitrage away anomalies will always be a powerful force in any market. If a particular market arrangement is a barrier to efficiency, you can be sure that there will be great pressure to remove that impediment because there will be arbitrage profits available to those who help remove it. Today's barrier to arbitrage may not exist tomorrow, as institutional and market arrangements and instruments are continuously evolving to overcome obstacles and exploit opportunities to make money. Tomorrow there may be other anomalies, and old ones may reappear, but it would be a great mistake to underestimate what Robert Merton, the University Professor Emeritus at Harvard University, and Zvi Bodie, the Norman and Adele Barron professor of management at Boston University, refer to as "the financial innovation spiral" that works to chip away at anomalies and inefficiencies.

8

Equities

The restless shape of the equity market

At the start of the 20th century, railroad stocks represented 63% of the US equity market and just 0.2% a century later. Russia and Austria-Hungary represented 11% of the global equity market in 1899 and less than 1% 117 years later. In the past 35 years in the global equity market, the weights of Japan, technology stocks and banking stocks have risen and then fallen, and in the years since the late 1980s the weight of the emerging markets has increased from around 1% of the global market to around 13% in 2017. The scale of these changes is a powerful challenge to anyone suggesting that investors should passively accept whatever changes may occur in the market. An autopilot approach to investing in either domestic or global equities over long periods is not credible. All investors need to be responsive to changes in the structure, risk and opportunities of the marketplace.

Concentrated stock positions in private portfolios

The analysis so far has assumed that any equity exposure reflects the risk characteristics of the equity market. Frequently, though, equity holdings are concentrated in a way that increases risk-taking. Sometimes this arises from an executive's successful career with a listed company. In the United States, concentrated positions in employer stock within company-sponsored 401(k) defined-contribution pension plans used to be common, though these have declined in recent years.

The prescriptions of traditional finance are clear on this issue: there is no premium return, only increased risk, offered for a lack of diversification.

Increasing awareness, legislative change and the threat of litigation are moving practice in the same direction.

Concentrated holdings within defined-contribution pension accounts are separate from the concentrated stock positions that executives may accumulate as a reward for success through corporate remuneration schemes. The pension plan holdings reflect a deliberate decision by the individual to acquire, or to retain, the stock. Executives' concentrated stock holdings reflect involvement in business through employment or entrepreneurship. The exposure was acquired to align the interests of an individual with those of the company. In an executive stock compensation scheme, if the company and the individual have been successful, significant wealth may have been accumulated. At that stage issues of wealth and risk management become relevant. They are not relevant at the outset of the process. For this reason, concern about how best to manage an executive's concentrated stock position is an "enviable dilemma".

An executive's stock position is often subject to formal or informal selling restrictions. When a restricted holding represents a substantial part of an investor's wealth, a financial adviser may recommend borrowing against the security of that holding to allow investing elsewhere. If the concentrated position is unhedged, the borrowing will not reduce risk-taking. It will increase the potential for wealth accumulation by gearing the investor's overall portfolio, but at the cost of even greater volatility of that wealth. The likelihood of a sudden diminution of wealth is increased, not reduced, by borrowing against an unprotected concentrated stock holding and investing the proceeds of that borrowing in a diversified stockmarket exposure.

Assisting in the tax and wealth management of concentrated stock positions is an important role for many financial advisers. The risks of such positions need to be taken into account when allocating other financial investments. This is because the total wealth is dominated by their volatile exposure to the equity of their business.

Stockmarket anomalies and the fundamental insight of the capital asset pricing model

Despite the extraordinary changes in the shape of the global equity market, an annually rebalanced, passive approach to investing in US, UK or global equities, if it had been available, could have performed extremely well over the past 12 decades (see Chapter 4). However, the belief that it should be possible to do "better" than to match the performance of the stockmarket is supported by a wide body of research (even though simple arithmetic tells us that this cannot be true for all stockmarket investors). This research has focused on extensive analysis of stockmarket "anomalies", which are well-established patterns of stockmarket performance that do not conform with the predictions of the original simplified theory called the capital asset pricing model (CAPM).

In its original form, the CAPM said that the performance of any stock should be expected to reflect two things: the extent to which the stock is a geared or a diluted "play" on the market as a whole; and a considerable amount of company-specific volatility. The first represents a stock's exposure to systematic risk (measured by its "beta") for which investors should expect to be compensated. An example of a stock which would be a "geared play" on the stockmarket, or a "high beta" stock, would be the stock of an equity money manager whose fee income, reflecting assets under management, would rise and fall in line with the stockmarket and whose profitability would be highly geared to this influence. Systematic risk cannot be diversified away in an equity portfolio. The second is "noise", or idiosyncratic or diversifiable risk. This should cancel out in a well-diversified portfolio, but it reflects the scope for an individual stock, or a portfolio of stocks, to perform differently from the market (or, more precisely, from the beta-adjusted market return).

There have been numerous refinements to the CAPM to reflect research indicating that there are a number of sources of risk for a particular share price in the stockmarket which can help to explain share price performance. These include interest-rate and foreign exchange exposure, corporate balance-sheet data, income and dividend information, as well as company capitalisation, industry and geographical location. An understanding of these sources of risk can help in the construction of equity portfolios, particularly if an investor has a view that a particular source of risk-taking is likely to produce good results in the period ahead.

However, the fundamental insight of the CAPM – the division of portfolio risk into undiversifiable, systematic market risk and diversifiable, idiosyncratic risk – has stood the test of time. It provides an invaluable framework for understanding how the activities of portfolio managers alter a portfolio's systematic and idiosyncratic risk exposures and so affect the performance and risk of that portfolio. An understanding of this insight, as well as its strengths and weaknesses, is an important aspect of the interface between finance theory and practical investment.

Among the weaknesses of CAPM is that it is now accepted that the original simplified theory does not fully explain the pattern of performance between different stocks. Low beta stocks, with supposedly diluted exposure to the market, do not systematically underperform the stockmarket as the original theory suggested that they should. Furthermore, stocks with smaller market capitalisation, certain measures of "value" stocks and recently successful, "momentum", stocks have shown an apparent persistence of superior performance that is inconsistent with the simplest versions of the theory.

There are two possible explanations:

■ These patterns reflect the impact on market prices of irrational investor behaviour such as investor fashions and a widespread desire to own shares in "good" companies and to avoid "dogs" (for example, historical stockmarket underperformers). If so, the anomalies would disappear only if sufficient weight of long-term investor money recognised the irrational behaviour of other investors, leading the "rational" investors to reorganise their portfolios to profit from these anomalies. This would bid up the prices that had been expected to outperform (removing the outperformance) and depress the prices of expected laggards (improving their subsequent performance). If enough investors responded in this way, the anomalies would disappear. But if they persist, "informed" investors who are aware of the anomalies should adjust their portfolios to profit from them.

■ The old measures of risk-taking may be wrong. If this is correct, those who seek to exploit the anomalies may simply be gearing up their risk-taking. For example, small cap (see below), some categories of "value" stocks and emerging-market stocks may be riskier than they appear to be. If so, it may be rational that they should trade at a discounted price to leave room, on average, for superior performance to reflect the extra margin of risk.

If the first explanation is correct (that groups of stocks tend to be underpriced), cautious long-term investors might reasonably increase their exposure to these groups of stocks. But if the second explanation is correct, this would be inappropriate. Investors need to know that there is no agreement among finance experts on this and that when faced with uncertainty, it is reasonable for cautious investors to err on the side of caution.

John Campbell of Harvard University and Tuomo Vuolteenaho of the National Bureau of Economic Research have argued that the traditional measure of market risk exposure, beta, is clouded by combining two different measures of risk. The first is the responsiveness of a stock to a change in the market's discount rate. As explained in Chapter 6 in the discussion of "good" and "bad" price declines, a fall in price caused by a rise in the market discount rate should be recouped by faster subsequent performance. For a cautious long-term investor this is not a major source of concern. The second element is the response of a stock price to a change in expectations for corporate earnings. This is what has been described as "bad beta", because there is no mechanism for ensuring a recovery of the lost performance in response to a downgrade of earnings growth expectations.

In studies of US equity performance, it was found that value stocks and small-company stocks are more sensitive than the market as a whole to changes in market-wide earnings expectations (bad beta) than growth stocks and large-company stocks, which are more sensitive to changes in the market's discount rate (good beta). Any investor should want to receive a premium return for incurring bad beta risk, and it seems that normally such a premium has eventually been paid to value and small cap investors, but it should not be taken for granted.

"Small cap" and "large cap"

In the early 1980s, Rolf Banz published research which highlighted the surprising superior performance of smaller companies compared with larger companies. This result has been replicated on numerous

FIGURE 8.1 **Cumulative return of US small cap and large cap stocks**
Total returns, before expenses, taxes and inflation, Dec 1925–Sep 2017, Dec 1925 = 1

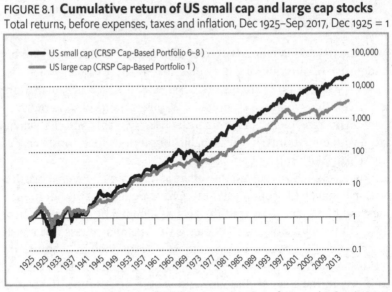

Data series: CRSP US database indices, Centre for Research in Security Prices,
University of Chicago, Booth School of Business.
Source: Bloomberg LP

occasions since for the United States, the UK and other countries, with a general pattern that the smallest, or micro-companies, have outperformed small companies, which in turn have outperformed large companies. The historical outperformance of smaller companies is the "small cap effect" or the "small cap anomaly", because, although small companies tend to be more volatile than large companies, the degree of outperformance could not be explained by the original simplified CAPM model.

A sense of the small stock "anomaly" is gained by looking at the historical performance of small and large capitalisation companies. Figures 8.1 and 8.2 make use of the comprehensive database maintained by the Center for Research in Security Prices at the University of Chicago's Booth School of Business. They contrast the performance from 1925 to September 2017 of the largest US companies (represented by the largest 10% of New York Stock Exchange listed domestic companies, as well as companies from the other leading US exchanges which are allocated

FIGURE 8.2 **10-year rolling geometric returns for US small cap and large cap stocks** Before fees, taxes and inflation, Dec 1935–Sep 2017, %

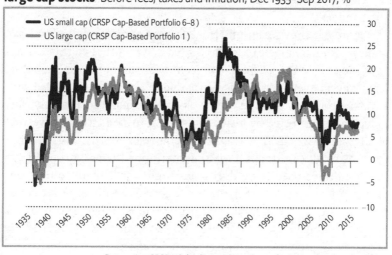

Data series: CRSP US database indices, Centre for Research in Security Prices,
University of Chicago, Booth School of Business.
Source: Bloomberg LP

to the same size bands) with the performance of small companies, indicated by those companies falling within the sixth to eighth decile bands of the same grouping. The cumulative outperformance of small cap since 1925 is impressive, with an initial $1 investment growing (before allowing for inflation, or expenses and taxes) to $20,600 by September 2017, compared with $3,500 for an investment in the group of largest companies. (Over the same period, consumer prices increased 14-fold.) This translates into an annualised performance of 11.4% per year for the small cap stocks, compared with 9.3% for the large cap stocks (and 2.9% per year for inflation).

A similar pattern is evident from research in the UK by Elroy Dimson and Paul Marsh, although as for the United States the margin of outperformance by small companies depends on the period chosen and the definition of small cap that is used. Their work lies behind the Numis Smaller Companies index, which has measured the performance of companies within the bottom 10% of the UK market capitalisation since 1955. Over the 62 years to the end of 2016, this index gave an annualised return (before fees, taxes and other costs) of 15.1%, which is 3.4% per year above the broad UK market, measured by the FTSE All-Share index.

Figure 8.2 shows a number of ten-year periods when small cap underperformed large cap in the United States, although this has not happened since 2003. The most recent persistent episode, including almost every overlapping ten-year period in the 1990s, coincided with a widespread view that the earlier observed "small cap anomaly" had indeed been corrected by heavy investment in small cap by investors bidding up prices as they tried to exploit the anomaly. In fact, since 1925, US small cap stocks have underperformed large cap stocks (on the definitions used here) during just under 30% of all rolling ten-year periods. Such relatively frequent periods of underperformance by small stocks are sufficient to caution most long-term investors against holding much more than a significant minority of their equity investments as strategic holdings in small cap stocks.

An understanding of what is meant by "small cap" is needed before a decision can be made on allocations. For example, different small cap managers may have different investable universes of stocks. Many money managers would regard stocks in the United States or Europe of less than $5 billion market capitalisation as small cap (though $2 billion is also quoted as a break point), and a market cap range of $5 billion–$15 billion as mid cap and anything above that as large cap. The index providers divide the market into proportions of the market. Large cap might be the top 70% or 80%, mid cap the next 15% or 10%, and small cap the remaining 15% or 10%. So 10% of total equity investments represents an allocation to small cap that could, if well diversified, constitute a neutral global allocation. Allocations of materially more or less than these amounts should reflect a decision to differ from the market.

With any equity investment programme, exposure to small cap stocks should be carefully monitored. It is almost always a mistake to approach small cap investing in an ad hoc, piecemeal fashion. This is more likely to be an issue with a private investor than an institutional investor, but the rule should be that exposure to smaller companies should be obtained through dedicated small-company portfolios or funds. In any event, there is a tendency for active investment managers to drift into small-company holdings (partly because they may be less well researched by competitors). For this reason, it is not sufficient to aggregate the benchmarks given to different money managers to arrive at a measure of exposure to different segments of the market. Active managers may vary significantly within loosely defined investment remits, and selected passive managers may have been appointed to manage money against index benchmarks that do not reflect the market. Wherever possible, management information should be obtained by aggregating underlying exposures to individual companies and then comparing them with the broadest possible measure of the market.

Will it cost me to invest ethically or sustainably?

Many investors have a strong preference to avoid investing in companies that transgress their personal codes of ethics or religion, so-called "sin" stocks. "Ethical" investors differ in their categorisation of sin stocks, but common industry groupings include weapons, tobacco, alcohol, gambling and pornography. A common supposition is that sin stocks will trade at a discount since they are shunned by many investors, in which case such stocks should be expected to outperform the market and ethical investors will pay a price for their ethical standards. The evidence for this is mixed, but it seems that investment managers often undermine the case for ethical investing by loading high fees onto ethical funds, which then underperform market indices and the most inexpensive index funds. But Jacquelyn Humphrey and David Tan, researchers at the Australian National University, in a 2013 *Journal of Business Ethics* article, "Does it Really Hurt to be Responsible?", have shown that responsible investing (for example, by screening out categories of "sin" stocks) need not lower expected risk-adjusted returns from investing in equities.

The track record for ethical investing, as illustrated by the FTSE4Good series of equity indices, has underperformed the broad market since its launch in 2001 (see Figure 8.3). The FTSE4Good index provides a benchmark for investors to identify and invest in companies that meet pre-set criteria. The index screens out companies that are tobacco producers, weapons producers, or nuclear power operators. To be

FIGURE 8.3 **Ethical investing, cumulative returns** $, Jan. 2001–Sep. 2017, Dec 1990 = 1

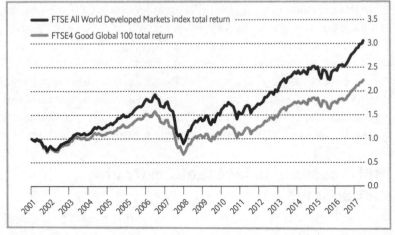

Source: Bloomberg LP

included, a company must adhere to specified standards for combating bribery, working towards environmental sustainability, ensuring good supply chain labour standards, promoting positive relationships with stakeholders and supporting universal human rights.

Analysis by the FTSE suggests that this past underperformance is explained by the company size and industry differences between the FTSE4Good index and the broad market. Specifically, the FTSE4Good index underrepresents the oil and gas, materials and utilities sectors, while overweighting technology and financials. There would seem to be no reason to expect this underperformance to continue for the indefinite future, although significant differences from market performance should not be a surprise.

Investors who favour "sustainable investment" are often seeking not to promote a particular moral code but rather to address a potential market failure, which is the likelihood that markets will fail to price appropriately externalities which impose medium- or long-term costs on the economy and society. One example would be a company that relies on inexpensive and plentiful fresh water, the supply of which is likely to become more difficult and so expensive over time, thereby undermining the company's business model. Other examples could involve waste management. Promoters of sustainable investment look to the integration of environmental, social and governance issues in investment decision-making. Some institutional investors are embracing such approaches as a way of fulfilling their desire to be responsible investors. Typically, they also anticipate that this will deliver superior risk-adjusted returns as the market gradually takes account of the costs of wasteful processes and corrects substandard governance arrangements. Such approaches have been supported by academic analysis of the corporate and social responsibility engagements with US companies between 1999 and 2009 by a leading institutional investor. This found that shareholder action by this large investor to improve the governance standards of companies on average does subsequently lead to an improvement in share price performance.

Don't get carried away by your "style"

Equity investment managers have particular investment approaches and philosophies, which lead to differences in style of investing. These characteristics are often as ingrained as any personal belief. Investors need to know and understand these differences. They will often find that some approaches are more appealing than others because of the sort of person they happen to be. Investors should be careful not to let these preferences result in unwitting risk biases in their investment strategy.

Philosophically, value and growth managers are quite different. Value managers have in common that they believe that markets repeatedly overreact as investor enthusiasm or alarm becomes detached from investment reality. As a result, value managers are contrarian individuals who are likely to make a virtue of implementing unfashionable investment decisions. Their analysis suggests that market prices oscillate around their fair values and that the turning point, when valuations become extended, is unpredictable. Value managers will try to persuade their clients that what is required is patience, as eventually the strategy is sure to be rewarded. In practice, clients are particularly attracted when a value manager has experienced recent good performance. This is when a value manager would naturally want to caution that such performance cannot be sustained indefinitely and that lean times might lie ahead.

The particular vulnerability for value managers who believe that "what goes around, comes around" is changes in long-term macroeconomic relationships. According to Sir John Templeton, a notably successful investor, "The four most dangerous words in investing are 'it's different this time'." But sometimes, particularly in the prospects for individual companies, things are different, for either good or ill. A growth manager is likely to criticise value managers for looking back and not identifying potential. For growth managers, analyses of technological and commercial change, and how this can transform the earnings prospects of individual companies, provide the cornerstone of their pursuit of new investment opportunities and understanding of business prospects. A growth manager's portfolio will consist of a variety of such investment prospects.

A crucial discipline for any manager will be when to sell out of a profitable investment position. This will often be much more instinctive for a value manager than for a growth manager, with the likelihood that a value manager may sell a profitable investment "too early" whereas a growth manager may be more likely to err on the side of selling it too late. This helps to shed light on some of the different risks faced by value and growth managers and their clients.

A close relative of the value style of investing is represented by wealth or fundamental weighted equity indices. Stockmarket indices are almost always constructed by giving different companies weights which reflect their comparative stockmarket valuation. These are the market capitalisation weighted indices such as the S&P 500 index for the US equity market. A criticism of these traditional indices from those who believe that the stockmarket is prone to overreaction caused by fads and fashions is that they overweight companies which are overpriced, but underweight companies which are underpriced. An alternative methodology has been suggested to reflect the contribution of each listed company to wealth creation, as indicated by their profit generation, cash flow and shareholders' equity (book value). If the underlying premise of this type of market overreaction is correct, these wealth-weighted indices should be expected to outperform the market capitalisation indices over time.

Value and growth managers

Value managers commonly have an investment process that starts with statistical screening of stockmarket databases for companies whose share price, earnings, dividend and balance-sheet data meet certain characteristics. A value stock will be one that has some combination of:

- higher than average dividend yield;

- lower than average ratio of the stock price to earnings per share or of the stock price to the book value of the company's assets per share;

- lower than average ratio of the company's valuation to sales or of valuation to cash flow.

These are some of the ratios that are used in constructing "value" indices of stockmarket performance. Individual managers will use different combinations of these and other indicators to screen for value in the stockmarket. Apart from purely quantitative managers, this screening process is best seen as a step towards reducing the potential universe of investable companies to a manageable number, which the investment manager can then research qualitatively in detail. This stage, involving management, product and industry research and ad hoc analysis, will often be the most important part of the investment process. But the screens are also important ingredients in describing a manager's investment style, and they will define the universe of stocks that the manager may then research further. As stock prices evolve, managers should be able to relate their actual portfolios back to those screens to demonstrate that the portfolios remain true to the managers' descriptions of their investment style.

Value managers divide into two camps:

- "Deep" value managers invest in stocks that meet their qualitative and quantitative criteria irrespective of how unrepresentative the resulting portfolio may be of the market as a whole. In particular, they are happy to have a zero weighting in parts of the stockmarket where the value screens suggest that all stocks offer poor value.

- "Relative" value managers manage the risks of their portfolios relative to the market as a whole, and so have disciplines that force the portfolio to hold some less expensive stocks in sectors that the screens suggest are absolutely expensive.

Money manager business leaders (who dislike the instability of assets under management that can be associated with deep value strategies) and investors who are particularly aware of "regret risk" generally feel more comfortable with relative value than with deep value management styles.

Growth managers are particularly concerned to exploit and profit from the relationship between earnings growth and stock price performance. Companies generally do not post unusually strong earnings growth results year after year. But as the market discounts the strong earnings of those companies that are growing rapidly, their stock prices can rise very strongly. This puts a premium on primary research into companies that may demonstrate unexpectedly rapid earnings growth in the future.

Many growth managers also use statistical screening of databases, but this is generally a less powerful tool than successful qualitative industry or thematic research. But such research is notoriously difficult to undertake successfully and consistently. The statistical screens used by the index compilers to define "growth" stocks are earnings per share growth, sales growth and the ratio of retained earnings to equity capital (the internal rate of growth).

Should cautious investors overweight value stocks?

Over the longest periods of time, by most measures, value stocks are shown to have outperformed growth stocks (see Figure 8.4). Despite this, by the traditional measure of risk, the volatility of returns, value stocks (in aggregate) have often appeared to be "safer" or at least "less risky" than growth stocks (see Figure 8.5), although noticeably this was not the case following 2008.

Investors who wish to tilt their investments to profit from the potential for value investments (or high income producing stocks) to outperform need to be able to withstand prolonged periods of underperforming the market. During the late 1990s growth stocks outperformed value stocks by more than 60% in just over two years, a process that was reversed in the subsequent 18 months, but then repeated in 2007–09 when value stocks (influenced by bank stocks) underperformed growth stocks by a cumulative 25% (see Figure 8.6). Few investors have the confidence to withstand being entirely on the

FIGURE 8.4 **Cumulative total return performance of US growth and value equity indices** Dec 1978–Jun 2017, Dec 1978 = 1

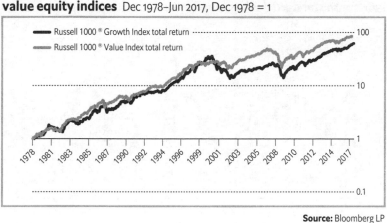

Source: Bloomberg LP

wrong side of such swings without making a mistaken reaction that would cost them dearly. As most equity investors now appreciate, maintaining balance is a prerequisite to sleeping easily.

Meanwhile, the possible risk explanations for the outperformance of both value as a style of equity investing and smaller company stocks cast doubt on the suitability of biasing cautious investors' portfolios in favour of value (or small cap stocks). This reinforces the case for a broad market approach to investing. To overweight value stocks or smaller company stocks then becomes appropriate for more aggressive investors.

Fashionable investment ideas: low-volatility equity strategies

In recent years there has been an enormous number of research papers published by academics and investment managers on stockmarket "anomalies". The holy grail for investment managers is a strategy that offers the prospect of higher returns (and so high fees) at no higher or, even better, lower risk. Largely based on the finding that value stocks (which are often low-volatility stocks) have delivered higher returns than would be expected by the original capital asset pricing model

FIGURE 8.5 **Volatility of US growth and value equity indices, 36-month standard deviations of return** Dec 1981–Jun 2017

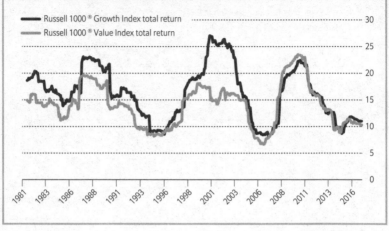

Source: Bloomberg LP

FIGURE 8.6 **US value and growth indices, 5-year rolling returns**
% per year, Dec 1983–Jun 2017

Source: Bloomberg LP

(CAPM), strategies have been designed to exploit these anomalies. This has led to a proliferation of minimum volatility equity strategies which select portfolios of stocks for their ability to deliver lower portfolio volatility than the equity market as a whole.

It is a characteristic of these approaches that they tend to overweight low beta stocks. These strategies are often sold on the premise that it is an anomaly that low beta stocks perform better than would be expected by the simplified CAPM. However, as discussed above, there may be systematic sources of risk that are not reflected in the volatility or beta of a stock. If so, investors ought to be, and normally are, rewarded for taking such risk. "Bad beta" (see the discussion on stockmarket anomalies above) would be one explanation.

Equity dividends and cautious investors

Cautious investors should follow cautious strategies. In so far as their caution allows them a margin of equity investments, equity risk should not be magnified by following an undiversified approach to equity investing. A focus on dividend yield can easily result in amplified equity risk. The disadvantage of relying on a stock portfolio for essential income is that it will not provide the element of insurance that is available from government bonds as it provides a less certain source of income. High dividend-yielding equities are likely to be particularly vulnerable to company-specific and economy-wide disappointments in earnings growth and threats to the level of dividends.

In conclusion, treat sceptically any suggestion that investing in dividend-paying equities represents a sound investment strategy that is likely to deliver both dependable growing income and accumulating capital values. However, if well diversified, such an approach can contribute towards a reasonably reliable source of regular income. An aggressive investor who has a need for income might emphasise higher-yielding equities and fixed-income investments. For a cautious investor, any such tilt should be modest. Such a strategy is not a magic solution for constrained finances, especially in an era of unusually low yields on government bonds.

Fashionable investment ideas: momentum strategies

A path-breaking 1993 study titled "Returns to buying winners and selling losers: Implications for stockmarket efficiency" found evidence of persistence or reversal in the relative performances of assets. The original research by Narasimhan Jegadeesh, chair of finance at Emory University in Atlanta and Sheridan Titman, professor of finance at the University of Texas at Austin, led to numerous subsequent papers by other researchers on persistence over successive time periods. These time periods are called by the experts who design investment strategies to exploit this effect the "formation" and "holding" periods. An example is a cross-sectional momentum strategy (CSM). This sorts the returns from a group of assets over a formation period, and maintains a portfolio over the holding period consisting of an equally weighted long position in the best-performing assets and equally weighted short position in the worst-performing assets. Such strategies have become popular in practice, due mainly to the fact that they have often delivered positive returns.

Since anomalous returns from momentum-based investment strategies might be thought to be contrary to the assumption of market efficiency, the returns generated by these strategies have been the subject of considerable empirical research spanning extensive asset classes, jurisdictions, and investment periods.

The reason why we hesitate to claim that this is contrary to market efficiency is that picking high-return stocks in the formation period may simply be picking stocks that are high risk. Most theories of finance argue that high-risk stocks should compensate holders of those stocks with high expected returns and the fact that high returns are found in the holding period may simply reflect that the stocks selected remain high-risk stocks with associated high returns. More behavioural explanations of momentum are based on over- and under-reaction to information, but these stories are not entirely convincing as there are not the same momentum effects in different markets. There is a broad belief that if momentum is driven by irrationality, then we might find more momentum in markets with a higher proportion of retail investors.

Can retail investors benefit from momentum? If we look back at the definition in the first paragraph of this section the CSM definition requires shorting the low return assets. This will prove expensive or virtually impossible for many retail investors. However, most of the profitability seems to come from the long part of the portfolio which can be replicated relatively easily. Indeed, certain versions of this, such as picking the best five stocks of the S&P 500 or FTSE-100 over the last six months and holding them for six months constitutes a momentum strategy which would be straightforward to implement (though of course at the mercy of the performance of the stockmarket as a whole). We do not endorse such a strategy, but readers can check for themselves if such an exercise would have performed well in the past, assuming they can access the appropriate data.

Home bias: how much international?

In recent years, investors around the world have allocated a growing proportion of their equity investments to international markets. Despite this, equity investors in almost all countries still have a strong bias towards domestic investment. The reasons for this have been debated widely. Any suggestion that domestic equities provide a better "match" for domestic currency obligations has little substance. The appropriate measure of "mismatch" is how well risk assets (such as domestic equities or foreign equities) correlate with the risk-free asset, which for a long-term investor is the domestic inflation-linked government bond. Although domestic equities may correlate better than international equities with domestic government bonds, they do not constitute any sort of "safe-haven" asset for long-term investment. But the reassurance of familiarity and habit, together with misunderstandings about the contribution of currency risk, largely explain the continuing home-country bias.

In most countries, this home-country bias is a significant risk management issue. However, the size and breadth of the US market, representing 52% of the world market in September 2017 according to MSCI, an index provider, means that well-diversified investors in US equities will have already achieved the bulk of the diversification gains that are offered by a global approach to investing. For investors in most countries international equity diversification matters a lot, but for US investors it matters less.

A recurring theme of this book is that investment strategy should be broadly appropriate for an investor's objectives, risk tolerances and preferences. Except for some cash flow matching bond portfolios, precision in identifying a suitable strategy is a pipedream. International investing is an area where strongly held differences of view on strategy are often indistinguishable within the range of broadly appropriate investment strategies. Despite this, when the performance numbers come in the differences can be large. This leaves a considerable margin of flexibility for an investor's gut preferences to influence policy legitimately. In international investing there is a range of appropriate diversified strategies and it would normally be inappropriate to suggest that a particular strategy is expected to be demonstrably superior to all others. For example, the diversification benefits of international investing are always subject to diminishing returns. Doing a little may get an investor a long way towards whatever is reckoned to be an "optimal" strategy.

Figure 8.7 shows (from a US perspective) the scale of the differences that can exist between US and international investing. After 1989, the United States substantially outperformed foreign markets, as much because of the prolonged weakness of the Japanese market as the strength of the US market. This pattern was reversed after 2002, and then in recent years reversed again, as the US stockmarket has outperformed. Figure 8.8 shows the UK has likewise experienced periods of marked outperformance or underperformance by international equities.

There are two reasons for investing internationally: opportunity and diversification. The natural starting point, from a textbook perspective, is the global market, with consideration being given to the possibility of hedging direct foreign currency risk. A global approach to investing should be appropriate for all equity investors. Other, domestically oriented approaches can also be appropriate; however, even for US investors there are demonstrable diversification benefits and increased opportunities to be gained from international equity investing.

The easiest way to assess the benefits from international equity diversification is to examine how it affects the measured risk of equity investing, using the conventional measure of risk: the volatility or standard deviation of returns. This metric is also used as the guide to the expected gains from international investing, because the prudent (and consistent) assumption is that the same expected rate of return will apply to international and domestic equity investments. The outcome will not (except by chance) be the same, but in setting strategic

FIGURE 8.7 **US and international equities, 5-year rolling performance**
% per year, $, Dec 1974–Sep 2017

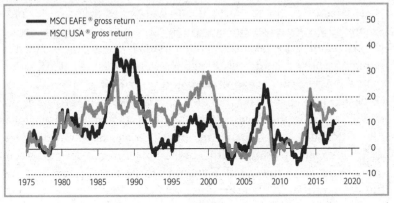

Note: The MSCI EAFE Index is widely used in the United States to measure international
equity market performance. It comprises the MSCI country indices.
Source: Bloomberg LP

FIGURE 8.8 **UK and international equities, 5-year rolling performance**
% per year, £, Dec 1974–Sep 2017

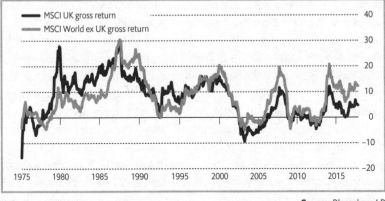

Source: Bloomberg LP

allocations, it is safest to assume that we do not know in advance which
equity market is more likely to do best.

This sidesteps the issue of whether there are any taxes or additional
management costs that apply to international equity investing but not

to domestic investors. If these are noticeable, they should be taken into account in determining international allocations. In what follows, this issue is ignored, and the focus is on volatility as the proxy for risk. Several strong messages emerge, which vary a bit with the time period chosen for analysis. For smaller equity markets, more can be gained in reducing equity volatility by following a well-diversified global rather than a purely national approach to equity investing. The result that consistently emerges is that the US stockmarket provides US investors with a level of equity diversification close to that achieved by global diversification. Other smaller national markets have not provided their domestic investors with comparable diversification, except over particular periods, which should not be extrapolated into the future. Nevertheless, there are still gains to be made by international diversification for US investors, though they are less compelling than for investors from other markets.

Figure 8.9 shows the volatility trade-off between domestic and international equities for the United States, greater China and India in more detail. The difference in the lines shown for the three countries tells a story. From a US dollar perspective, there is little apparent benefit in terms of reduced volatility from international investing. For Indian investors in particular, the historical data show a clear pattern, with equity volatility potentially being almost halved for investors who invest 80% of their holdings in well-diversified holdings outside India. These exercises also illustrate the impact of diminishing returns on the process of diversification: the biggest contribution to diversification comes from the initial foray into (diversified) international equities.

The scale of the potential diversification gains from international investing depends on the volatility of the international equities and on how highly international prices correlate with those of domestic equities. The higher the correlation, the less well international equities will diversify domestic equities, and the less will be the scope for reducing overall equity volatility by adding international equities. It should be no surprise that the degree of correlation is unstable, as is the level of volatility. Critically, at times of crisis measures of correlation and volatility often "jump" upwards. But just because correlations increase, it does not necessarily follow that the benefits of international diversification are diminished if at the same time volatility increases.

FIGURE 8.9 **Who needs international equity diversification?**
Volatility of equity investments from a US, Chinese and Indian
perspective % per year

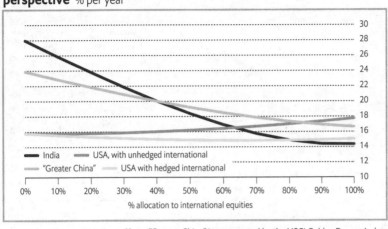

Note: "Greater China" is represented by the MSCI Golden Dragon Index,
which includes China, Hong Kong and Taiwan.
Source: Authors' calculations using MSCI indices

This will, however, mean that systematic or undiversifiable risk from equity investing has increased.

Figures 8.10 and 8.11 show movements in correlations of domestic and international equities from the perspective of US and UK investors. The message that emerges is that in benign times (the mid-1990s, ahead of the financial crisis, and in the years following 2014) rolling correlations between domestic and international equities (and especially with emerging market equities) can be reassuringly low. However, in 2014–15 the impact of the unusual decline in oil prices, and its differential impact between countries was also a factor. In bad times though, the reasonable expectation is that correlations (and volatilities) will increase, but even then, international equities should still provide valuable diversification benefits.

Who should hedge international equities?

This discussion of international equity investing has ignored the impact of currency risk (which is discussed further in Chapter 9).

FIGURE 8.10 **Correlations between US equity market, international equities and emerging-market equities** 36-month rolling correlations, Dec 1990–Sep 2017

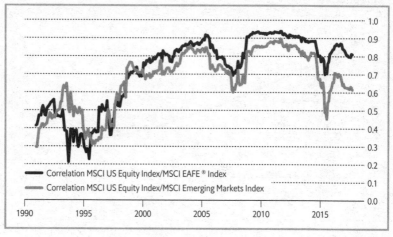

Source: Bloomberg LP

FIGURE 8.11 **Correlations between UK equity market, international equities and emerging-market equities** 36-month rolling correlations, Dec 1990–Sep 2017

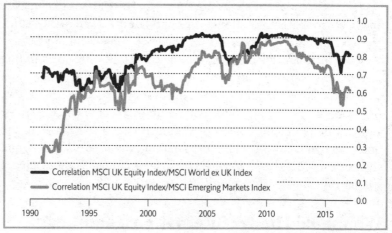

Source: Bloomberg LP

The reliable rule of thumb is that currency exposure in international equities generally adds little to the risk of equity investing (this is in contrast to international bonds, where currency hedging almost always achieves a significant risk reduction – see Chapter 9). But recent research has shown that this generalisation needs qualifying to allow for the tendency for safe-haven currencies to move against equity markets, which is a particularly valuable characteristic at times of equity market stress. Research by John Campbell, Karine Serfaty-de Medeiros and Luis Viceira published in the *Journal of Finance* in 2010 has shown that between 1975 and 2005 holdings of the US dollar, the Swiss franc and the euro (and before that the Deutschmark) diversified global equity risk. This means that US, Swiss and German (and then euro) investors would have profited at times of global equity market weakness if they had hedged their international equity exposure for currency risk. Hedging international equities for currency exposure does not much affect the volatility of international equity investing, but it does affect the pattern of equity returns. For investors from safe-haven currencies the research showed that it reduced losses (as compared with not hedging) at times of equity market weakness. An investor with a currency which tends to move with equity markets (for example, strengthening in bull markets and weakening when equities weaken) reduces risk by not hedging, and is likely to reduce losses in times of market stress. Historically, this has applied particularly to the Canadian and Australian currencies, and to a lesser extent sterling.

However, a currency can represent a safe haven in one period but not in another. The changing views of sterling, and also the euro, suggest that before drawing on this research to inform a decision to hedge or not to hedge international equities, a separate view needs to be taken on whether the investor's base currency is likely to have "safe-haven" status in the period ahead. Nevertheless, for investors with safe-haven base currencies (or whose currency is linked to a safe-haven currency), foreign currency hedging can provide an element of valuable (and inexpensive) insurance which is likely to provide a pay-off at times of crisis. Inexpensive insurance policies that are likely to pay out in "bad times" are particularly attractive to investors.

Consistent with the findings of academic research, unhedged international equities have been less volatile than hedged international

FIGURE 8.12 **US perspective on impact of hedging international equities, 36-month rolling standard deviation of returns**
$, % per year, Dec 1990–Sep 2017

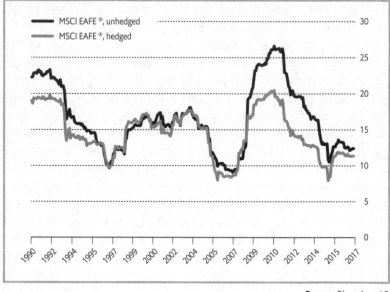

Source: Bloomberg LP

equities for Australian and Canadian investors. For Japan, Switzerland and the United States, currency hedging noticeably reduced international equity volatility. For the UK and the euro zone the reduction in volatility was scarcely noticeable. This is also reflected in Figures 8.12 and 8.13 which show the volatility over time of unhedged and hedged international equities from a US and then a UK perspective.

How much in emerging markets?

Over the past 25 years "old world" developed markets have (in aggregate) declined in weight in global equity markets as the so-called emerging markets, particularly of Asia, have grown in importance. Emerging markets, as classified by MSCI, include such comparatively developed economies as the Czech Republic, Chile, South Korea, Taiwan, the United Arab Emirates and, with effect from November 2013, Greece. The

FIGURE 8.13 **UK perspective on impact of hedging international equities, 36-month rolling standard deviation of returns**
£, % per year, Dec 1990–Sep 2017

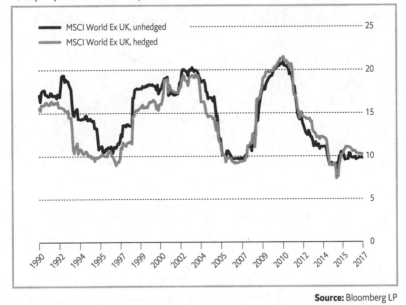

MSCI World Ex UK, unhedged
MSCI World Ex UK, hedged

Source: Bloomberg LP

MSCI Emerging Markets Index represented less than 1% of the world market in 1988, a figure that had grown to around 12% by October 2017. That proportion is growing further, not least as the index providers over time broaden their inclusion of domestic Chinese stocks ("A-shares"). In September 2017, China already represented 30% of the MSCI Emerging Markets Index. Changes to index inclusion policy could see this rise over the years ahead.

Opinions about the role of emerging markets in global equity portfolios differ. Some favour emerging markets because of their increasing importance in the global economy, their impressive track record, their diversification benefits and the prospect of higher rates of return. Faster GDP growth in these markets is often cited as a reason for expecting superior returns from emerging markets, but this is controversial, and history shows that the link between a country's

FIGURE 8.14 **Volatility of world and emerging-market equities, 5-year rolling annualised standard deviation of returns**
$, % per year, 1992–2017

Source: Bloomberg LP

economic growth and the domestic equity market can be more tenuous than is often supposed.

There are several reasons for this. First, much economic growth can reflect the activity of the government sector, the unlisted private sector, or of companies which are listed in other countries. In addition, even in emerging markets, domestic listed companies may earn much of their profits from abroad. Elroy Dimson, Paul Marsh and Mike Staunton of London Business School have examined the relationship between economic growth and stockmarket performance across 19 countries over more than 100 years and a further 40 countries with more than 25 years' stockmarket performance record and "find no evidence of economic growth being a predictor of stockmarket performance". However, they do think it is reasonable to expect higher performance from investing in emerging markets rather than developed markets, not because they are growing faster, but because they are riskier.

Figure 8.14 shows that emerging markets are more volatile than developed markets. In part this reflects inferior diversification in the emerging markets (which is not a risk that should systematically lead

FIGURE 8.15 **Performance of emerging-market equities in best up months for world equities** Jan 1990–Sep 2017, %

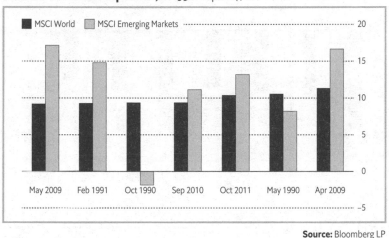

Source: Bloomberg LP

to higher returns), but also it reflects emerging markets behaving as if they provide a geared exposure to world markets (which leads to higher expected returns).

Figures 8.15 and 8.16 show that in the months when developed markets have performed best, emerging markets have tended to do even better, and that when developed markets have recorded their worst results, emerging markets tend to perform even worse. This high beta characteristic (see also Figure 8.17) is a reason to expect premium returns from emerging markets, but it is a reward for risk-taking and investors need to consider whether they will be sufficiently patient to weather the inevitable periods of disappointment to harvest that longer-term premium return.

Since the late 1990s, the emerging markets have consistently had a high (though recently, seemingly declining) beta with respect to world equities, averaging 1.3 between January 2000 and September 2017 (see Figure 8.18), suggesting it ought to be rewarded, if it is expected to be maintained, with an extra premium return of perhaps 1% per year, if markets operate efficiently and are fairly priced.

Figure 8.18 shows that prolonged periods of disappointing

FIGURE 8.16 **Performance of emerging-market equities in worst down months for world equities** Jan 1990–Sep 2017, %

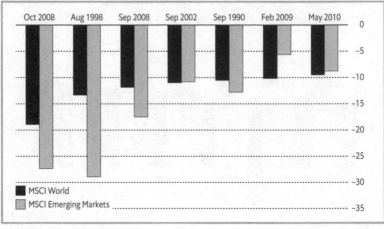

Source: Bloomberg LP

FIGURE 8.17 **5-year rolling beta* between MSCI Emerging Market Index and MSCI World Equity Index** Dec 1992–Sep 2017

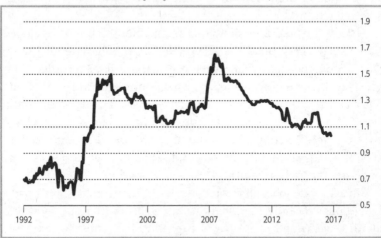

Note: *See Appendix 1
Source Bloomberg LP
:

FIGURE 8.18 **10-year rolling returns from developed and emerging-market equities** Dec 1997–Sep 2017, % per year in $

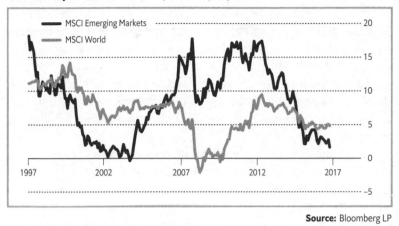

Source: Bloomberg LP

performance are evident even in the short period covered by the MSCI Emerging Markets Index. In the 20 years since the MSCI index started at the beginning of 1988, the rolling ten-year performance record has been equally divided between periods with developed markets outperforming emerging markets and periods when emerging markets outperformed. A predecessor index (covering years when emerging markets were much smaller as a share of global equity markets) shows emerging markets underperforming in the previous decade. Emerging markets may offer the prospect of superior performance to compensate for higher risk, but investors need to be able to withstand prolonged periods of underperformance.

For investors who are sure that they have the capacity and the inclination to act as risk-tolerant, long-term investors, Campbell Harvey, J. Paul Sticht professor in international business at Duke University's Fuqua School of Business, argues that the undiversifiable risk characteristics of investing in emerging markets go wider than the observation that emerging markets provide a geared exposure to global markets. These wider systematic factors include illiquidity, the scope to exploit inefficiencies in pricing which are still reflected in segmentation of emerging equity markets, as well as a negative skew of returns, and the exposure to "tail risk" that is exacerbated by exposure of emerging markets to contagion and the risk of explosive volatility due to "regime changes". Harvey argues that these should be regarded as "known unknowns" of emerging-market investing. Emerging markets also benefit from the strong link between liberalisation of finance and subsequently lower discount rates and faster growth. A patient long-term investor should have the ability to "time diversify" these risks, but also needs to be aware that, often because of institutional failings, not all emerging markets can take advantage of their growth opportunities.

For a long-term investor with the appetite and capacity to stomach these risks, Harvey says that the allocation within global equities to emerging markets should take as a point of reference not just the weight of emerging markets in global equity markets (around 10% at the end of 2016) but also their weight in world GNP (around 37% in 2011, according to Goldman Sachs).

Fashionable investment ideas: frontier markets

In international investing, it is easy for investors to be drawn into the latest "fashionable" theme. What is fashionable is often potentially illiquid, with surprisingly low measured volatility and attractive diversification characteristics. Sometimes these characteristics will indicate inefficiencies and opportunities for active managers. They also indicate potential liquidity issues that could arise in a flight to quality. At such times, as investors learned in 2008, previously reassuring correlations between risk assets typically increase rapidly and investment vehicles whose diversification qualities were touted by eager salesmen suddenly detract from rather than add to portfolio balance. Frontier emerging markets are a likely candidate for such promotion.

Figure 8.19 shows rolling three-year correlations between emerging markets, frontier emerging markets and the MSCI World Equity Market Index. The Frontier Emerging Market Index (whose largest country exposures at the end of October 2017 were the Philippines, Argentina, Kuwait, Peru, and Colombia) shows a persistently lower correlation with world equity markets than does the mainstream emerging-markets equity index. But a more detailed examination of the returns series for frontier emerging markets shows a greater degree of stickiness of prices (serial correlation), negative skew and liability to extreme returns (excess kurtosis) than is the case with the broad emerging-markets index. As with emerging markets, an investment in frontier markets should be justified by a long time horizon, an appetite for taking risk and an expectation of long-term reward for taking risk. Any diversification story is most unlikely to be helpful when it is most needed.

FIGURE 8.19 **World, emerging and frontier markets, 36-month rolling correlations** Dec 2008–Sep 2017

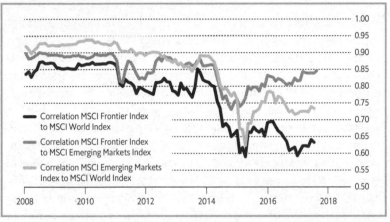

Correlation MSCI Frontier Index to MSCI World Index

Correlation MSCI Frontier Index to MSCI Emerging Markets Index

Correlation MSCI Emerging Markets Index to MSCI World Index

Source: Bloomberg LP

Credit

THE CREDIT CRUNCH OF 2007–09 showed many bond portfolios to be less well diversified than their managers believed them to be. It also reminded all investors that creditworthy government bonds are usually by far the most reliable diversifiers of risk assets. Before the credit crunch most bond portfolios became increasingly complicated as managers embraced new ways of packaging, and they thought diversifying, credit risk. The bond managers who performed best in the "bad times" of 2008 included those who were previously dismissed as irredeemably old fashioned by some for not adopting what were widely seen as new and better ways of managing portfolio risk. Table 9.1 shows the performance of government bonds in the United States, Germany and the UK in 2008–09 and that of corporate credit and equities. It shows government bonds diversifying best when diversification is most needed, that is in "bad times".

A holding of government bonds should have been, and for many investors was, sufficient to mitigate materially the damaging impact on investor wealth of the collapse in risk asset prices in 2008. Most bond funds have always exploited the premium yield (in excess of government bonds) offered by exposure to credit and this undermined the diversification offered by bond holdings in 2008.

Many lessons have been learned, but the most important lesson is that bond portfolios do not need to be complicated, though they often are. This chapter provides an overview of credit and credit ratings and why investors may not receive the premium return seemingly promised by superior yields. It also introduces "securitisation", which is the process of turning pools of bank loans (such as mortgages) into marketable securities, and gives a brief introduction to the world of

TABLE 9.1 **Government bond and equity markets in 2008–09**
Diversification doesn't come much better than this
% annual total return

	2008	2009
Bloomberg Barclays US Treasury Index	**13.7**	–3.6
Bloomberg Barclays Municipal Bond Index	–2.5	12.9
Bloomberg Barclays US Corporate Investment Grade	–4.9	18.7
Bloomberg Barclays US Corporate High Yield	–26.2	58.2
MSCI USA All Equity Index gross return	–37.1	28.8
Bloomberg Barclays German Government Bond Index	**11.2**	2.9
Bloomberg Barclays Euro Aggregate Corporate Investment Grade	–3.8	15.7
Bloomberg Barclays Pan Euro High Yield	–34.2	76.1
MSCI EMU Equity Index gross return	–44.3	28.7
Bloomberg Barclays Sterling Government Bond Index	**12.9**	–1.0
Bloomberg Barclays Sterling Aggregate Corporate Bond Index	–10.0	14.7
MSCI UK Equity Index gross return	–28.5	27.7

Source: Bloomberg LP

credit derivatives, which are, and will continue to be, used extensively in the management of credit portfolios.

However, a useful starting point for thinking about credit is an elementary review written by John Maynard Keynes, one of the world's greatest economists, in 1925 of a study of long-term returns from equities and bonds in the United States between 1866 and 1922. The study showed a substantial outperformance of equities over bonds in periods of both deflation and inflation. Keynes found this counter-intuitive, his expectation being that a period of deflation would be better for bonds than equities. He suggested a number of reasons for the inferior performance of bonds:

- The asymmetrical threat of changes in the price level. While bonds can be eroded by inflation without limit, the scope for the price level to fall (which would benefit bond holders, so long as bond issuers have the ability to repay these higher real values) is more constrained.

- Although a bond may default, no bond ever pays more than its coupon.

- Company management sides with equity investors rather than with bond holders and, "in particular, management can normally be relied on to repay bonds at dates most advantageous to the shareholders and most disadvantageous to the bondholders".

- Retained earnings provide an element of compound growth beyond the dividend yield, and this eventually accrues to shareholders in higher prices (while also making existing bond holders more secure in their entitlement to a fixed income).

This underlies the message of many advisers and of a number of academics that the natural habitat for genuinely long-term investors is the equity market. Nevertheless, almost all investors do, and should, seek diversification away from equity risk. In Part 1 this was argued from the perspective of investing in government bonds. This chapter provides the background to other types of credit instrument, which introduce new aspects of risk in return for the prospect of new sources of excess performance. An important element in this is the trade-off between credit quality and performance.

Credit quality and the role of credit-rating agencies

Credit-rating agencies originated early in the 20th century to assess the creditworthiness and publish ratings of securities. In practice, the two related risks that matter are default by a borrower and a deterioration in the assessment of creditworthiness of a borrower who nevertheless continues to meet contractual obligations. Investors routinely use the ratings of the leading agencies to measure the credit quality of their portfolios and also as thresholds to specify the minimum credit quality eligible for inclusion in particular portfolios. In effect, this has enabled private investors and many institutional investors to outsource analysis of credit risk to these rating agencies.

Historically, a rating from an agency has often been a precondition for marketing a new security and the credit-rating agencies have had a major role in promoting market liquidity. The late Peter Bernstein wrote in 2007:

> *The rating agencies contribute (or at least have contributed) to market liquidity because they spare investors the trouble of carrying out their own credit research.*

Acute problems with the rating of some structured products, particularly those focused on subprime mortgages, rather than in the rating of corporate bonds, undermined confidence in the rating process. The long-term rating classifications used by the three main agencies – Fitch, Moody's and Standard & Poor's – are shown in Table 9.2.

An important break point in Table 9.2 is between investment grade securities and non-investment grade securities. The latter are commonly referred to as speculative or high yield. The ratings are intended to be objective assessments of the creditworthiness of borrowers or of

TABLE 9.2 **Long-term rating bands of leading credit-rating agencies**

	Fitch	Moody's	Standard & Poor's
Investment grade:			
Highest quality, extremely strong	AAA	Aaa	AAA
Very high quality	AA	Aa	AA
High quality	A	A	A
Moderate to good quality	BBB	Baa	BBB
Speculative grade:			
Speculative, marginal or not well secured	BB	Ba	BB
Highly speculative or weak	B	B	B
Poor quality or very weak	CCC	Caa	CCC

Note: Precise definitions vary between rating agencies. These can be checked on individual agencies' websites.

TABLE 9.3 **Corporate bond average cumulative default rates** %

Rating	One-year	Two-year	Three-year	Four-year	Five-year	Ten-year
AAA	0.11	0.22	0.34	0.47	0.59	0.97
AA+	-	-	-	-	-	-
AA	-	-	0.11	0.27	0.44	0.49
AA-	0.06	0.06	0.06	0.06	0.07	0.19
A+	-	0.09	0.19	0.25	0.35	0.7
A	0.05	0.24	0.42	0.65	0.88	2.04
A-	0.16	0.29	0.43	0.53	0.69	2.28
BBB+	0.12	0.22	0.42	0.73	1.06	2.03
BBB	0.09	0.47	0.94	1.5	2.03	4.07
BBB-	0.35	0.98	1.72	2.36	3.14	7.21
BB+	0.77	2.51	4.04	5.58	6.83	9.92
BB	0.66	2.25	3.95	5.59	6.94	12.26
BB-	1.45	2.85	4.03	4.94	5.72	8.67
B+	1.04	3.57	6.01	7.64	8.59	9.43
B	2.15	4.9	7.5	10.66	13.61	14.81
B-	2.79	5.07	6.61	7.15	7.95	7.84
B						
CCC - C	23.52	30.36	34.73	36.64	38.97	39.88
Investment	0.11	0.31	0.55	0.79	1.05	2.15
Speculative	2.74	5.09	7.1	8.75	10.17	12.85
All corporates	0.71	1.38	1.97	2.48	2.94	3.98

Source: Fitch Ratings Global Corporate Finance, 2016 Transition and Default Study

instruments and are reflected in the spreads that borrowers must pay to compensate creditors for the risk of default (or of a deterioration in credit rating).

Table 9.3 shows average default rates for periods of up to ten years for corporate bonds of differing credit rating based on experience from

FIGURE 9.1 **Default rate of Fitch-rated issuers of bonds**
% of rated issuers

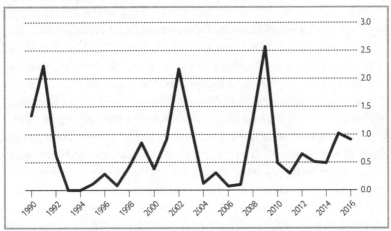

Source: Fitch Ratings Global Corporate Finance, 2016 Transition and Default Study

Fitch over the period 1990–2016. The table demonstrates that the rating agencies perform at least reasonably well in assessing the likelihood of different corporate bond issues defaulting. It suggests, for example, that investment grade corporate bonds had a ten-year likelihood of default of 2.2% while subprime(speculative) corporate bonds had 12.9% likelihood of default. These default rates are averages for Fitch-rated corporate debt.

Figure 9.1 shows that the incidence of bond defaults is cyclical. It reflects the default experience of all issuers of Fitch-rated corporate bonds, whether they have been rated investment grade or speculative. Indeed, the overwhelming majority of defaults by rated companies were ascribed a speculative rating before they defaulted. For example, Fitch reports that all 28 of its rated bonds which defaulted in 2016 were bonds which Fitch had rated as speculative grade at the start of 2016.

The pattern shown in Figure 9.1 is consistent with the pattern over much longer time periods. A 2011 article by four financial economists, Kay Giesecke, Francis A. Longstaff, Stephen Schaefer and Ilya Strebulaev, "Corporate bond default risk: A 150-year perspective", found that default experience is highly clustered and that on average in the United States,

1.5% of corporate bonds defaulted each year between 1866 and 2008. However, the authors report, based on other research, that investors probably recovered on average around 40–50% of the amounts due, suggesting an annual loss rate to investors in all types of corporate bonds of around 0.75% per year. Over the long term, the authors found that "credit spreads are roughly twice as large as default losses, resulting in an average credit risk premium of about 80 basis points".

Table 9.4 shows how spreads over US Treasuries have varied with differences in credit rating. These spreads follow the ordering of formal credit-rating assessments, suggesting that the financial markets broadly share the assessments of the rating agencies as yields paid increase as ratings deteriorate. It also shows average performance of the corporate bonds with different ratings. Note that the premium returns earned (column 4) tend to be noticeably less than the average yield spread on which they will have been purchased (column 2). This discrepancy is discussed below.

TABLE 9.4 **US Corporate bond yields, spreads and performance**
Aug 1988–Sep 2017

	Average yield	Average spread over Treasuries	Average total return	Premium over US Treasuries
	Column 1	Column 2	Column 3	Column 4
Bloomberg Barclays indices:	Under-10-year maturity bonds			
US Treasury debt	4.3	0.0	5.7	0.0
AAA corporate debt	5.4	1.0	6.1	0.4
AA corporate debt	5.4	1.1	6.3	0.6
A corporate debt	5.8	1.4	6.5	0.8
BAA corporate debt	6.4	2.1	7.0	1.3
Corporate high yield bonds*	10.0	5.7	8.3	2.6

*All maturities
Source: Bloomberg LP

FIGURE 9.2 **US corporate bond spreads** % per year, Feb 1987–Sep 2017*

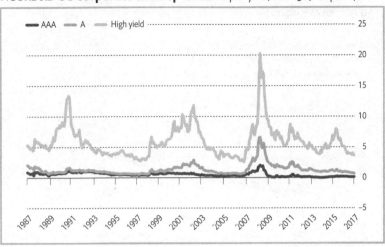

* Bloomberg Barclays Intermediate-term bond yields, relative to US Treasuries.
Source: Bloomberg LP

Figure 9.2 shows that credit spreads are, like the default rate, cyclical. However, the detailed research by Giesecke and her colleagues found that movements in credit spreads were a poor predictor of future default experience. Instead, they found that movements in credit spreads were best explained by movements in financial variables such as the stockmarket (spreads narrow as the market goes up), and of its volatility (spreads increase as stockmarket volatility increases), and by changes in the short-term Treasury bond rate (spreads generally increase as the risk-free rate falls). These results matter for investors as they suggest that a generalised increase in spreads is more likely to reflect adverse changes in market liquidity, for example, which a long-term investor should be able to withstand, than to be a reliable forecast of the likelihood of default. This is consistent with the recovery of credit markets after the severe widening of spreads in 2008.

Although credit spreads have more than compensated for the default experience of corporate bonds, it does not follow that investors have necessarily been adequately rewarded for investing in corporate bonds. Figure 9.3 shows the performance for the Bloomberg Barclays

FIGURE 9.3 **Cumulative performance of US under-10-year Treasury and corporate bonds** Jan 1987–Sep 2017, Jan 1987 = 1

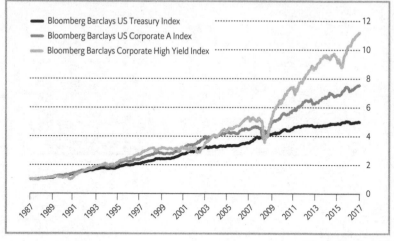

— Bloomberg Barclays US Treasury Index
— Bloomberg Barclays US Corporate A Index
— Bloomberg Barclays Corporate High Yield Index

Source: Bloomberg LP

US Treasury bond index alongside that for single A-rated corporate bonds and also for high-yield corporate bonds. This shows the superior performance of single A bonds and also highlights the risks and volatile performance associated with high-yield bonds.

Table 9.4 shows how the performance of investment grade credit has persistently delivered a smaller premium return over Treasury bonds than would be suggested by the spreads implied by redemption yields on the bonds. In the table this is shown by the difference between column 2 (the spread investors could have bought into the index) and column 4 (the more modest excess return earned over Treasury bonds, before any allowance for fees).

Some performance gap should be expected from the impact of occasional defaults. But their impact has been too small to account for the performance gap between the columns in Table 9.4. Fitch, one of the three leading international rating agencies, reports that the average five-year cumulative default rate for Fitch-rated investment grade bond issuers averaged 0.9% between 1990 and 2016, or 0.18% per year. However, actual losses will have averaged less than this as a result of recoveries of, probably, around 40% of amounts due.

Defaults of investment grade bonds therefore cannot explain the failure of the spreads at which investors buy such bonds to translate into corresponding premium performance. Other possible causes of performance difference include a movement of credit spreads between the start and end of a period of comparison and the likelihood that the corporate bonds and government bonds have different durations, and so respond differently to movements in government bond yields over a particular period. These can be important over short periods of time, but over the 29-year period covered by Table 9.4 this cannot be material (not least because the Bloomberg Barclays intermediate indices used in the table comprise bonds with less than ten years' remaining maturity).

Instead the reason is institutional and related to index composition rules. Investors commonly have credit-quality guidelines for their portfolios or the funds in which they invest, and the managers of investment grade bond portfolios are typically obliged to sell when bonds get downgraded to a high-yield or speculative rating, and perhaps when the bonds have less than one year to maturity (and so are excluded from the index).

Antti Ilmanen, the author of *Expected Returns, An investor's guide to harvesting market rewards*, and Kwok-Yuen Ng and Bruce Phelps, authors of a 2011 *Financial Analysts' Journal* article, "Capturing the Credit Spread Premium", have highlighted the asymmetry between a bond's underperformance before it is downgraded from investment grade and a bond's (possibly the same bond) outperformance before it gets promoted to investment grade from high yield. An investor with a credit-quality guideline which requires the sale of any speculative grade bond will lose out by suffering the underperformance before the downgrade and also by missing the outperformance of soon-to-be-upgraded bonds. The investor will also suffer from the much larger transaction costs that are paid when downgraded bonds are sold. A low-fee index tracking fund which is mirroring an investment grade bond index will suffer these performance penalties, while an actively managed bond fund which tries to exploit the phenomenon confronts a steep performance penalty from high fees. In their detailed analysis, Ng and Phelps estimated that a buy-and-hold approach to downgraded bonds would have improved investment performance on average by

0.38% per year between 1990 and 2009. The risk of default, which increases the longer the maturity of a bond, emphasises the need for any buy-and-hold approach to investing in corporate bonds to be well diversified.

Corporate bonds and stockmarket volatility

One way of looking at a corporate bond is to see it as an investment in a safe government bond at the same time as writing or selling an option (a put option) on the company. Normally, the investor in the corporate bond gets a reward equivalent to the return on the government bond plus a premium which is paid to the corporate bond investor as payment for the option that has been granted to the firm's creditors. Seen in this way, the option expires worthless if the company survives and is able to repay the corporate bond in full at maturity. Meanwhile the value of the option will vary according to the time to maturity of the corporate bond; the worth of the company in relation to its debt (in other words, whether it seems at any point of time easily able to meet its bond payments, that is, its creditworthiness); and also the volatility of the value of the underlying stock, which in turn will be a combination of the volatility of the stockmarket and the extent to which the stock might provide a diluted or leveraged exposure to market risk (in other words, the stock's "beta").

Perhaps counterintuitively, this results in a close relationship between stockmarket volatility and the spread, or premium yield, offered by corporate bonds over government bonds. This is shown in Figure 9.4. Expressed another way, since put options become more valuable when volatility increases and corporate bond investors are selling the put which will increase in value, corporate bond spreads are expected to increase as stockmarket volatility rises, and to fall as stockmarket volatility falls.

This leads to some important messages for investors. First, any corporate bond fund should be expected to underperform when stockmarket volatility increases. Equally, if stockmarket volatility is unusually low, then the spread over safe government bonds for investing in corporate bonds is likely to be unusually low. As was seen in 2008–09, investors should not rely on corporate bonds to have stable capital values at times of stockmarket turmoil. Equally though, the income from diversified corporate bond funds is likely to be more resilient than the fluctuations in prices of corporate bonds might suggest.

FIGURE 9.4 **Stockmarket volatility and corporate bond spreads**
Apr 2004–Oct 2017

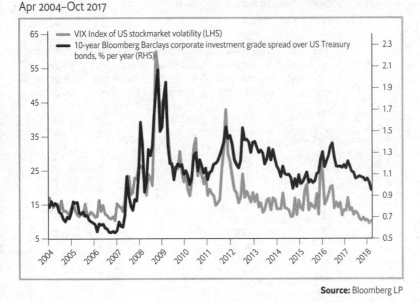

Source: Bloomberg LP

Portfolio diversification and credit risk

The words that rating agencies use to describe sub-investment grade debt, such as "speculative", "highly speculative" or "poor quality", fairly describe the risk of individual issues when treated in isolation.

For a long time it has been evident to investors in well-diversified corporate debt that the performance of the market is much less volatile than the performance of an individual issue, and that when the market is performing well, good performance can be provided by a portfolio of well-diversified high-yield bonds. So, it is inappropriate to regard a portfolio of high-yield bonds as if it had the risk characteristics of an individual sub-investment grade bond. Equally, the strong language that rating agencies use to describe the risk of individual high-yield bonds should remind investors that the only sensible way to invest in such credit risk is through a well-diversified portfolio. Diversification among a portfolio of high-yield bonds will reduce the risk of an adverse event affecting a particular issue. However, while a fund will diversify

TABLE 9.5 **Performance of selected debt markets in months of extreme US equity performance**
Jan 1994–Sep 2017, total return in $

	MSCI US Large Cap 300 Index	Bloomberg Barclays US Government Bond Index	Bloomberg Barclays US Investment Grade Corporate Bond Index	Bloomberg Barclays US Corporate High Yield Index	JP Morgan Emerging Market Bond Index Plus
Worst months for US equities					
Oct 2008	−16.2	−0.3	−6.4	−15.9	−13.8
Aug 1998	−14.3	2.6	0.5	−5.5	−28.7
Sep 2002	−10.8	2.3	1.9	−1.3	−3.7
Best months for US equities					
Oct 2011	10.7	−0.7	1.8	6.0	4.4
Oct 2002	9.3	−0.8	−1.3	−0.9	7.7
Apr 2009	8.9	−1.3	3.5	12.1	5.1

Source: Bloomberg LP

the idiosyncratic risks associated with individual high-yield bonds, it does nothing to reduce the systemic risk that can drive all prices in the market.

Table 9.5 compares the performance of the US government bond and investment grade credit indices with that of the high-yield and emerging-market debt markets in the months of most extreme US equity market performance since 1994. Debt issued by sovereign (or corporate) borrowers of emerging markets offers an alternative source of debt-based risk-taking. This debt may be denominated in US dollars or in the currency of the issuer (but see Local currency emerging-market debt box below). Such debt performed well in the years after the liquidity crisis of August 1998. In that month, the JPMorgan emerging-market debt index fell by 29%, more than twice the amount it fell in October 2008 (see Table 9.5). The 1998 experience revealed the undiversifiable risk of contagion in the market for emerging-market debt. This risk may have lessened as more emerging markets have repaid debt, accumulated foreign exchange reserves, acquired investment grade credit ratings and evolved towards joining the group of developed financial markets. In the years leading to 2007, performance of the market relied heavily on spread compression. But the danger of systemic setbacks leaves emerging-market debt exposed to the risk of occasional extreme negative performance, which has historically been a characteristic of the marketplace.

Local currency emerging-market debt

Early investors from developed markets who invested in emerging-market debt almost always invested in debt denominated in US dollars, or in other major currencies such as the yen or the euro. At the time there was little local currency debt available for international investors (which was a major structural weakness for debtor countries). This was attractive to many investors because they did not wish to compound the credit risk of investing in emerging-market debt with the currency risk associated with emerging markets.

In the past 20 years a growing number of emerging-market governments have issued debt in their own local currency, which has been targeted at international investors. These steps are responding to a market opportunity that suits both investors and borrowers.

A well-diversified portfolio approach to investing in local currency emerging-market debt can be attractive to a range of investors because:

- yields may be more attractive than comparable dollar debt (though this varies between countries);
- it enables investors to position strategy to take advantage of a view of the relative performance of the US dollar and emerging-market currencies;
- it may provide one source of efficient investment diversification for any investor (although the basis for any such calculation needs careful consideration).

Such investments may be particularly attractive to investors from emerging economies who have their investment accounts measured and reported in US dollars, and yet their base currency is to a degree ambiguous (see Chapter 1). The attitude to currency risk of these investors is less clearly defined than it is, for example, for a US resident. For some of these international investors, a portfolio of well-diversified emerging-market debt may offer an attractive way of mitigating some of their exposure to the US dollar.

The available benchmarks for emerging-market debt illustrate that these markets have been highly volatile in the past. Although diversification between countries is a major benefit, the impact of the 1997 Asian currency crisis shows how extreme the performance of individual markets can be, and even with a diversified approach, strong negative returns have been recorded at times of crisis. The JPMorgan local currency emerging-market liquidity index declined in US dollar terms by 15.7% between July 1997 and January 1998 and by 20% between July 2008 and February 2009. However, the 2008–09 decline owed much to movements in the US dollar and was just 2% when measured in euros and 9.5% in Singapore dollars (Singapore's currency floats with reference to a basket of trading partners).

Securitisation, modern ways to invest in bond markets, and the credit crunch

In recent decades, innovations in securities markets have transformed investment markets and bank balance sheets. Securitisation was for a number of years welcomed as enabling banks to better manage their credit exposures by separating their lending decisions from their need to manage the risks of their balance sheets. This was possible because standardised arrangements evolved which enabled the banks to offload their risk exposures to other banks, to hedge funds or to long-term investors.

Securitisation was a major innovation and it is a process that can facilitate risk management in the financial sector. But it also lies at the heart of much that went wrong in the financial sector leading up to the credit crunch of 2007–09. With hindsight, it seems as though banks used the invention of a series of useful risk management devices as an excuse to take much more risk, rather than to manage better the risks that they were already taking. Behaviour and incentives lay at the root of this. Securitisation encouraged bank executives with sales targets to achieve to take less responsibility for the quality of their lending decisions, which they knew would no longer stay on their banks' balance sheets. Thus a mechanism that was heralded as a means of dispersing risk instead led to much greater and hidden concentrations of risk. Securitisation itself was a good idea, but it was applied in ways that encouraged, while providing no mechanism to rein in, much looser standards in banking.

Mortgage-backed securities

Securitisation was an influence in financial markets much earlier than is widely recognised. William N. Goetzmann, Edwin J. Beinecke Professor of Finance at Yale School of Management, and a former student Frank Newman, describe in their 2010 paper, "Securitisation in the 1920s", how the issuance of commercial mortgage-backed securities fuelled the boom and then over-development of skyscrapers in New York and Chicago in the 1920s. More tall buildings (of over 70 metres) were built in New York during the ten years after 1921 than in any other decade before or since. Although taller buildings offered the hope of higher total rent income, many of these buildings were speculative builds which were then unable to find tenants to justify the inflated rents which had secured their financing and construction. Heavy losses for investors swiftly followed. Real estate bonds represented almost one-quarter of US corporate debt issued in 1925 and almost zero by 1934.

A major modern advance, which has some parallels with the mortgage bonds of the 1920s, came in 1970 with the introduction of a mortgage-backed security by the Government National Mortgage Association (Ginnie Mae), whose cash payments to investors represented a direct "pass-through" of the cash flows of the underlying household mortgages. Previously, mortgage-backed bonds had represented claims on the issuing bank, with a further claim on the underlying mortgages should the bank default. The principal investment feature of pass-through bonds is that they expose the investor to prepayment risk, because household mortgage holders in the United States can generally prepay fixed-rate mortgages without penalty. Prepayment risk is the main differentiator of mortgage-backed securities as investments. Individuals prepay for a number of different reasons, but the principal driver is the opportunity to refinance at a lower interest rate and cut monthly mortgage payments, after allowing for the fees involved. So prepayment risk is directly tied to changes in the level of interest

FIGURE 9.5 **Yields on US mortgage securities** % per year, Jul 2000–Sep 2017

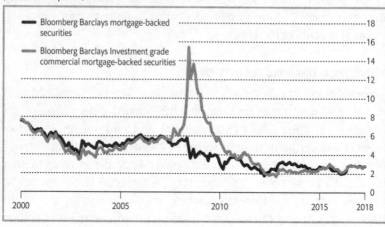

Source: Bloomberg LP

FIGURE 9.6 **Cumulative performance of agency mortgage-backed securities and commercial mortgages** Jul 2000–Sep 2017, Jun 2000 = 1.0

Source: Bloomberg LP

rates. A defining feature of the US residential mortgage market is that interest and principal payment obligations of mortgage-backed securities issued by the three federally sponsored mortgage agencies are guaranteed by those agencies.

This differentiates mortgages that conform to the loan quality guidelines of the federal mortgage institutions from those that do not – for example, because of their size ("jumbo" mortgages), a high loan to house value ratio or the low credit score of the borrower, or because some other qualitative guideline is breached (these are known collectively as "subprime" mortgages). Mortgage-backed securities based on pools of conforming US mortgages did not have the dramatic spike in yields experienced by other credit securities during the credit crunch, but damage was inflicted on bank and investor portfolios by securities based on pools of commercial mortgage-backed securities (see Figures 9.5 and 9.6) as well as non-conforming home equity loans.

By the mid-1980s the pass-through mortgage market led to the development of the collateralised mortgage obligation (CMO). The CMO arranges for the payments from a pool of mortgages to be split into a series of tranches, which are exposed to different elements of mortgage prepayment risk. These developments in the US mortgage market transformed the portfolios of investors in US dollar-denominated bonds. In the years before 2008, the repackaging of conforming mortgages provided the model for related but increasingly convoluted and often ill-fated innovations in other areas, where the credit-quality guidelines that have always applied to mortgage-backed securities were absent.

The role of mortgage-backed securities in meeting investment objectives

Mortgages that are subject to prepayment risk represent a peculiar investment which has become mainstream for many institutional investors. An investor, conscious of the need to meet particular objectives at dates in the future, is unlikely to have thought of an investment with the pay-out profile of a mortgage as a candidate for a core investment to meet those objectives. However, investors venture out of their safe-haven, minimum-risk investment strategy in anticipation of a premium yield in return for accepting prepayment risk. The benefits of the mortgage market for issuers is clear. It provides liquidity and has increased access to additional capital, both of which have probably lowered costs to borrowers. The outstanding volume of US mortgage-backed securities was around $5.7 trillion at the end of 2012 compared with $11.6 trillion of outstanding US Treasury debt.

For an investor, replacing government bonds with mortgage bonds, which are subject to prepayment risk, introduces uncertainty to a previously low-risk investment strategy. When long-term interest rates fall, homeowners will refinance their mortgages. This will be reflected in prepayments on a mortgage bond, which will reduce the bond's ability to support a given level of income in the future because the prepaid income has to be reinvested at the lower rate of interest. In this environment, mortgages should be expected to underperform government bonds. By contrast, when long-term interest rates rise above expectations, homeowners will want to retain their current lower level of mortgage payment, and repayments are likely to be lower than expected. In other words, mortgage securities, which are subject to prepayment risk, prepay more when investors want less, and may prepay less when investors want more. They represent a source of dynamic mismatch risk in trying to meet long-term objectives.

In return for these undesirable features, investors in mortgage securities collect an insurance premium, which is the extra yield that mortgage-backed securities offer over conventional bonds (after making appropriate adjustments to ensure fair comparison). This represents the premium that borrowers must pay investors for the option to prepay their mortgages ahead of the maturity date of the loan. This insurance premium represents a source of performance for investors in mortgages.

The phenomenon just described is known as negative convexity and is in general an unattractive characteristic for an investor. However, for long-term investors whose future obligations are subject to uncertain timing (for example, an individual whose retirement date is unclear or a foundation whose expenditure profile is not fixed), introducing an element of negative convexity through investing in mortgages might not increase uncertainty about the ability to meet future objectives, and might, thanks to the additional expected premium income, modestly reduce it.

Table 9.6 compares the returns on the major components of the Bloomberg Barclays Aggregate Bond index since 1987. It shows that over this 30-year period, on average, conforming mortgages did reward investors with a modest

TABLE 9.6 **Performance and volatility of components of Bloomberg Barclays Aggregate Bond Index**

Nov 1987–Sep 2017

	% weight in Bloomberg Barclays Aggregate Index Sept 2017	Geometric mean	Standard deviation	Maximum monthly decline
		% per year	% per year	%
Bloomberg Barclays US Aggregate Bond Index*	100%	6.4%	3.7%	−3.4%
Bloomberg Barclays Government Bond Index	37%	6.1%	4.4%	−4.4%
Bloomberg Barclays Mortgage-backed Securities Index	28%	6.4%	3.1%	−2.6%
Bloomberg Barclays Credit Index	26%	7.2%	5.2%	−7.8%

* Components shown do not total to 100 as they exclude commercial mortgage-backed securities and asset-backed securities.

Source: Bloomberg LP

premium return over government bonds, and they did experience lower volatility and lower drawdown when interest rates increased.

The position of mortgages in an investor's strategy should depend on analysis of the superior risk-adjusted return expected from mortgages, its uncertainty and how it correlates with an investor's other sources of systematic return. Furthermore, since mortgages represent a source of systematic risk-taking and government bonds (of an appropriate maturity) provide a safe-haven investment, the appropriate balance between government bonds and prepayment mortgages (as one of a variety of risky assets) should be guided by the investor's tolerance for risk-taking rather than the composition of market indices.

Quantitative investment

This is a term used to describe processes or strategies that are principally based on mathematical techniques. The term is often abbreviated to "Quant", which is then used as an adjective or as a noun to describe investment professionals who use mathematics in their investing life.

The advantages of using mathematical models in finance may not be apparent to practical people, but they allow decisions to be made in an emotionless way. Behavioural finance (see Chapter 2) has shown that investment decisions are easily contaminated by a variety of psychological issues, and so a rules-based decision process can have definite advantages. Of course, it may well be that psychological quirks are to some extent embedded in the model's own quantitative rules.

Quant was blamed for much of the global financial crisis. One strand of argument essentially says that quants were to blame because their bosses did not understand the models devised by the quants. This has some substance since the skills acquired or possessed by senior managers very rarely involve mathematics.

An extension of this argument is provided by an often quoted 2009 article by the financial journalist Felix Salmon "Recipe for Disaster: The Formula That Killed Wall Street". It went even further and seemed to blame the entire collapse of the global economy on a single formula. This seems scarcely credible, but it is a good example of the sorts of attacks made upon quants.

> In the mid-'80s, Wall Street turned to the quants – brainy financial engineers – to invent new ways to boost profits. Their methods for minting money worked brilliantly... until one of them devastated the global economy. ... And [one] formula will go down in history as instrumental in causing the unfathomable losses that brought the world financial system to its knees.

That formula was the Gaussian copula family of models that were used to estimate the risk of losses on collateralised debt obligations (CDOs), whereby payments from pools of loans (one example being subprime mortgages) were divided up into different tranches, reflecting the order in which payments were received from debtors in to the pool. These tranches were given different credit ratings, by the rating agencies, with the first tranche of receipts naturally being rated higher than the next tranche and so on. These tranches were sold to investors who will have taken their credit ratings to be a guide to probability of losses. In the event, the modelling which underlay the ratings on such structured products turned out to be woefully unreliable.

Quant and equity; quant and bonds

Felix Salmon's article challenges investors to ask when quant might be expected to work and when it might be expected to not work. This can be explored by looking at how quant can be applied to equity and bonds.

In the valuation of equity, there is a fairly common practice which is based essentially on two variables. The first is the ratio of dividends to corporate earnings; the second is the discount rate. While there are different types of stocks, a fairly homogenous group such as the S&P500, can be treated all in the same way and valued based on a common approach to the (approximately) 500 assets being valued. Experts in the field will point to subtleties that emerge even in this example, but the key idea here is homogeneity; the more similar different assets are, the more they can be valued by the same formula.

In contrast to equities, bonds are much more heterogeneous (a generalisation which often surprises non-professionals). This is reflected in the nature of quant bond models. These usually require many more resources to build and have far more component parts. In some cases a separate yield curve is used for each company's corporate bonds. While in an equity model, there may be one or possibly two such curves. Furthermore, different models are needed for different types of bonds; these include corporate, municipal, government and so on.

This helps explain why it is hardly surprising that the special formula alluded to by Felix Salmon's often quoted article might not work in practice. The objects being valued included a very wide range of very disparate financial contracts, which were extremely heterogeneous in nature. There is no reason to believe that one formula (actually, to quants, a very simple one) should work in all these different cases.

Retail investment and quant

It is important for individual investors to be financially literate. Most of that literacy is essentially basic quantitative investment. Understanding how portfolio returns are calculated, understanding simple notions of risk, understanding the time horizon of investment, are all ideas that can be explained with simple mathematics and are also easily capable of intuitive understanding.

Gaining such an understanding equips investors with the ability to challenge and assess external financial advisers, many of whom may not have much financial literacy themselves. Furthermore, given the fees and incentive structures financial advisers operate within, the advice retail investors receive is always liable to be contaminated by the advisers' self-interest. Being able to check some of the underlying calculations and to challenge some of the underlying assumptions oneself gives one a great deal of autonomy. As a general rule, quant managers are more likely to be well on top of this aspect of their investment business.

Equally though, the needs of individual investors can also be met by low-fee, very simple strategies that are tailored to their own particular circumstances.

International bonds and currency hedging

For all investors, foreign government bonds represent a way of diversifying yield curve risk and of seeking opportunities to add value beyond a domestic government bond benchmark. In Chapter 1, the ambiguity of the notion of a "home" currency for many international executives or families was discussed, and the importance was emphasised of carefully thinking through the currency composition of "safe-harbour" investments, such as cash or government bonds. Similar issues often apply to international investment funds, such as sovereign wealth funds. For textbook investors with a clear home currency, investing in foreign currency government bonds involves foreign exchange risk, which need not be a problem so long as that risk is properly managed. Otherwise the rationale for making a particular investment may be overwhelmed by the impact of currency fluctuations.

Currency risk is a manageable risk. It is also a big risk, which incorrectly handled can lead to windfall losses (or gains) of 20% or more over a 12-month period. Currency hedging is the way to manage this risk in international investments. The intuitive way of understanding currency hedging is to remember that it is equivalent to placing cash on deposit in the investor's home currency (for example, US dollars) and borrowing the equivalent amount in a foreign currency (for example, euros) to finance a foreign investment. In this way, fluctuations in the exchange rate will wash out, having an equal and opposite effect on the foreign investment and the foreign debt. The investor's investment return will be the performance of the foreign investment in foreign currency, plus the interest rate on the domestic currency deposit, less the interest rate on the foreign currency debt.

The more conventional way to describe this is to say that foreign currency risk can be neutralised through foreign exchange "hedging", where an investor contracts to sell foreign currency at a date in the future (or "forward") at the current exchange rate. The contract allows for differences in interest rates between the two countries. Typically, the contracts are for one or three months. They are then rolled forward and adjusted as needed to reflect any changes in value of the underlying investment, to make sure that it and any capital appreciation (or decline) remain fully hedged.

What does it achieve?

Currency hedging is interesting because it enables management of currency risk and, for many investments, it provides a marked reduction in the volatility of international investments. This is most clear in investment grade bonds, where a pattern of a marked reduction in volatility is evident when high-quality modest duration international bonds are hedged for whichever market over whichever period where there are liquid forward currency markets. For investments of moderate volatility, such as well-diversified high-yield bond funds or many hedge fund strategies, the arguments in favour of hedging currency risk remain strong. However, difficulties arise if the underlying investments are illiquid (see below). For more volatile markets, such as equities, currency hedging alters the profile of investment returns, but has a much more modest effect on volatility. The summary message, which can be replicated time and again is shown in Table 9.7.

What does it cost?

Three types of costs may be incurred in foreign currency hedging:

■ Transaction costs. Foreign exchange markets are among the most liquid markets in the world, and the transaction costs of putting

TABLE 9.7 **Hedging significantly reduces bond volatility but not stock volatility**
Sep 2000 –Oct 2017, annualised volatility of returns

	MSCI World Equities		Bloomberg Barclays Global Aggregate Bond Index	
	Unhedged	Hedged	Unhedged	Hedged
$	15.1%	13.5%	5.7%	2.7%
£	14.2%	14.4%	8.4%	2.8%

Source: Bloomberg LP

in place and particularly of rolling forward hedges in the principal currencies are tiny – a small number of basis points each year. But it is important to check whether there are any supplementary transaction costs that over time could materially reduce the attractiveness of hedging. For currencies that are subject to occasional liquidity crises, the "spread" levied in the foreign exchange market between forward purchases and sales – which would be expected to reflect the difference in short-term interest rates – can widen sharply at times of market crisis. This will dramatically increase the cost of hedging in those currencies. For this reason, an investor should not normally hedge investments denominated in currencies that may, at a time of crisis, become illiquid.

■ Cash flow costs. There are regular cash flows associated with currency hedging. These represent the currency gains and losses on the hedge that should be offset, perfectly with a perfect hedge, with currency losses and gains on the hedged investment. In an investment account, the gains and losses of the hedge will often be painfully evident, while the foreign exchange gains and losses on the foreign investment will be less obvious. Where the investment is illiquid – for example, if a US investor is hedging a European private equity investment back to dollars and the US dollar depreciates against the euro – the scale of the depreciation will be felt as a cash outflow associated with the hedge as the dollar depreciates. (See Chapter 10 for a discussion of foreign currency risk and illiquid investments, especially real estate.) Foreign currency hedging is best suited to highly liquid investments, such as government bonds. The cash flows associated with hedging can be both embarrassing and, for illiquid investments, painful.

■ Opportunity cost. This is closely tied to regret risk, that is, the risk that the decision to hedge an international investment will be regretted because subsequent currency movements would have made it more profitable not to have hedged. In this case, the investor's accounts may show a negative cash flow impact of the hedge and encourage statements such as "this hedge has cost me ...". Investors need to reflect on the reasons for the hedged investment when making these statements.

Sometimes, as with international equity investing, hedging decisions are finely balanced (see Chapter 8). Frequently, though, the appropriate rule of thumb is that certain types of international investment should not be made unless they are to be hedged. The obvious examples are investments in foreign bonds. Furthermore, many hedge fund strategies should be either managed or hedged to the investor's base currency. This is because exposing bond and hedge funds to unmanaged currency risk transforms the performance pattern that should be expected from the investment and this will often undermine the role that the investment is supposed to have in an investment strategy. If an investor likes the foreign bond market and likes the currency, a critic might ask: why hedge? The answer is that since currency volatility will contribute much more to the risk of losing money than bond market volatility, the position should be seen as a foreign currency view and not a bond market view.

How easy is foreign exchange forecasting?

Central banks, which ought to be well informed about the nature of currency markets, sometimes admit that they do not know how to forecast exchange rates. With hindsight it may appear that a particular exchange rate was "bound" to trend in a particular direction. With foresight it is never that easy. One of the most dangerous things an investor can do is to take unstructured foreign currency bets. These almost always degenerate into "bet the ranch" gambles, which make nonsense of any considered risk-taking that might until then have characterised investment strategy. This is because foreign exchange is a source of significant volatility with, on average, no expected pay-off. Nevertheless, carefully managed foreign exchange risk can have a role in any strategy where an investor uses a team that has both insights and a track record, and where the risk management process reassures the investor that the downside risk for when things go wrong – which is inevitable from time to time – is acceptable.

10

Alternative investments

ANY INVESTOR CAN FIND a suitable mix of investments to meet their needs from domestic and international equities and bonds. Most commonly investors will also have some exposure to property. Traditionally, "alternative investments" is the term used to describe direct investments in unlisted assets, such as private equity and hedge funds as well as property. They also include investments in infrastructure, venture capital and natural resources. The boundaries between these groups have become increasingly fuzzy and arbitrary, and the main categories are taken here to be direct investments in real estate, private equity and hedge funds. Not being listed on a stock exchange, they are often illiquid and also typically expensive for investors (but see below).

Illiquid alternative investments are not suitable for short-term investors. In addition, illiquidity restricts an investor's flexibility, and so should not be incurred unless there is confidence in superior returns or better diversification. Illiquidity also places a premium on information and the importance for investors of convincing themselves that they have a credible edge that enables them to perform at least averagely well in these markets. In liquid equity and bond markets, passive investing enables any investor to have confidence in being able to earn the market return (for good or ill). In private markets, performance is strongly influenced by the skill of managers, the extent of leverage that the managers use to amplify their returns, and the level of fees that they charge. These are markets where salespeople boast of their funds' superior past performance, but where in reality, and unlike with investments in stocks and bonds, investors cannot presume that they will be able to perform even averagely well. The key to unlocking returns in private markets is information, and investors have to believe that their managers have an edge that enables them to deliver at least market returns. Investing in an arrangement that lacks this edge will incur premium costs and condemn the strategy to inferior performance.

However, alternative investments are not always illiquid. In recent years, both pension funds and private wealth managers have made significant allocations to liquid strategies which give exposure to manager skill and sources of investment risk and return that are not readily available from stock and bond markets and so are intended to give better risk diversification and new sources of investment performance. Some of the largest multi-strategy hedge funds (see below) feature as core holdings in these allocations to "liquid alternatives". In addition, these allocations can include exposure to property through listed Real Estate Investment Trusts (REITs) and can access infrastructure, private equity and venture capital exposure through listed private equity companies (see below). These liquid alternative strategies may be packaged as alternative mutual funds (so-called alternative "40 Act funds") in the US or as UCITS hedge funds in Europe and give investors much more ready access to liquidity and sometimes lower fees than less liquid hedge fund or private equity strategies. However, although their promoters will not volunteer this, their price transparency also facilitates easy comparison with the volatility and performance achieved in the past by strategies of index matching equities and bonds offered by managers of passive funds.

PRIVATE EQUITY: INFORMATION-BASED INVESTMENT RETURNS

The appropriate place for private equity in investment strategy is straightforward. Private equity is what it says. It is equity, and so if included in strategy it should form part of an investor's allocation to equity. It is also private, and so unquoted and illiquid and not suitable for short-term investors, and its illiquidity will add inflexibilities and opportunity costs into any investment portfolio. Investors need to satisfy themselves that they can expect a premium return to compensate for these costs. All the comments about diversification by style, by size and by geography for investing in quoted equities (see Chapter 8) can be applied to private equity. However, since private equity is only part of an investor's allocation to equity, there is no requirement to include in a private equity portfolio all the diversification that can be obtained from the private equity market, when it can also be obtained inexpensively and with confidence from the quoted equity market. The key for investors is to be driven by a dispassionate assessment of their ability to gain access to skilled managers. The investor has to attempt to separate the impact of skill from that of leverage on the manager's track record. Having done this and become comfortable with the manager's approach to gearing the investments, the investor can then decide whether to make an allocation. The next step is to ensure that the total equity allocation (public as well as private) has the degree of diversification with which the investor is comfortable.

Since much private wealth has a shorter and less predictable time horizon than institutional wealth, most private investors are likely to be less willing than institutional investors to make long-term commitments to private equity or venture capital funds. As one wealth manager quoted in the Money Management Institute's 2012 annual report put it:

> We don't use private equity much. This is great for Yale or Harvard. But it is illiquid, and clients just don't get it. Death and divorce are too disruptive.

Despite this, families with very substantial wealth often do make significant allocations to private equity. According to Preqin, a database provider and consultant on alternative investments, family offices on average allocate around 25% of their assets to private equity. Most private investors, even if wealthy, have more modest wealth, and it is more telling and perhaps more typical that private wealth managers seem to allocate little to direct private equity, in contrast to their more significant allocations to hedge funds (see below).

What is private equity?

It is useful to think of the market in two distinct parts. The first is start-up venture capital. The second is the market for leveraged buy-outs of existing businesses. The market is commonly divided further, with venture capital differentiated between seed capital and early-stage venture capital, while the later stages of investing differentiate between buy-outs and expansion capital.

Expansion capital may take the form of "mezzanine" financing, which is the riskiest form of debt obligations. It will often have options to convert into equity if the firm fails to meet the terms of its debt, which will be priced to deliver a high rate of return. Mezzanine finance is expensive for companies. Management buy-outs occur when an existing management team is supported with external private equity, for example when a family business is sold, or a larger firm decides that an existing division is no longer a core business for the parent company.

The word "leverage" in a leveraged buy-out (LBO) refers to the financing of the deal, when the new private equity owners will have leveraged their equity ownership. This may occur, for example, through the issue of asset-backed loans or the sale of high-yield bonds, or, where bond or loan covenants are weak, by restructuring the company's balance sheet such that existing debt becomes devalued, and so higher yielding. This focus on the use of leverage is the principal reason private equity should, in general, be regarded as more risky than quoted equity.

Private equity firms transform the businesses they acquire through financial engineering, through changing the incentives facing managers, through more direct management of the governance of firms (than, for example, is possible with a shareholding in a listed company) and by deploying industry expertise to transform the operational management of the business. Buy-outs are also often associated with restructuring, which includes the divestment of non-core activities and also the acquisition of related businesses.

FIGURE 10.1 **Volatility of private and public equity, proxied by 3i share price and FTSE 100 index** % per year, Oct 1994–Sep 2017

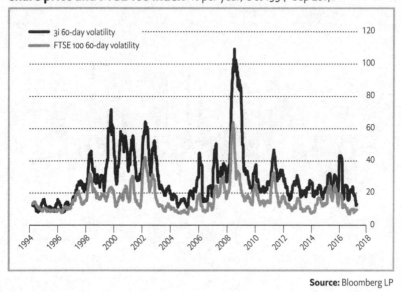

Source: Bloomberg LP

Private equity market risk

In all countries there is a wide variety of private companies, of which most are small, but some are large enterprises. In the years before the credit crunch, the development of private equity groups controlling large amounts of investor money led to the emergence of substantial private industrial and commercial conglomerates controlling private companies across different sectors of the economy throughout the world. These have branched out into new areas of investing, which have caused the boundaries between private equity, hedge funds and real estate funds to become blurred.

Private companies often look similar to the quoted companies with which they compete. However, this does not mean that the risks for investors are comparable with those of the stockmarket. Alongside leverage, a principal risk is illiquidity, and the great difficulty of selling a part ownership in a private company and the impossibility, other than at infrequent intervals, of rebalancing the allocation to private equity.

FIGURE 10.2 **Volatility of private and public equity, proxied by 60-day volatility of 3i relative to UK stockmarket** % per year, Oct 1994–Sep 2017; UK stockmarket volatility = 100

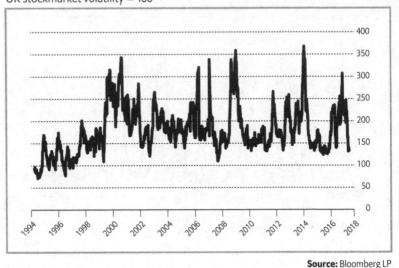

Source: Bloomberg LP

Another risk is that there are systematic biases in the characteristics of private companies compared with quoted companies (for example, private companies will have a bias towards small and medium-sized companies). Nevertheless, it might be thought that the inherent risk or volatility of their aggregate value should be broadly comparable to that of quoted companies. Leverage normally means that this is not true. Furthermore, even if this was the case, illiquidity would mean that it was not an adequate measure of risk.

One perspective on the intrinsic volatility of the private equity market is given by the volatility of diversified listed private equity firms. An example is provided by the 3i Group, which has been listed on the UK stockmarket since 1994, and was for a number of years the world's largest quoted company whose core business is the management of a diversified private equity portfolio. The evolution of the volatility of the 3i share price and that of the UK stockmarket is shown in Figures 10.1 and 10.2. Since the late 1990s, 3i has always had a volatility significantly higher than that of the UK stockmarket; between November 1994 and

September 2017 this was on average 80% higher (see Figure 10.2). This would not be the case for a diversified portfolio of listed UK stocks.

Some systematic differences apart from smaller size should be expected between the types of firms that are included in buy-out and venture capital funds and those that dominate the stockmarket. These biases will vary over time, with venture capital inevitably reflecting a bias towards whatever is the latest "new, new thing". Innovative technology will always be a characteristic feature and risk of early-stage venture capital investing.

Researchers have used a variety of more or less satisfactory ways of getting a handle on private equity volatility. These include examining the volatility of returns earned from private equity funds and using indices of smaller company stocks as a proxy for private equity.

Individual venture investments will always be subject to considerable stock-specific risk and, to diversify this risk, venture portfolios tend to hold more positions. However, manager expertise may still lead to focused risk exposures. In 2017, the troubled experiences of two large venture funds managed by Enervest, a Houston oil and gas company, highlighted the risks that can be focused on leveraged funds with exposure concentrated on one industry, and in this case, on one volatile commodity price, oil.

Financing structures are critical to the risk of LBO investments. For this reason, the intrinsic volatility of the private equity market, however well diversified, is probably significantly higher than that of the quoted equity market. Investors should not be satisfied with an expected return that does not compensate them for this leverage. Moreover, it makes no sense to pay performance fees simply to leverage an investment portfolio. Any investor can achieve this at minimal cost by buying equity index futures or a levered equity tracker fund. Few seem to choose to do so.

The process of allocating investment capital requires some rules of thumb for the risk of private equity. Here are some suggested guidelines:

- A major risk for both investors and managers of private equity portfolios is to act on inferior information. Do nothing in private equity unless you can access a credible information advantage.

- A broad-brush fund of funds approach that combines exposure to buy-outs and venture capital can be severely undermined in adverse markets by a combination of leverage and rising risk premiums, even if great skill has been applied in selecting the underlying companies in which the funds are invested.

- Investors need to ask what information advantage a well-diversified fund of funds arrangement is likely to have.

- An assumption that a well-diversified fund of funds has a volatility approximately twice that of the quoted market is probably reasonable. For a more concentrated approach, an assumption of a volatility three times that of the market might be used.

- In so far as private equity is a leveraged version of quoted equity, investors should require a premium return for the additional risk and should benchmark their private equity against a leveraged quoted equity index. However, investors should be aware that the level of leverage, and so the level of risk-taking, in buy-outs is cyclical.

These magnitudes matter because investors need to have a feel for how an allocation to private equity is changing the risk that is already present in their allocation to quoted equity. A diversified allocation to private equity of, say, 10% of an investor's equity allocation is likely to have a noticeable but not transforming effect on the volatility of the overall equity portfolio. However, if the allocation comprises one or more private funds, it will introduce illiquidity and so a degree of rigidity to asset allocation, which can probably only be unwound at significant cost.

Listed private equity

The traditional way for institutions to invest in private equity or venture capital is through buy-out or venture capital funds, or through funds of funds that invest in these funds. Typically, they have a high minimum subscription. Wealthy individuals often obtain exposure to ventures through less formal business angel (see Appendix 1) arrangements, as only the wealthiest have been able to subscribe to partnerships

TABLE 10.1 **Geographical spread of Standard & Poor's Listed Private Equity Index**
Oct 2017

US	54.5%
UK	12.5%
Canada	10.5%
France	8.2%
Switzerland	6.1%
Germany	3.4%
Japan	2.2%
Sweden	2.0%
Belgium	0.5%
Other	0.1%

Note: Index covers largest listed private companies that meet size, liquidity, free float and other eligibility criteria.

Source: Bloomberg LP

or to funds. The emergence of the listed private equity sector within mainstream equity markets offers an additional route to obtain private equity exposure. In the years before the credit crunch, this sector of the market expanded rapidly as private equity firms including Blackstone, KKR and Brookfield, a Canadian firm, obtained stockmarket listings for parts of their private equity investment businesses. In the UK, the globally diversified private equity business 3i has been included in the FTSE All-Share index since 1994, and in Japan, Jafco has been listed in the first section of the Tokyo Stock Exchange since 2001.

There are estimated to be over 100 listed private equity companies spread around the world. The geographical breakdown of the S&P index is given in Table 10.1 and Figure 10.3 shows the cumulative performance of this global index of listed private equity companies since 2003. The correlation between the broad equity market and the listed private equity sector is apparent, as is a leveraged relationship between private equity and global equities.

The listed private equity sector enables private investors with modest resources to establish exposure to private equity through the

FIGURE 10.3 **Cumulative performance of global listed private equity companies and global equities** Nov 2003–Sep 2017; Nov 2003 = 100, log scale

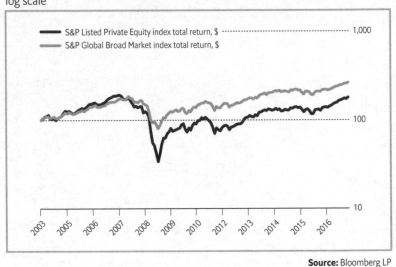

Source: Bloomberg LP

quoted market. It also provides a market price that shows either a premium or a discount to the appraisal values at which private equity funds are otherwise valued. This premium or discount to appraisal net asset values "marks-to-market" those valuations and so gives a benchmark that could be used as a check against appraisal values.

However, the premium or discount of listed private equity combines several factors. One is the valuation of business prospects of underlying companies. A second is the assessment of the management of the private equity firm, and whether it will improve the efficiency of the underlying firms by more than it weighs them down with added fees and, for example, whether it will successfully manage the cash flow needs of its underlying firms during a recession. The share prices of the listed private equity companies will incorporate more up-to-date information about these factors than are reflected in appraisal values.

A third, most important, influence on the premium or discount is liquidity. It reflects the price that buyers and sellers of a listed private equity firm pay for the ability to trade immediately (at least for small amounts) while investors in funds (which may have the same or similar underlying investments) normally are committed to their investments for years. When liquidity is highly prized (such as during a credit crisis), listed private equity vehicles will trade at a discount to net asset value, as sellers pay for the ability to exit their investment. This may represent a buying opportunity for long-term investors who have convinced themselves of the quality and sustainability of the underlying portfolio.

Private equity portfolios

An old adage in private banking says that you should concentrate investments to get wealthy (at the risk of losing your shirt), but that having become wealthy, you should diversify to maintain the wealth that you have already accumulated. This has parallels with the safety-first and aspirational portfolios described by behavioural finance (see Chapter 2). Private equity is about exploiting information advantages by identifying entrepreneurial skill. It is not about being financially conservative. It may form a component of an efficient diversified approach to investing, but within that it clearly forms part of an aspirational strategy to accumulate wealth.

This leads to several conclusions:

- Well-diversified fund-of-funds arrangements are likely to diversify away precious elements of information advantage, which will be further eroded by the burden of high fees.

- If high leverage persists across the funds, intrinsic volatility may still be surprisingly high even with a well-diversified fund of funds.

- It can be entirely appropriate to have a modest allocation to a small number of funds (even from just one team), so long as the combined allocation to private and quoted equity is reasonably balanced.

- A common danger in private equity investing is to fail to diversify private equity over time. Once a preferred arrangement has been selected, it makes sense to maintain a commitment to the market over time, most probably staying with the same team (or teams).

Otherwise, risks that were particularly prevalent in the market at a particular point in time (for example, high leverage or exposure to particular themes in venture capital investing) will unduly characterise the investor's experience of investing in private equity.

Private equity returns

Before making an investment in private equity, investors need to be confident that it is likely to be worthwhile. It is not sufficient that private equity firms should improve the financial performance of the companies they hold in their funds (research suggests that on average they do). Private equity funds need to raise performance to a degree that rewards investors adequately for the additional risks they encounter including illiquidity and leverage. A major self-imposed hurdle private equity funds have to overcome is the high level of direct and indirect fees charged by the private equity firms that manage buy-out and venture capital funds. Another, which is related, is the asymmetry of information that always confronts investors in their dealings with investment managers in private equity.

Private equity performance data suffer (as do those for private equity risk) from the absence of market indications of the value of private businesses. They need to rely on appraisal estimates which smooth the reported performance included in published calendar-year performance results. Appraisal valuations are still useful as they provide important management information for investors on what is "work in progress". However, the only private equity performance data that really matters is the internal rate of return (IRR) earned on investments. This combines the amount invested, the amount received back and the interval of time in between. In substance, these are the only financial magnitudes that the investor eventually knows for certain when investing in private equity (or any private investment). The IRR is the standard rate of return reported for funds and individual investments, but it is important to note that unrealised investments will be included at an appraisal value in reports of fund IRRs.

Industry data often report IRRs for funds started in a particular "vintage" year. This information does not reveal the volatility of those returns or enable like-for-like comparison with stockmarket performance. Such information is often broken down in marketing material to show the attractive performance of better-performing managers (for example, the top 25%), with the message that it is important to select a manager who will be in the top quartile in the future. It is always desirable to select winners, but the issue is whether the historical performance data of private equity managers provides a useful guide to future performance.

In mutual fund investing it is agreed that past performance in league tables is a poor predictor of future league table performance (but see Chapter 4). But in private equity there have long been suggestions that success is repeatable. There is some evidence from academic research that this may be the case, though more recently the phenomenon seems to have been less evident. However, research published by Robert S Harris, Tim Jenkinson, Steven N Kaplan, "How do private equity investments perform compared to public equity", in 2016 by using cash flow data for 1800 North American buy-out and venture capital funds found that buy-out funds, on average, consistently outperformed the S&P 500 index between 1984 and 2006, but that this relative performance appears to have tailed off since 2005. A more marked record of on average outperformance was found for venture funds, but without the consistency found for buy-out funds. Such comparisons are fraught with difficulty. As with mutual funds (see Chapter 4) there seems to a tendency for buy-out and venture fund performance to decrease as the aggregate amount of capital allocated by investors in that vintage year increases.

This research highlights the importance of a number of themes emphasised earlier in this chapter. First, the hurdle of fees is high, particularly when an investor can gain exposure to global stockmarkets through low-cost passive funds. Ludovic Phalippou of Oxford University's Saïd Business School, in a 2011 report for the Norwegian Ministry of Finance, said:

> A buy-out fund with a return after fees equal to the historical average return of the US stockmarket (over the last 30 years, ie, 11% per annum) would charge 6% fee per year.

This is after taking into account headline fees (typically 2% per year plus 20% of total return in excess of the hurdle rate, often 8%) and any consulting and advisory fees that may be charged by the buy-out fund to the companies in its portfolio. It probably should not be a surprise that investors in private equity have not, after fees, on average earned a premium reward to compensate them for the extra financial gearing or illiquidity involved in private equity.

A second theme is that investors need to convince themselves that they can identify better-than-average managers. Skill is essential. Investors cannot profit from market returns in private equity through a passive, market-matching strategy, so they should not expect to do even averagely well unless they can gain access to skilled managers, which requires more than reliance on a possibly out-of-date track record. Without skilled managers, investors will be condemned to underperform unless, for a period, they happen to get lucky. The problem is that it is most likely that a private equity manager who presents to an investor will be able to claim upper quartile performance. In the same report, Phalippou included an appendix, "Is there any fund that is not top quartile?" He starts by saying that "the oft-repeated private equity quip that '75% of funds claim to be in the top quartile' may indeed be true". The good news, he goes on to say, is that no evidence has been found of managers systematically mis-stating their own performance. Instead, the flexibility was found in their choice of benchmark, and the ambiguity that exists about when a fund properly opens for business.

HEDGE FUNDS

Hedge funds are another category of, knowledge-based, expensive investment vehicles. Some hedge fund strategies are quite illiquid, and their managers typically require quite long commitments from their investors. Other hedge fund strategies, particularly where the underlying investments are highly liquid contracts in derivatives or currencies, can be bought or sold more or less at will. Both liquid and illiquid strategies can give access to sources of return and diversification which are otherwise largely unavailable. But, as with private equity, no one needs to invest in hedge funds.

In the last 30 years, hedge funds have grown from being fringe

FIGURE 10.4 **Cumulative performance of hedge fund index and equities** $, Jan 1993–Aug 2017, Dec 1993 = 1.00, log scale

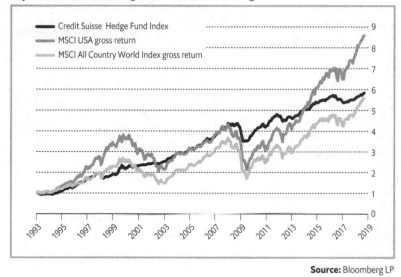

Source: Bloomberg LP

investment vehicles, managing money for some enterprising private investors as well as the hedge fund managers themselves, to mainstream investments for many institutional investors. In between, they also became a staple for investment of private wealth managers. In the early years, they built up a reputation with investors for being able to manage money successfully even when traditional investments did poorly. With notable exceptions, this reputation took a battering in 2008, when performance and assets under management declined sharply, but since then, hedge fund assets have grown strongly as they became a core holding for many institutional investors (see Figures 10.5 and 10.6).

In the crisis year of 2008, many hedge funds were confronted with a mismatch between the liquidity they had offered their investors and the illiquidity of many of their underlying investments. Performance losses were particularly acute in illiquid strategies. Funds of funds, where a portfolio of professionally selected hedge funds are marketed as a single fund, used to be a mainstay of private wealth involvement

FIGURE 10.5 **Hedge fund industry assets under management**
$bn, 1997–2017

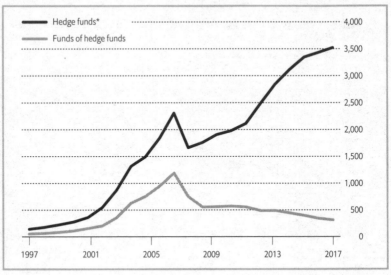

* Including managed futures funds (CTAs).
Source: BarclayHedge Ltd, www.barclayhedge.com

in hedge funds before the financial crisis. However, having represented around half of all hedge fund assets, according to BarclayHedge data, they have since declined, to around 10% in late 2016. In part this has been led by a renewed focus on fees, transparency and the marketing of managed accounts of hedge funds rather than funds of funds by the same managers. In aggregate, hedge fund assets reached $3.5 trillion in mid-2017 (see Figure 10.5), according to BarclayHedge, a hedge fund industry research and database provider. According to the hedge fund consultant, Preqin, around 70% of hedge fund assets are managed in the United States, with UK-based managers coming a distant second with 14%. In recent years there have been some well-publicised redemptions of hedge funds by institutional investors (especially pension funds), but at the time of writing aggregate allocations appear stable. In aggregate, institutional investors now account for around 60% of hedge fund assets, according to Preqin.

What are hedge funds?

Hedge funds are best understood as private entrepreneurial investment companies that operate with few constraints. Their investment strategies can be sorted into generic types. They have historically been lightly regulated, though this position has changed in recent years in both the United States and Europe. All hedge funds have in common remuneration structures that are exceptionally favourable to the hedge fund managers when their fund performance is good, though fee schedules have come under marked pressure in recent years. Three other characteristics are the investment of a substantial part of the managers' net worth in their own fund; their ability to have short positions in investment portfolios; and the secrecy that has often surrounded their underlying investment positions. They are also distinguished in being designed to generate positive returns, rather than to beat or match a stock or bond market index. The illiquidity of the underlying investments of a number of hedge fund strategies has always meant that those strategies are not suitable for short-term investors – something that investors were reminded of in 2008 when many funds delayed or "gated" redemptions to protect the interests of other investors.

Alternative sources of systematic return and risk

Hedge funds offer a range of sources of risk and return. Some of these have direct parallels with long-only stock and bond portfolios. Hedge funds typically attempt to isolate manager skill by reducing the influence of market returns on the portfolio, although funds still have a significant exposure to market risk. The origins of hedge fund investing in the late 1940s were represented by such funds, which today would be known as long-short equity funds.

But other funds offer completely new opportunities, for example the ability to treat market volatility as an investment to be bought and sold and to exploit trends in its pricing. Others include a number of market efficiency raising arbitrage strategies, including merger arbitrage, statistical arbitrage (exploiting short-term momentum in markets), fixed-income and convertible arbitrage. There is no long-only equivalent to the technical skill and market timing involved in such strategies, which are sometimes called "alternative beta" strategies. Each of these represents a potential source of systematic return, although the hedge fund industry's casual use of the word "arbitrage" must not be taken to mean that these strategies are low risk. Correspondingly, macro and commodity trading advisers (CTAs, also known as managed futures funds) are other strategies that have no long-only parallel. In these and other areas, hedge funds provide a risk transfer and liquidity service which in previous times either was not systematically provided or was provided by commercial banks. Hedge funds need considerable skill in providing these services, but the return that investors might expect from these services derives primarily from the market return to such risk-taking. It became clear in 2008 that many of these rely on ready access to liquid markets as well as a stable regulatory regime.

"Do hedge funds hedge?"

Figure 10.4 shows that the index of hedge fund industry performance (net of fees) has performed creditably against the US and global stockmarket indices (before fees) since the early 1990s and with evidently less volatility. The prospect of being able to earn superior risk-adjusted returns from diversified investing in hedge funds has always been one of the principal attractions of such funds.

This argument was cemented in the minds of many investors during the equity bear market of 2000–02, when hedge fund indices comfortably outperformed equity market indices. This helped to lay the foundations for the enormous growth of the hedge fund industry in the following five years. In 2008 the modest margins by which hedge funds in aggregate outperformed collapsing equity indices will have satisfied few investors. Although around one in five hedge funds did report positive returns for 2008, the experience of that year will be etched on investors' collective memory: hedge funds may help to diversify equity market risk, but they are risk assets and they provide no safe haven. This is not a new revelation. Best practice among private client and institutional advisers has for years been that hedge funds represented an interesting way of diversifying, but not of avoiding, equity risk.

TABLE 10.2 **Hedge fund performance during calendar quarters of equity market crisis**
1994 Q1–2017 Q3, % total return in $

	MSCI World gross return	Bloomberg Barclays US Treasury total return	Credit Suisse Hedge Fund Index
2008 Q4	−21.7	8.8	−10.2
2002 Q3	−18.3	7.4	−0.4
2011 Q3	−16.5	6.5	−4.8
2008 Q3	−15.2	2.3	−10.3
2001 Q3	−14.3	5.5	0.1

Source: Bloomberg LP

For investors who accepted that hedge funds were risk assets, the role of hedge funds in diluting equity market risk, while offering the prospect of additional sources of return, may even be confirmed by the experience of 2008.

Many equity hedge fund managers adjust their exposure to what they see as trends in markets, raising exposure after market rises and cutting after market falls (see the box in Chapter 8 on momentum strategies.) The 2000-02 equity bear market was unusual in being long and drawn out. That experience probably misled investors to expect hedge funds to be able to hedge in the event of sharp equity market reversals. During 2007–09, the credit crunch forced deleveraging and asset sales, whether or not hedge fund managers would have preferred to act differently. Table 10.2 shows the performance of an aggregate hedge fund index during the most disappointing equity market calendar quarters since the index started in 1994. These figures emphasise that investing in hedge funds may mitigate market risk, but it does not avoid it.

The quality of hedge fund performance data

The quality of hedge fund performance data is a subject that arouses considerable debate. This was brought to the forefront again by the Madoff scandal. The Dow Jones Credit Suisse indices are asset weighted to show the performance of the average dollar invested in the Dow Jones Credit Suisse sample for that strategy. Other index providers use a simple average of the returns of each fund (of whatever size) that qualifies for their index.

The focus of much commentary on hedge fund performance is that published indices overstate the actual experience of investors. One historical example was the 1998 failure of Long-Term Capital Management (LTCM), the largest hedge fund that would then be described as following a fixed-income arbitrage strategy. However, its failure is not reflected in the hedge fund industry performance numbers because from the outset LTCM, a highly secretive organisation, did not wish to share its performance numbers with anyone apart from its investors. Participation in databases of hedge fund performance is in part voluntary and the indices are not comprehensive.

The LTCM example is an illustration of incomplete reporting distorting the performance of hedge fund indices. However, consistent non-reporting by individual funds is not an obvious reason for the index numbers to overstate performance. Some have argued that the opposite may be true as consistent non-reporters may be among the group of successful, historically well-performing funds. Other data issues might bias the numbers. One is that new hedge funds are able to "backfill" their performance numbers in databases of hedge fund performance after they decide to start reporting performance (the disappointing "incubator" results may not get reported at all). However, reporting data to a database says nothing about the rules for eligibility for inclusion in an index; these are generally designed to exclude backfill bias by ignoring data for months before the date the data are first reported.

The consensus is that hedge fund indices do suffer from some element of survivor bias, which causes reported performance to be higher than the average experience of hedge fund investors. Furthermore, the track records that investors are shown ahead of new investment decisions are almost always subject to bias – investors do not invite the poor performers to make new business presentations. However, investors should not take investment decisions based on past performance alone. The key is always the expected future performance (and its source), how a fund might perform in "bad times", how this relates to the pattern of performance expected from the investor's other assets, and whether the investor can access that source of performance and risk from anywhere else. An understanding of these issues should be much more important than historical reported performance numbers in informing investors' decisions.

Are hedge fund fees too high?

Hedge fund fees need to be kept at the forefront of investors' minds. The traditional headline fee payable on an individual hedge fund often used to be "2 and 20". In other words, 2% a year of the value invested levied as a base fee and 20% of the return earned each year would be retained as a performance fee, so long as the return is positive and exceeds the previous "high watermark" or maximum level of performance. In recent years, base fees have been under some pressure, and in 2016 are estimated by Preqin to have averaged 1.6%, but it seems that typical performance fees have remained close to 20%, with both base fees and performance fees tending to be higher, the larger the fund. For more liquid strategies which are packaged as mutual funds or unit trusts fees tend to be lower.

The existing fee structure is already sufficiently rich to weaken (but not remove) the case for investing in hedge funds. For a fund of hedge funds arrangement, which involves an extra fee, the comparable figures would be even higher. These are generous takes by any reckoning, and not surprisingly have been under pressure.

The importance of skill in hedge fund returns

There is an abundance of research and practical experience that testifies to the scarcity of unusual skill in managing traditional investment portfolios. This is demonstrated by the difficulty of identifying managers who are likely to outperform in the future.

However, hedge funds give skilled managers greater scope to implement their skills, although they also need to find additional competencies. The extra latitude offered by hedge funds arises from the fewer constraints they face (compared with long-only investing). The first is the ability to establish leveraged positions through borrowing. The second is the ability to establish short positions, and to make money from their negative investment views (long-only managers

FIGURE 10.6 **Hedge fund assets under management by type of strategy** $bn, 1997–2017

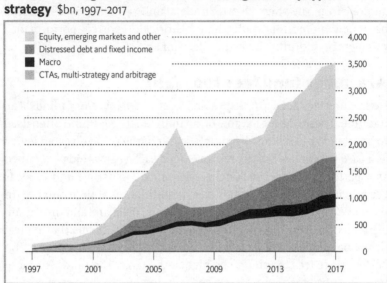

Source: BarclayHedge, www.barclayhedge.com

have to pass up such opportunities). These extra flexibilities require additional investment risk management and back-office operational skills. However, they do not make it easier to assess the skill of a hedge fund manager than that of a long-only manager. This is probably more difficult because hedge fund strategies are less transparent.

It is a mistake to think that unusual manager skill is the only element of performance that should attract investors to hedge funds. Hedge fund performance is a reflection of manager skill, leverage and market returns. Sometimes the exposure to market returns generated by hedge funds represents exposure to equity or credit market returns that can be obtained at much lower cost by investing passively in equity or credit markets. There is no need to pay hedge fund fees to access such returns. However, there are other types of market returns that cannot be accessed efficiently through traditional investment manager mandates and which represent investment performance paid for providing valuable services. These liquidity and risk transfer services are offered by a number of hedge fund strategies.

The shape of the hedge fund market

Figure 10.6 shows BarclayHedge data over the past 20 years, while Table 10.3 shows the detailed allocation by strategy in 2017, highlighting the marked decline and subsequent recovery in equity hedge funds in 2008 and the generally steadier growth in other strategies.

TABLE 10.3 **Hedge fund industry: assets under management**
June 2017, $bn

Hedge fund industry *	$3,179	
Fund of funds industry	$312	
Sectors		
Convertible arbitrage	$22.80	0.7%
Distressed securities	$111.30	3.5%
Emerging markets	$296.80	9.3%
Equity long bias	$290.10	9.1%
Equity long/short	$251.80	7.9%
Equity long-only	$170.20	5.4%
Equity market neutral	$90.10	2.8%
Event driven	$156.80	4.9%
Fixed income	$586.80	18.5%
Macro	$242.10	7.6%
Merger arbitrage	$78.90	2.5%
Multi-strategy	$391.20	12.3%
Other **	$337.00	10.6%
Sector-specific ***	$153.40	4.8%
Total	$3,179	100.0%

* Excludes fund of funds assets and managed futures funds (CTAs).
** Other: Includes funds categorised as Regulation D, equity short bias, mutual fund timing, statistical arbitrage, closed-end funds, and without a category.
*** Sector-specific: Includes sector funds categorised as technology, finance, real estate, metals & mining, and miscellaneous oriented.

Source: BarclayHedge Ltd, www.barclayhedge.com

Hedge fund replication and "alternative betas"

The enormous growth of the hedge fund industry in the past few decades and the combination of high fees and the apparent competitive performance of some hedge fund indices have attracted much academic analysis. Two strands of this research stand out for investors. One is the analysis of what can be deduced about the risks of hedge fund investing from the patterns of monthly returns for different types of hedge fund (see later in this chapter). The other related area of research has been to estimate the extent to which the performance of hedge funds can be explained by different market risk exposures (which may take significant expertise to access) rather than pure manager skill. If the performance of hedge funds can be replicated, so the argument goes, by combinations of inexpensive, easy-to-access market returns, it should be possible to obtain the benefit of hedge fund investing less expensively, with more liquidity and transparency, than by investing in hedge funds. Harry Kat and Helder Palaro, working at Cass Business School, London, in 2005, and then Jasmina Hasanhodzic and Andrew Lo, both academics at MIT (Kat and Lo are also investment managers), were among the first to suggest such a liquid alternative to hedge fund investing. So-called hedge fund replicators have since been marketed by a number of banks and asset managers. They have, however, been subject to criticism, not least because the lacklustre aggregate performance of hedge fund indices in the years up to 2017 (when risk asset markets were generally strong) meant that the replicators also suffered dull performance. Furthermore, a number of the replication strategies, though offering liquidity and transparency, nevertheless levied fees in excess of the charges that might be expected for such a commoditised (though technically sophisticated) product.

The analysis of hedge fund performance highlighted that investing in hedge funds often includes a large degree of exposure to equity, credit and interest-rate risk, as well as other easy-to-access exposures such as smaller companies and foreign exchange risk. Investors do not need sophisticated products to access these risks. However, hedge fund investing has two principal attractions. One is to access the performance benefits of unusual and exceptional investment management skills, which are rare, difficult to find and command a premium price. Another is to access alternative sources of market returns, so as to better diversify investment portfolios which are otherwise dominated by equity, credit and interest-rate risk, each of which can be accessed inexpensively using passive investments. Some of these alternative sources of return, also called "alternative betas", include collecting insurance premiums (and so risk suffering occasional large losses), which are represented, for example, in volatility and event-driven hedge fund strategies. (Volatility strategies may collect premiums in effect for providing insurance against stockmarket crashes.) Other strategies seek to capture systematic returns offered by momentum strategies. These sources of risk and return are recognised to be underrepresented in most investment portfolios and the techniques of hedge fund replication offer the prospect of being able to access them inexpensively. This is different from an attempt to replicate the performance of broad hedge fund indices (which research has shown to be dominated by equity, credit and interest-rate risks). Suitably tailored to offset the risk exposures already present in an investment portfolio, this offers the prospect of helping investors to diversify, a bit, the risks in their strategies to achieve a better overall balance between risk and return.

There are a number of different ways of grouping together different hedge fund strategies. One is to categorise fund strategies by whether their performance follows markets or is essentially independent of markets. This is helpful in interpreting the performance of a fund and considering its place in an investor's overall strategy. Long-biased equity hedge funds for example would be expected to follow the direction of the stockmarket, whereas an equity-market neutral fund or an arbitrage fund would not (though in practice it might). A completely different broad categorisation would be to consider the liquidity of the fund. This is set by three constraints. The initial "lock-up" period to which a new investor must commit, secondly, the length of notice that needs to be given to redeem units, and finally, the frequency of potential redemption dates. The less liquid the underlying investments, the more inflexible the redemption process. For example, distressed-debt funds have a focus on long-term investing and, according to Preqin, an initial lock-up of 15 months would be typical (but even then, funds might be unwilling to welcome investors who might wish to redeem so quickly). Other strategies are much more liquid. Managed futures funds (CTAs) and macro funds give investors quick access to their capital. CTAs for example may impose no lock-up period and require notice of redemption of less than one week. The liquidity of a fund and of its underlying investments will be key criteria which determine whether a hedge fund is suitable for different types of investors. Private wealth managers are often particularly attracted to more liquid hedge funds as a source of alternative investments for their clients.

Directional strategies

Global macro

In the early 1990s macro funds were the dominant type of hedge fund. Their importance has diminished in the past two decades as the range of other hedge fund strategies grew.

A macro fund may use leverage to exploit a diverse range of opportunities, investing in individual companies, equity or bond markets, commodities or currencies. The instruments a macro fund uses range from long and short positions in highly liquid (and potentially highly leveraged) currency or futures markets through quoted securities to illiquid investments in private equity or direct loans to companies. Historically, investment banks were able to replicate this range of opportunistic investing, but few other investment vehicles can come close to a macro hedge fund for the diversity of its entrepreneurial risk-taking. Performance comes from manager decisions: the changes in their market exposures mean that there may be no persistence of such exposures, and that little comfort should be taken from the low average correlation between macro funds and the equity market shown in Table 10.4. The flexibility of a macro fund's strategy means that sometimes it will diversify market risk and sometimes it will amplify it. The macro fund's investors probably will not know until after the event how the fund was positioned during turbulent market conditions.

Equity hedge, equity long/short and equity market neutral

The hedge fund business is traditionally considered to have started with the partnership set up by Alfred Jones in the late 1940s (though there are other claims for earlier antecedents). It would be recognised today as an "equity long/short" or "equity hedge" fund. It incorporated short selling of overvalued stocks alongside holdings of undervalued stocks. In this way its exposure to market movements was reduced and its exposure to manager skills was emphasised.

TABLE 10.4 **Selected hedge fund strategies: correlations with global equity market**
Jan 1994–Sep 2017, % total return in $

	MSCI World
Credit Suisse Hedge Fund Index	
Long-short equity	0.71
Global macro	0.23
Managed futures	−0.03
Short bias	−0.74
	MSCI Emerging Market Equity Index
Emerging markets	0.79

Source for underlying data: Bloomberg LP

Equity long/short funds normally have some positive exposure to equity markets and are considered to be directional funds. This is confirmed in Table 10.4, which shows that between 1994 and 2017 the correlation between the index of equity long/short hedge fund manager performance and that of the world stockmarket was 0.71. Furthermore, the pattern of returns generated by these funds often indicates that the stocks that they "short", or sell, tend to be easy-to-borrow liquid large cap stocks or even index futures contracts, whereas the stocks that they purchase (or go long) have tended to be less liquid, smaller company stocks. This pattern introduces a distinctive element of systematic risk into many of these hedge funds, which may have a leveraged exposure to the performance of small companies relative to large companies.

Equity long/short hedge funds typically have much less diversified portfolios than conventional long-only portfolios. Some of these equity hedge funds seek to neutralise market risk exposures and to offer an investment return that, as near as possible, reflects only the investment manager's stock-picking skills. These, called equity market neutral, form a minority of the equity hedge funds.

Short-selling or short-biased managers

Short-selling managers sell stocks that they expect to decline in value in the expectation of being able to buy them back at a later date at a lower price. These directional funds should perform particularly well when the stockmarket declines. How well a short-selling fund provides this insurance will depend upon how well it is diversified. In practice, the average performance of the short-selling strategy in calendar quarters of equity setback has been strongly positive.

Table 10.4 indicates that the correlation between short-biased hedge funds and the US stockmarket has been around −0.74. Short-selling funds are particularly used by fund of hedge fund managers to reduce the overall equity market exposure of their portfolios of hedge funds. In practice, the money managed by short-selling funds is normally modest.

Long-only equity hedge funds

These do exist. They do not hedge, but they call themselves hedge funds and during the bull market before 2007, they represented a way for hedge funds to diversify their business. The principals own a significant equity stake and typically they invest opportunistically in smaller quoted and perhaps some unquoted private companies. The fee arrangements are much more attractive to the managers of these funds than those for their close relative, the small cap mutual fund. Furthermore, they are given a greater degree of investment flexibility by being in a stronger position (than a mutual fund) to manage the terms on which clients can exit from the fund.

Emerging-market hedge funds

As the name suggests, these funds exploit opportunities in emerging markets. They are directional funds which invest in both equities and bonds. It can be difficult to borrow stock in these markets and one means of altering market exposure is by leveraging the entire portfolio through borrowing, or by scaling back exposure through building up holdings of cash. Their performance is often highly correlated with emerging-market equities (see Tables 10.4).

Fixed-income hedge funds: distressed debt

"Distressed debt" conjures up images of the obligations of companies that are close to bankruptcy. This is the traditional fishing pond for hedge funds specialising in distressed debt. This group of hedge funds also includes some significant hedge funds which can resemble "private debt funds". The risk for investors is a function of the underlying investments, of the leverage and of the illiquidity of the fund. The largest of these have much in common with large private equity funds. For an investor, there is likely to be an overlap in terms of the underlying investments with the much less expensive, well-diversified, high-yield corporate debt fund.

Nevertheless, a distressed-debt fund is quite distinct from a high-yield mutual fund. First, the hedge fund managers may be the bankers extending loans to their investee companies and generally a distressed-debt fund is likely to embody more leverage than a high-yield mutual fund. The hedge fund managers will have a much more direct sense of ownership for their holdings, and greater scope to influence corporate management, than the best-informed high-yield manager. Second, the hedge fund can impose lock-up periods on investors and so can gain the advantage of time and be in better control of flows of liquidity into and out of the fund. This can provide an investment advantage to a distressed-debt hedge fund compared with a high-yield bond mutual fund.

Arbitrage strategies

Before the credit crisis, arbitrage hedge fund strategies commonly used significant leverage and often had illiquid holdings. The crisis put such funds under severe pressure. A number of them closed, but those that survived adjusted to operating with the lower levels of leverage and often higher levels of margin payments requested from the banks.

Fixed-income arbitrage

Fixed-income arbitrage strategies exploit pricing anomalies in fixed-income instruments while managing exposure to interest-rate risk. Fixed-income arbitrage funds establish long and short positions in closely related fixed-income markets or securities. Where the offsetting positions are close substitutes, leverage may be used, though the degree of leverage was curtailed by the credit crisis. Short positions are generally highly liquid and long positions may be less liquid. These strategies will often be positively affected by a narrowing of credit spreads and vice versa, although the hedge funds can equally easily bet on credit spreads widening as narrowing.

Merger arbitrage

Merger arbitrage (sometimes simply called "risk arbitrage") funds provide an insurance which previously was left as unsought risk by long-only equity managers. When an intended merger or takeover is announced, the share price of the target company moves close to the announced takeover terms. Its new share price is normally (unless a higher bid is anticipated) less than a cash bid price. The amount of the discount will reflect the probability that the bid will succeed, as well as the intervening rate of interest. Merger arbitrage funds provide insurance against the risk that the announced merger might fail by acquiring the target company and hedging that by selling the acquiring company. As well as potential restrictions on fund leverage or short selling, this strategy is vulnerable to two risks that can undermine positions: company-specific issues could cause the merger to fail; or a severe equity market decline could cause a renegotiation of the terms of the deal. In common with other difficult-to-diversify insurance arrangements, merger arbitrage provides a steady flow of income with the risk of occasional large losses.

Convertible arbitrage

Hedge funds were said in early 2005 to hold around three-quarters of outstanding convertible bonds, such was the popularity at that time of convertible arbitrage strategies. Convertible bonds pay a low coupon (or low yield) because they have the added benefit that they can, at the discretion of the investor, be converted into equity. They provide the upside potential of equities and the downside protection of a bond. They offer a natural opportunity for hedge funds seeking to exploit any technical anomalies in the pricing of the debt, convertible bonds, warrants (that is, options on equity) and equity of a particular issuer.

In principle, these strategies should be able to deliver steady profits. However, illiquidity can cause anomalies to become more exaggerated before the date at which the arbitrage profit should be crystallised. If the fund is subject to severe redemptions as investors respond to disappointing performance, forced sales can easily have a cumulatively negative impact on performance. In 2008, the impact of this was compounded by the need to cut positions as margin requirements were raised, and by the impact of bans on short selling. These contributed to an unprecedented negative return for this strategy. Nevertheless, in principle there can be clear arbitrage profits for patient long-term investors, and hedge funds provide the obvious vehicle to exploit such anomalies.

Statistical arbitrage

There are a number of arbitrage strategies that may be used by relative value hedge fund managers and that may be found within multi-strategy funds. These include liquidity arbitrage trades to exploit (and correct) the short-term impact on market prices of securities of large market trades. Historically, another type of trade was the observed positive or negative impact on stock prices of companies joining or leaving an index that is widely used as an investment benchmark. This declined in profitability as new money chased the unusual profits that had previously been earned by exploiting these phenomena. Both these types of statistical arbitrage trades show how hedge funds can improve the efficient functioning of markets by reducing the scale of these short-term anomalies. But they also illustrate how anomalies can be eroded by a weight of money, leaving few if any profits for latecomers.

Multi-strategy funds

From the beginning of the hedge fund industry, larger funds have often managed their own risks and their investors' risks by having more than one team of portfolio managers, each dedicated to a different investment strategy. This enables the hedge fund's management to take responsibility for allocating resources as opportunities in the different strategies change. Multi-strategy funds provide strong competition with fund of hedge fund arrangements and even traditional combinations of stocks and bonds.

Multi-strategy funds include some of the largest hedge funds. Some multi-strategy funds have developed expertise in corporate finance, to facilitate involvement in corporate takeovers and management buyouts.

Commodity trading advisers (or managed futures funds)

Commodity trading advisers (CTAs) provide one of the most interesting absolute return strategies. Their investable universe is provided by the world's futures, options and foreign exchange markets. The dominant group of CTAs is systematic traders who are highly quantitative followers of trends ranging from a few days to several months in the futures markets covering agricultural commodities, industrial and precious metals, currencies, government bonds and equity indices. These are generally highly liquid and easy to value. Some investors are nervous of the opaque, model-driven (black-box) approach to investing in systematic CTAs. One concern is that the highly qualified quantitative analysts building the models in the different firms may unwittingly identify the same trends and lead to hidden concentrations of positions held by CTA funds in individual futures contracts. Discretionary CTAs, which rely on manager judgments of when to trade, accounted for just 8% of CTA assets in mid-2017.

CTA strategies have been subject to extensive statistical analysis, which shows that, on average, they have demonstrated strong diversifying characteristics and a tendency to perform well at times of equity market crisis when other hedge fund strategies often underperform. The pattern of returns shown by indices of CTA manager performance during calendar quarters of equity market weakness (see Table 10.5) is quite different from the corresponding figures for other hedge fund performance. With the exception of dedicated short strategies, the overriding message from hedge fund data is that hedge funds do not provide short-term insurance against extreme poor equity market performance. On average, CTAs have provided some such hedge. This continued in 2008 when the Credit Suisse Managed Futures index returned 18.3%, compared with a negative return of 19.1% for the broad

TABLE 10.5 **Managed futures fund (CTA) and commodity index performance during calendar quarters of equity market crisis**
1994 Q1–2017 Q3, % total return in $

	MSCI World gross return	Bloomberg Barclays US Treasury total return	Credit Suisse Managed Futures Index	Credit Suisse Hedge Fund Index
2008 Q4	–21.7	8.8	10.9	–10.2
2002 Q3	–18.3	7.4	14.2	–0.4
2011 Q3	–16.5	6.5	3.5	–4.8
2008 Q3	–15.2	2.3	–7.1	–10.3
2001 Q3	–14.3	5.5	6.4	0.1

Source: Bloomberg LP

index. There is no assurance that this pattern will continue, and the performance of individual CTAs can be very different.

There are various possible explanations for the apparent insurance against equity market setbacks that CTA strategies have provided. It may be down to luck that in the relatively small number of quarters (or months) with large negative equity returns the average CTA manager has delivered a somewhat surprisingly strong performance. Or, more likely, CTAs have provided insurance against equity market setbacks when their models have been able to identify a change in market direction, which has subsequently proved to represent a change of trend that the CTAs have successfully exploited. Sometimes this will work and sometimes, when markets are affected by a sudden setback, it will not. Nevertheless, an investment that offers the prospect of good performance during bad times is rare and valuable to investors.

Hedge fund risk

Madoff, hedge fund due diligence and regulation

Hedge fund risk should feature prominently in any assessment of hedge fund investing. There have been well-publicised examples of hedge fund fraud and apparent fraud, and it is likely that the entrepreneurial, cottage-industry nature of some parts of the hedge fund industry have made it more prone to elementary process weaknesses. The scale of the multibillion-dollar fraud at Bernard L. Madoff Investment Securities, which was revealed in late 2008 (see Chapter 1), was particularly shocking as it was far removed from any idea of a cottage industry. It exposed the shallowness of ways in which many private clients appeared to have chosen hedge funds – often being led by personal recommendations and a review of historical performance data, together with a confirmation of the evident esteem and reputation of the principals.

Rigorous due diligence is different. Many investment firms avoided dealing with Madoff, not least because they were willing to admit to themselves that they did not understand how his firm earned its returns, and so were unwilling to invest.

Illiquid hedge fund investments and long notice periods

Many hedge funds find promising opportunities in unquoted and illiquid investments. Typical examples include private loans to corporations, which may be investment grade or distressed debt, and unquoted or illiquid equity opportunities. These are precisely the sort of opportunities that an entrepreneurial investment company would be expected to exploit.

However, 2008 exposed the long-established weakness of the hedge fund industry, which is a mismatch between the illiquidity of underlying investments and the frequent opportunities to redeem. This has always been a concern because errors in valuing illiquid investments when hedge funds are bought and sold give rise to windfall transfers of wealth among fund participants. In 2008 these issues led to the widespread imposition of restrictions on redemptions of hedge fund holdings by funds that were unable, or unwilling, to meet their regular schedules of dealing dates. In March 2009, Credit Suisse estimated that 17% of hedge funds (by assets) were "impaired" by having put restrictions on, or suspended, redemptions or had frozen investors' share of hard-to-value investments in a separate portfolio. This illustrates that investors in illiquid hedge fund strategies should not object, indeed should demand, that fellow investors are subject to early redemption penalties (to accrue to the fund) that properly reflect the underlying illiquidity of the hedge fund. Long lock-up periods, seemingly inflexible redemption arrangements or wide bid-offer spreads for hedge funds with illiquid underlying investments can be in the best interests of all investors in those funds.

Lies, damn lies and some hedge fund risk statistics

There are other problems that arise with those hedge fund strategies which hold unquoted or illiquid assets. Any price for an unquoted investment will be an appraisal price. Appraisal prices unavoidably smooth and lag changes in underlying market prices. Consequently, appraisal prices are less volatile than market prices. This means that the volatility of monthly appraisal prices should not be used as a guide to the risk of a strategy that involves a significant element of appraisal prices in its valuations. The same smoothing of volatility can arise with little traded quoted investments. Where the price data are smoothed, calculations for volatility and for risk-adjusted returns (such as Sharpe ratios, see Appendix 1) will be distorted, with risk looking lower than it is and risk-adjusted performance better. Appraisal prices can provide useful management information, but they must be used with care.

There has been extensive research into the issue of illiquidity and the unavoidable smoothing of some hedge fund returns, and the implications of this for measures of hedge fund risk. The results tend to be uniform in establishing the importance of the issue and the way that it is focused on illiquid hedge fund strategies. The affected categories include distressed debt, convertible arbitrage, event-driven and emerging-market strategies. The strategies that are not normally affected by this valuation-smoothing phenomenon are the generally liquid strategies: equity long/short, macro, short-biased and especially CTA or managed futures funds.

In private equity, where issues with illiquidity always arise, appraisal valuations of underlying investments provide management information, but not normally dealing prices. It is understood that the only performance that matters is the internal rate of return calculated from the amount of cash originally invested, the cash subsequently paid back to investors and the passage of time in between (see earlier in this chapter).

Another danger that hedge fund investors should look for is where there is a combination of price smoothing and the pursuit of an investment strategy involving the collection of option or insurance premiums which happen not to have been reflected in periodic poor performance, so far. Clifford Asness, co-founder of AQR Capital Management, wrote in 2004:

> Combining some lags in marking to market with invisible option writing can produce one heck of a historical Sharpe ratio, but with a potentially toxic combination going forward.

"Perfect storms" and hedge fund risk

Money managers often attribute unusual poor performance to a highly improbable confluence of events. Nowhere is this more true than in hedge fund investing. Events that are described by hedge fund managers as "being expected" to occur only "once in a million years" seem at times to be so common as to be unremarkable. In 2008 the combination of the evaporation of market liquidity and regulations restricting short selling made it seem as if no matter how insightful was a fund's investment process, events were conspiring to undermine its endeavours. But an apparently unusual frequency of extreme events always has accompanied hedge fund investing.

This can be illustrated with the historical anecdote from the car industry described in Chapter 7. On that occasion groups of hedge funds found themselves on the wrong side of offsetting positions in GM securities that they thought were good hedges for each other. A similar example arose in 2008, when Volkswagen shares were squeezed when it became known that Porsche owned much more of VW than had previously been believed. The GM episode was described by one hedge fund (which was caught short) as an "eight standard deviation event", which should almost never happen if markets behaved as simple models would suggest they should. However, the apparent frequent occurrence of "bad news" in hedge fund performance reflects a particular characteristic of many hedge fund strategies that investors must understand. Since they are often comparable to investment insurance-type arrangements, hedge funds often provide steady returns most of the time, as the insurance premiums are collected,

FIGURE 10.7 **Monthly performance of Credit Suisse arbitrage and multi-strategy hedge fund indices** 1994–2017, %

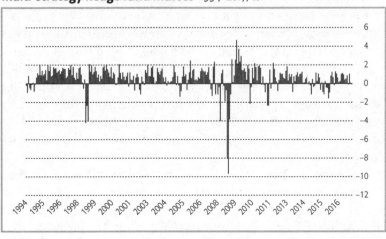

Note: Chart shows equally weighted performance of Credit Suisse convertible arbitrage, event-driven, fixed-income arbitrage and multi-strategy hedge fun.
Source: Bloomberg LP

while being exposed to the risk of occasional large losses, when the insurance policy must pay up.

This is illustrated in Figure 10.7, which combines the monthly performance for the multi-strategy and arbitrage strategy indices as reported by Credit Suisse. It vividly reflects this combination of modest positive returns most of the time, with occasional large negative returns.

As Bill Sharpe, the Nobel Prize-winning originator of the standard measure of risk-adjusted returns, said in an article in August 2005 in the *Wall Street Journal*: "Past average performance may be a terrible predictor of future performance." This pattern of returns is particularly common in some hedge fund strategies that offer investors the prospect of systematic market returns for bearing this insurance risk.

Managing investor risk: the role of funds of hedge funds

Investors need to have an understanding of the role they expect an exposure to hedge funds to play in the risk and return of their overall asset allocation. This may mean selecting one multi-strategy fund to complement their holdings of stocks, bonds and perhaps real estate or it may mean investing in either a portfolio of separate hedge funds or a fund of hedge funds. Fund of hedge fund managers perform two critical roles: one is portfolio construction and overall investment risk management; the other is hedge fund manager due diligence. Ahead of the financial crisis of 2007–09, these funds of funds used to account for around 50% of total hedge fund investments. In mid-2017, according to BarclayHedge, they represented just 10%. This decline is partly explained by concerns about an additional tier of fees paid to the fund of funds manager, and partly by competition from individual multi-strategy hedge funds.

Investors need to try to satisfy themselves that the due diligence process they are using is thorough. But there will always be a risk of a surprising investment performance or operational mishap and of investors saying to their due diligence team: "I thought you were supposed to check on that."

How much should you allocate to hedge funds?

You do not need to allocate anything to hedge funds, and you should not unless you think that you can access a hedge fund arrangement which complements your other investments. Paying higher fees for a diluted version of your equity investments is wasteful. There should be an element of extra skill or access to rewards that are not available elsewhere to justify a decision to invest in hedge funds.

A common weakness with a fund of funds approach to hedge fund investing is that it is typically structured in ignorance of the investment risks that are present elsewhere in an investor's strategy. With some aspects of hedge fund performance and risk being close substitutes for those available elsewhere and others being unique, asking how much to allocate to hedge funds ceases to be a sensible question. Instead, the investment issue is how much should investors wish to allocate to different types of systematic risk? Thus there is a strong argument in favour of the approach of some managers of funds of hedge funds, which is to offer combinations of funds segregated into different categories or "buckets" of risk-taking. For example, some hedge fund strategies (such as equity hedge funds) offer combinations of equity market risk and manager skill exposures which are obvious alternatives to, or competitors with, the risks and opportunities that investors expose themselves to when they select conventional equity managers. The same principles apply to hedge funds that specialise in, for example, emerging markets or some credit market strategies: the allocation to such managers should be considered at the same time as decisions are made to allocate to emerging-market debt or equity or, for example, sub-investment grade corporate debt (allowing for the different elements of diversification provided by each).

More interesting is how to decide what to allocate to hedge funds which offer sources of investment performance and risk that are different from those found in equity and bond markets. This is the reward offered to hedge fund investors for providing a variety of insurance services, most commonly through the provision of liquidity and intermediation services in different markets. These include the range of "alternative market beta" strategies, loosely described as arbitrage strategies, each of which also has a strong component of manager skill. The process of determining how much to allocate to these strategies should be driven by a view of the risk associated with them and how well it is diversified by other investments, and by an informed opinion on how much reward is expected to be earned from allocating capital to them.

From an investor's perspective this is where difficulties arise, because this is still relatively uncharted territory, particularly in respect of return expectations. Nevertheless, several conclusions would be broadly agreed:

- The diversification benefits of a number of these strategies appear well established (although they are not robust in all periods).
- It is reasonable to assume that the market should reward these services since other market participants are demonstrably willing to pay for them.
- The diversification benefits are such that the required premium return (above the return on safe-haven investments) needed to justify an allocation to these alternative hedge fund strategies is modest.

This leads to the two final conclusions:

■ The uncertainties involved mean that an allocation to these alternative betas should err on the side of caution by not dominating an investor's strategy.

■ For most investors, some such allocation can normally be justified. However, appropriate strategies for any investor can consist of stocks, bonds and cash, with no allocations to hedge funds.

REAL ESTATE

The experience of investors in real estate is determined by three things: the performance of the market; the skill of their advisers; and the degree of leverage involved in the vehicle they use to access the market. This, in turn, is influenced by the level of interest rates and whether the rent generated by the properties can cover the debt interest payments. It is a routine weakness in appraising real estate managers to fail to account properly for the impact of leverage on performance and risk.

Developments in the US public market for real estate investment trusts (REITs), a US innovation dating from the early 1970s, and parallel developments elsewhere in the world, have made the public market for real estate comparable to the rest of the quoted equity market. Investors can obtain, at low cost, exposure to the real estate market. The REIT market is a leveraged market and in the years before 2007 many new investors were introduced to the power of leverage. This was when debt interest costs were lower than the income received from real estate rents, the underlying market conditions appeared benign and performance was strong. During the real estate crisis of 2007–09 and the credit crunch, investors were reminded that an income yield higher than the debt service cost is a necessary but not sufficient condition for financial success with a levered property portfolio.

Property investments can be either private or public. Private investment involves the direct ownership of properties. The public market involves ownership through a public commingled fund, or through stock exchange listed vehicles, most commonly REITs. REITs grew substantially in the years before the global financial crisis and in the United States their aggregate market capitalisation reached $438 billion at the end of 2006, declining to $192 billion at the end of 2008, and then rebounding to $1,019 billion by the end of 2016. Similar entities have been introduced in over 35 countries, including Australia, Brazil, Canada, France, Hong Kong, Japan, the Netherlands, Singapore and the UK. In the United States, individual REITs specialise by sector of the market, with a minority investing primarily in mortgages.

The principal difference between a REIT and a conventional company, whose business is investing in and managing properties, lies in their tax treatment. Generally, REITs are exempt from profit or corporation tax and, in the United States, have a guideline that at least 90% of their income must be distributed to investors as a taxable dividend. Guidelines vary between countries. The equivalent in Australia is the large, long-established listed property trust market.

The main differences between listed real estate vehicles, such as REITs, and direct investments in property are that the former are securitised, have daily prices and are typically leveraged to some degree through borrowing. They are ideally suited to giving diversified exposure to real estate for modest levels of investment. Since they have daily prices, appraisal valuations of underlying properties help analysts construct estimates for the net asset value of REITs, but they do not set the terms on which investors transact.

What is real estate investing?

Home ownership

Everyone needs a home and for many, the wealth committed to their home represents their most valuable investment, typically representing the largest investment in any one type of asset (such as cash, stocks or bonds in their pension or other accounts). Economists frequently ask (as only economists could) why do they not hold a more diversified portfolio? The answer is that home ownership (unlike purely financial investments) serves two roles: it is an investment, but it is also what economists call a "consumption good". Everyone needs a roof over their heads, and if it is not owned, it must be rented. If it is rented, then the individual has a commitment or obligation to pay rent in the future. Again, in the language of economists, someone who rents their home is "short" the housing market. One of the attractions of home ownership is that it provides a hedge against this obligation and against unfavourable future house price movements. So although house prices (especially, the prices of an individual house) are volatile and risky, an investment in housing provides something of a safe harbour and is in some respects less risky for an individual than the investment in other risky assets that might be in their savings and investment portfolio. In the words of Laurent Barras and Sebastien Betermier, both associate professors of finance at McGill University, Montreal, in a 2016 research paper entitled, "The predominance of real estate in the household portfolio", "the portfolio share of real estate is bound to be large as a result of the homeowners' consumption decisions irrespective of whether it is a good investment". Homeowners always need shelter, but the extent of their need often follows a life cycle. Young families will typically need a larger investment in housing than will their grandparents. This provides a rational economist's justification for suggesting downsizing to free up financial resources to facilitate a more efficiently balanced portfolio of household wealth. However, customary lifestyle also follows a life cycle, and apparent housing needs may well have evolved with lifestyle over time. For many, "there is no place like home" suggesting a psychic return to home ownership, which has parallels with the rewards from owning collections of treasured possessions, such as works of art, discussed in Chapter 11.

Commercial real estate

It is common to divide the broader real estate market into segments such as those shown in Figure 10.8. In a number of international markets, private equity funds have become important participants in the real estate market. Private equity real estate funds brought a more aggressive attitude to leverage, with the introduction of high-risk, potentially high-return "mezzanine" debt into real estate transactions. These developments mean that investors have various ways of gaining access to real estate returns.

The underlying real estate market is divided into the main types of property: retail, office, industrial and residential. (Other categories include hotels and resorts and mixed category properties.) The REIT

FIGURE 10.8 **The four quadrants of real estate investing**

	Private Investments	Public or quoted Investments
Real estate equity	Direct properties Real estate commingled funds	Real estate investment trusts (REITs) Real estate operating companies (REOCs) Real estate mutual funds Listed property trusts Other listed property companies
Real estate debt	Individual mortgages "Mezzanine" debt	Commercial mortgage-backed securities (CMBS)

market provides access to each segment of the market. Two principal databases for institutional real estate are the National Council for Real Estate Investment Fiduciaries (NCREIF) in the United States and MSCI-IPD (formerly known as the Investment Property Databank). The US National Association of Real Estate Investment Trusts (NAREIT) is the source for information about US REITs. Table 10.6 gives a breakdown of the types of properties owned by investors in the United States and Europe.

What are the attractions of investing in real estate?

The traditional reasons for making investments in real estate equity include portfolio diversification, accessing premium and relatively secure income yields, and the potential for attractive total returns that should offer some protection from inflation.

Diversification

Appraisal valuations of properties unavoidably smooth changes in the level of property prices. This complicates an assessment of the diversification qualities of real estate. Smoothing performance often gives short-term comfort to private investors and pension fund trustees who do not need to be confronted with the reality of market prices except when they transact. This paucity of reliable price information does not provide a substantive reason for favouring real estate

TABLE 10.6 **MSCI data on direct real estate investments by type of property**

Region	UK *	Euro zone **	USA ***
	Sep 17	Dec 16	Sep 17
Retail	39.5%	24.2%	18.4%
Office	28.2%	45.2%	38.0%
Industrial	20.9%	6.0%	17.2%
Apartments / residential	2.4%	17.2%	24.5%
Hotel	2.8%	2.0%	0.6%
Other	6.2%	5.3%	1.3%
Capital Value (in billions US $)	205.7	362.6	334.0

* The data for UK represents the IPD UK Quarterly Property Index (GBP) as at September 2017
** The above data for euro zone includes the combined direct domestic investment property index datasets for euro zone nations (Austria , Belgium, Finland, France, Germany, Ireland, Italy, Netherlands, Portugal and Spain as at December 2016
*** The above data for USA represents the IPD US Quarterly Property Index (USD) as at September 2017
Source: MSCI

investment. The market for REITs gives a market valuation and a time series of transaction prices, which permits a market-based assessment of the contribution of real estate in an investment portfolio, although allowance has to be made for the value of the debt held in a REIT.

Income yield

A recurring argument in favour of real estate investing is the provision of a dependable income that can be expected to increase in line with inflation. The ability to gain access to seemingly reliable income becomes particularly attractive to investors at times of low nominal interest rates.

Table 10.7 compares the income return offered by different investment markets. Over the period, the income return for REITs has been comparable to that on investment grade bonds, which have, in aggregate, been subject to much less price risk. The income stream

TABLE 10.7 **Income yield from REITs, quoted equities and bonds**
1990–2017, % annual average income yield

	FTSE NAREIT North America REIT Index	MSCI US Index	MSCI EAFE ® Index	Bloomberg Barclays Credit Index*	Bloomberg Barclays Government Bond Index*	Bloomberg Barclays Municipal Bond Index*
1990–1994	8.6	3.4	2.0	7.9	6.6	5.9
1995–1999	7.4	2.4	1.9	6.7	5.8	5.0
2000–2004	8.2	1.5	2.1	5.5	4.0	4.0
2005–2009	4.9	2.1	3.1	5.6	3.5	4.0
2010–2014	4.4	2.0	3.3	3.2	1.3	2.8
2015–2017	4.1	2.0	3.1	3.3	1.9	2.3

*Redemption yields.
Note: There are important differences in the tax status of the investments shown in this table.

Source: Bloomberg LP

from REITs may appear stable, on average, but the price volatility has been comparable to equities. This means that REITs cannot be regarded as "low-risk" substitutes for a high-quality bond portfolio.

Inflation hedge

Real estate investments always have one clear advantage over investments in conventional bonds: while bonds are eroded by any unexpected inflation, rents from real estate should be expected to respond over time to inflation. This does not mean that rents will always keep up with inflation. A market with excess or obsolete capacity should expect to see rents fall. Nevertheless, it is reasonable to assume that rents will increase faster the higher is the rate of inflation. This in turn will be reflected in the value put on buildings, which should also respond to inflation. In this way, long-term investments in real estate provide an element of insurance against the biggest danger facing long-term investors in conventional bonds: erosion of wealth by inflation. (But see the discussion of rental income below.)

Styles of real estate investing and opportunities for active management

Entrepreneurial real estate managers have always liked real estate for the same reason that money managers of any asset class do: they see it as an opportunity to use their skills to make money for themselves and their clients. Since the real estate market is such a heterogeneous, lumpy and immobile market, it provides a natural habitat for well-informed, skilled managers to add value (and for other market participants to underperform). This, together with its other advantages such as long-term inflation hedging, helps explain why some investors have focused on developing an expertise and portfolio concentration in real estate investing.

Equity managers are often characterised by their style of investing, and this also happens with real estate managers. It has the advantage of helping investors understand better what to expect from a particular manager. Broadly, there are two approaches to real estate investing: a core approach, with an emphasis on the generation of steadily growing income from a balanced portfolio of well-let prime properties; and an opportunistic approach, which is more concerned with the prospects for price appreciation through redevelopment and exploiting changes in market trends and fashions. The first should deliver a less volatile, less exciting performance than the second. Real estate managers point to a third category, a distinctive "core-plus" approach for the more entrepreneurial commingled or institutional portfolios. The more aggressive, opportunistic approach is likely to be reflected in the real estate activities of, for example, private equity or hedge funds. These have become, and are likely to remain, major players in parts of the international real estate market.

What is a property worth and how much return should you expect?

One of the attractions of real estate investing is that it is often easy to analyse individual investments in direct property quantitatively. Although this is no guarantee of investment success, it helps to identify any opportunities that rely on unusually strong assumptions.

The financial appraisal of real estate requires assessment of a number of variables:

- today's government bond yield;
- market supply and demand forecasts as influences on prospects for rental incomes;
- tenant creditworthiness;
- property depreciation or obsolescence.

No real estate investment should be undertaken unless it is expected to perform better than the guaranteed return from high-quality government bonds. And any real estate investment should be sold if it is expected to underperform government bonds over some relevant time horizon.

Rental income

The return to be expected from a property is the discounted value of the expected rental income, net of expenses, plus the proceeds from selling the property at some date in the future. The key variables in this evaluation are the future rate of change in rents and the appropriate rate at which to discount that rental stream back to a present value or fair price for the property.

Just as forecasts of corporate earnings growth drive an analyst's valuation of a company, so in real estate investing the principal driver of valuation is the forecast change in a property's rental income. Detailed projections for local or regional real estate markets can provide the raw material for these calculations. When appraising these forecasts, it is often helpful to gauge how the rent forecast relates to a forecast for economy-wide inflation. This is because rents need to be forecast, either implicitly or explicitly, for long periods, if only to provide a basis for estimating the price at which the building might be sold in the future (which will itself be a function of expected rents).

This focus on rental income is important to avoid two common mistakes. First, the value of a property often has little to do with the cost of rebuilding it. It is the value of future rent that determines its value. Given the value of the property, this can be broken down into the

TABLE 10.8 **Direct real estate investment by type of property**

	Initial values	Subsequent values
Property value	$10m	$11m
Cost of rebuild	$9m	$9m
Land value	$1m	$2m

Source: Authors' illustration

cost of rebuilding, proxied by the insurance value put on the property, and a residual, which is the value of the land underneath the building. Second, a property is never expensive because the land underneath it is expensive. It is always the other way around. Land is expensive because rents are high, and because rents are high property is expensive. A third important feature for real estate investing follows from this: the price of land, the residual in property valuation, can be extremely volatile. A simple illustration is given in Table 10.8.

In this example, if the value of the property increases by 10%, and if rebuilding costs stay the same, the value of the land will double to $2 million. This is important both as an explanation for the speculative nature of development land and as a useful cross-check on valuations. Equally, the importance of the price of land will depend upon the scarcity of land. Where land is abundant and planning restrictions do not impede new construction, rents will tend towards reimbursing with a "normal" profit the marginal cost of new building, which may or may not keep pace with the general level of inflation.

So long as this situation persists, land will always be cheap. With technological progress in building, commercial properties risk becoming a commodity that individuals or corporations who need to use real estate (for homes, offices, industrial or retail space) must decide whether to own, rent or lease on the same basis as other financial decisions. So although rents, and the cost of land, will move with changes in supply of and demand for properties, there is no inexorable tendency for them to increase faster than inflation. Rents can lag behind inflation for a long time. For example, at the height of a boom in City of London property in 1973, rents were reported to have been in the region of £20 per square foot. Allowing for inflation, prime rents in the City of London almost half a century later are little more than one-third of that level. Property experts will point to a number of reasons for the underperformance of London City offices, such as the move of the fashion conscious to the West End and the drift of the large investment banks and the budget conscious to the new financial district in the docklands. The investment message though is to challenge any assertion that property rents will necessarily keep pace with inflation, and to emphasise that there is little reason to expect them to increase, as is sometimes suggested, in line with the rate of growth of the economy.

However, it may be reasonable to assume that the growth of equity dividends is ultimately related to the growth of the economy. It follows that real estate investors rely on rental income, rather than capital appreciation, as the principal source of investment performance. This also explains why the income yield from real estate investing is normally much higher than the income yield from mainstream equity investing.

It is not clear how much premium return over government bonds should be expected by financial investors in real estate in the long term. This required premium is reduced by the diversification benefits that real estate brings to a balanced investment strategy. It can be influenced by the degree of confidence that investors have in the quality of the investment process that they are able to deploy in investing in real estate markets. Most importantly, as with private equity, direct investors in real estate should not assume that they will earn the market return. The prerequisite is to put in place a demonstrably skilful investment process. However, the more skill that is assumed, the easier it will be to justify a large allocation to real estate. In this case, great caution needs to be exercised in assessing the basis for a belief that the investor can access unusual skill. Particular care is needed in interpreting past performance, in isolating the effects on performance of leverage during a rising market and in differentiating between skill and luck. As was emphasised in Chapter 6, in the presence of uncertainty, the prudent approach is to err on the side of caution.

Government bond yields as the benchmark for real estate investing

Using government bond yields as the benchmark for assessing real estate investments is helpful in several respects. It focuses on the only legitimate reason to move away from safe-haven investing: to achieve a superior return that more than compensates for the risk of a disappointing result. In real estate, the prospects for superior returns will be influenced by the state of the market and also by the quality of the contractual rental income. For this, the creditworthiness of the tenants, as well as other factors such as building depreciation, will be critical.

Tenant credit risk

A property with a government agency as a long-term tenant will be directly comparable with government bonds, although allowance should be made for the illiquidity of the real estate investment, as well as the likely existence of options to break the contract. Organisational issues may inhibit the ability of institutional investors to exploit fully the comparison between long-term holdings of government bonds and a long-term rental income from a government agency. Other investors such as hedge funds have no such inhibition, so long as they can access the liquidity needed to exploit the opportunity. Nevertheless, all real estate investors should make the effort to analyse opportunities in this way.

The spread over government bond yields paid by private-sector tenants needs to allow for the credit risk associated with those tenants, as well as the illiquidity of the contract. The credit risk is the risk that the tenant will fail to meet the terms of the lease; that there will be an interruption to rental payments; that there will be costs associated with attracting new tenants; and that a new tenant might be attracted at less favourable terms than the existing one. These potential costs will be influenced by the state of the market – in a buoyant market replacement tenants can be found more quickly and at less expense than in a depressed market. Corporate credit ratings can provide a guide to the credit risk spread that investors should demand from tenants. When a tenant fails, a replacement can normally be found in due course, and so it is unclear whether the credit spread should apply to the entire rental stream expected from the client.

Property obsolescence

The required yield also needs to allow for the expected depreciation of the property, which may be a very different cost from the actual outlay on property maintenance. This rate of obsolescence will be a major determinant of the rents that will be earned on the property in the future. Obsolescence is partly a matter of physical deterioration, but it is also accelerated by changes in the pattern of demand for particular types of building or location. Standard depreciation schedules rarely reflect actual experience, which is what matters for market investment values. Obsolescence is always subject to uncertainty, but it is uncertainty of a kind that can affect whole parts of a diversified real estate portfolio. As Green Street Advisors, a real estate consultancy, has said: "One of the real estate industry's dirtiest little secrets is the degree to which depreciation is a very real expense." This is why it is appropriate to allow a material risk premium for obsolescence.

Private and public markets for real estate

The parallel private and public markets for real estate invite comparisons of where it is cheaper to buy exposure to real estate: by buying REITs or by directly buying properties. This is the old stockmarket valuation question: are corporate assets valued below or above their replacement value? The ratio of the market value of a company to the replacement cost of its net assets is called Tobin's Q. In theory this ratio, if the underlying data are free from measurement biases, should tend towards 1. The greater liquidity of REITs might normally cause them to trade at a premium to net asset values, and on average they have done. In Figure 10.9, evidence from the United States is shown for the movement in this ratio for the real estate market in recent years and its average value. Substantial real estate investors in countries with a thriving REIT market have a clear choice between investing in direct property or through REITs, although for most private investors it is not realistic to seek to achieve a diversified portfolio in direct real estate.

The relationship between the two real estate markets in the United

FIGURE 10.9 **Is it cheaper to buy real estate on Wall Street or Main Street?** US REITs' share price compared with Green Street estimates of property net asset values
% premium or discount to Green Street estimate of NAV Jan 1990–Jul 2017

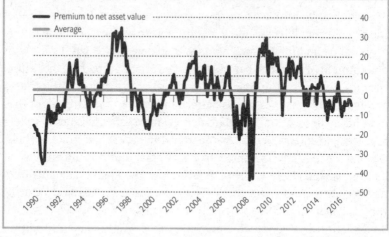

Source: Green Street Advisors

States shown in Figure 10.9 illustrates that over more than 25 years to 2017 the prices of REITs have (when taken together) ranged from a premium to net asset value of the underlying properties of 32.6% in 1997 to a discount of 43.6% in November 2008. Green Street Advisors, whose research is shown in Figure 10.9 (and whose UK and continental European research on REIT valuations shows a similar pattern though for a shorter time period), says that after the early 1990s bond and equity markets had a much more direct influence on property market developments than previously.

The stockmarket prices for REITS permit ready analysis of risk and return. In recent years considerable research has been undertaken to attempt to remove the smoothing features of appraisal based commercial property market indices. The transaction-based indices which use transaction prices to compute "more realistic" prices series for commercial real estate show more volatility than the appraisal-based indices. However, these new indices are still problematic, and unlike the widely used Case-Shiller transaction-based index for US housing markets, they suffer from the relatively small number of transactions in commercial real estate and methodological issues with the commercial transaction linked indices. Over time, the appraisal and transaction-based or linked indices for US and also for European institutional direct real estate investment appear to give similar results, and it is the short-term pattern of returns that can differ. For long-term investors, it may be thought that the difference is of little importance. This is not correct. Transaction-based indices offer the prospect of more accurate measures of the volatility of the direct real estate market and of how real estate correlates with the stock and bond markets. These should enable more reliable assessment of the diversification role of real estate in an investment strategy.

Research published in 2006 by Martha S. Peyton and Fabiana Lotito of TIAA-CREF, a US retirement fund for university staff, "Real estate: the classic diversifying asset", and separately a 2007 article in *Journal of Portfolio Management* by Shaun Bond, Soosung Hwang, Paul Mitchell and Stephen Satchell, "Will private equity and hedge funds replace real estate in mixed asset portfolios?", point the way to how illiquid investments are increasingly being modelled in asset allocation exercises. The key is to correct for the smoothing impact of appraisal values in illiquid investments, such as real estate, hedge funds and private equity (and to allow for the costs of illiquidity). Both studies are strongly supportive of the diversifying role of real estate, and the second article answers its title's question with its pithy subtitle: "Not likely".

Private investors access real estate through direct ownership of individual properties (which is difficult to diversify) and through the public market for REITs (which institutional investors often shun in favour of bricks and mortar). The potential diversification role of REITs in overall investment strategy was demonstrated during the equity bear market of March 2000–March 2003.

Figures 10.10 and 10.11 compare the performance and volatility of the US equity market and US equity REITs. The performance chart shows that REITs can behave very differently from the rest of the stockmarket, and so provide valuable diversification. This happened in the late 1990s and early 2000s, when REITs first missed out on the technology boom and then avoided the subsequent market downturn. However, REITs can at other times act as if they are a levered play on the stockmarket.

FIGURE 10.10 **Cumulative performance of US equities and REITS**
1984–2017, Dec 1984 = 1.0

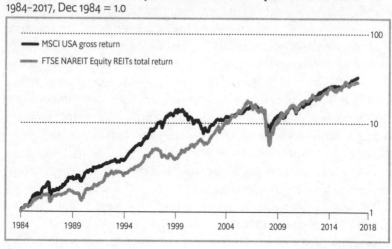

Source: Bloomberg LP

FIGURE 10.11 **Volatility of US equity REITS and US stockmarket, rolling 36-month standard deviations of return** 1987–2017, %

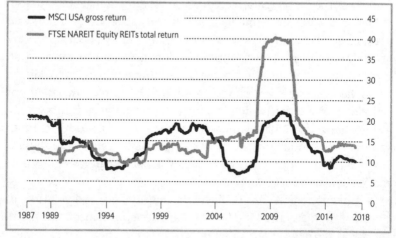

Source: Bloomberg LP

TABLE 10.9 US, UK and euro zone real estate market indices: volatility, and correlations with stocks and bonds
Jan 2007–Sep 2017

A. US	FTSE NAREIT Equity REITs
Standard deviation (% per year)	24.8%
Correlation with MSCI USA	0.75
Correlation with Barclays US Aggregate Bond Index	0.26

B. UK	FTSE EPRA UK REITs
Standard deviation (% pa)	22.4%
Correlation with MSCI UK	0.61
Correlation with Barclays UK Aggregate Bond Index	0.21

C. Euro zone	FTSE EPRA euro zone REITs
Standard deviation (% pa)	18.7%
Correlation with MSCI euro zone	0.74
Correlation with Barclays euro zone Aggregate Bond Index	0.23

Sources: Authors' calculations; data source: Bloomberg LP

In the years leading up to 2007, REITs experienced a strong bull market, fuelled by credit and the housing boom, and amplified the subsequent downturn and then recovery after 2008. These differences are also shown in Figure 10.11: for many years REITs, despite their sector focus and degree of leverage, had a volatility no more than the equity market, and often less. After 2007, their volatility was considerably more than the market as a whole, though in recent years, REIT volatility has been more similar to the market as a whole. These comparisons partly reflect the leverage inherent in REITS. Equity REITs are typically leveraged, around 30 to 50%. (About 10% of US REITs are mortgage REITs, which have a much higher level of leverage than equity REITs. The business of equity REITs is to invest in properties; the business of mortgage REITs is to invest in mortgages. Mortgage REITs are normally more volatile than equity REITs.)

Table 10.9 gives statistics for the REIT markets of the United States, UK and the euro zone. It shows the annualised volatility (standard deviation) of the indices for the period 2002 to 2017, and the correlation of each series with the stock and bond markets.

Research into the behaviour of UK property prices by Colin Lizieri, Stephen Satchell and Warapong Wongwachara in 2012 found that appraisal valuations and transaction prices seem to respond vigorously to stockmarket moves when those moves are strongly negative, a process which seems to reinforce serial correlation in appraisal property prices. In turn, this is one aspect of the rise in correlations between risk assets at times of great risk aversion.

International diversification of real estate investment

With the spread of REIT markets around the world, international diversification of real estate investing has never been easier. The word diversification implies risk reduction. But does international diversification of real estate reduce risk? It turns out that currency risk is a particularly knotty issue for international real estate investing.

Currency risk and international real estate investing

The guidelines on foreign currency exposure and the desirability of foreign currency hedging suggested in this book can be summarised as follows:

■ Lower volatility international investments need to be hedged for foreign exchange risk otherwise currency fluctuations will transform the risk and return of the underlying investments by markedly increasing their volatility.

■ Higher volatility international investments (such as equities) do not need to be hedged for currency risk because currency hedging will simply alter the pattern of returns, not materially increase or decrease the magnitude of volatility (but see Chapter 8 for a discussion of exceptions to this rule of thumb).

- It is easy to put in place foreign currency hedges between the major liquid currencies and to hedge liquid investments. It can be expensive or impractical to hedge the foreign exchange risks which involve one or more less liquid currencies.

- Foreign currency hedging involves frequent accounting for cash gains or losses on the hedged investment. These gains and losses are much easier to accommodate in an investment arrangement if the hedged investment is itself highly liquid. In these circumstances, for example, currency gains on an investment can be offset by investment sales to fund offsetting currency losses on the currency hedge. With an illiquid investment this is much more difficult to achieve. Accumulated cash flow losses from a persistent home currency depreciation can require additional injections of cash, which may be substantial. Investors should therefore not hedge illiquid and lumpy international investments, such as whole properties, unless they are sure that they can fund the potential liquidity drain from the hedge. (Note that an alternative is to raise a mortgage abroad to fund the foreign investment, and if need be to offset this with a cash deposit at home so as to reduce the scale of leverage. This would reduce the scope for liquidity pressures in managing the investment, and would hedge the greater part of the foreign exchange risk.)

The implications of this for international real estate diversification are as follows:

- Private market international real estate investments should not be hedged because the investments are illiquid and the holdings are generally indivisible.

- This means that the unhedged investments will be volatile and so should only be made for their opportunistic performance potential and not, for example, for the potential income yield. An exception to this arises if investors genuinely have an exceptionally long time horizon (and do not simply wish that they had). In this case, an investor may be justified in putting faith in an expectation that eventually currency movements will keep track with the relative purchasing power of different countries.

■ Investments in public market real estate securities (such as REITs) in international markets can easily be hedged. This will be necessary if investors intend to rely on the income from the overseas REIT. However, they should check whether the level of leverage in the REIT causes it to have a volatility that will swamp any cushioning effect from hedging. Nevertheless, hedged or unhedged, investors should expect the price of a REIT that invests in direct real estate equity to be volatile.

11

Art and investments of passion

"I WOULD RATHER MY FAMILY'S WEALTH was tied up in a Titian than in a bank share," one art consultant told one of the authors. Many people have collections of paintings, other works of art or items such as stamps, rare books, classic cars or fine wines on which they have expended significant amounts of money. Such collections are sometimes called investments of passion, but they are primarily treasured collections. Consistent anecdotes from a range of markets indicate that few acquire fine art or collectibles solely to earn a financial return. The prospect of earning an emotional, not financial, dividend from owning a beautiful work or a prized possession is almost always the catalyst for a decision to buy.

In the years following the darkest days of the financial crisis at the end of 2008 and the extraordinary easing of monetary conditions that followed, interest rates stayed close to zero and the prices of a wide range of risk assets recovered strongly. Investments of passion from classic cars to fine wines and also fine art shared in this and in many cases had never been so strong. Although it is difficult to verify, market participants and analysts agree that the monetary environment encouraged more spending and higher prices in these niche areas. With no interest being paid on cash, the opportunity cost of indulging in a passion for collecting had not been lower in living memory. As an article in the *New York Times* put it in April 2013, "Whether he intended it or not, or even realises it, Ben S. Bernanke has become a patron of the arts."

How monetary easing probably inflated the prices of fine art and collectibles

Any purchase involves choices. By purchasing a painting, a collector decides to forgo the interest that could be earned on a bank deposit or from a government bond of roughly the maturity in years that the collector might own the painting. Collectors buy paintings because they prefer the prospect of enjoying the art at least as much as they would benefit from the income that could be earned from cash or government bonds. The box in Chapter 5 ("How do investors invest?") reported evidence from the Capgemini "World Wealth Report" 2017 that the world's high net worth families may hold one-quarter of their financial wealth as cash, deposits or some other form of liquidity. This may seem surprisingly high, but it is a consistent finding from global surveys of investors. The income of these families will have been reduced by over $100 billion per year for each 1% cut in interest rates. When interest rates fall to almost zero, it is much easier to justify spending money on art (or on almost anything) rather than leaving the money in the bank. Easy money almost certainly increased the demand for and prices of fine art and collectibles.

This increase in demand for collectibles has occurred against the background of the internet having facilitated price discovery and, almost certainly, the liquidity of auction markets for collectibles. Websites such as eBay are much more accessible than traditional "bricks and mortar" auction houses, though investors may fear that counterparty risk is a bigger issue with online auction houses. Even the humblest auction house can now put its catalogues for forthcoming auctions online, and there are well-developed internet services which enable almost any local auction house to accept online bids. According to the consultant and data provider Artprice, 95% of the world's auction houses had an internet presence in 2015, compared with just 3% in 2005. It is easy to forget how difficult it was before the internet to access information that is routinely of interest and importance to a collector. Furthermore, online auction websites (which traditionalists argue are not suitable for many treasured possessions) are a powerful force for reducing transaction costs. This, together with easier price discovery and the enormously reduced "shoe-leather" costs of attending auctions should provide an enduring lift to demand for collectibles, even if the impact of ultra-low interest rates diminishes.

Psychic returns from art and collectibles

Collectors collect and art lovers buy art because they expect to enjoy their collections. This aesthetic or "psychic" reward is a dividend to be valued over and above any monetary return that they might hope to get when (or if) they eventually sell their collection.

A number of economists have attempted to estimate the psychic return from art. Some have used data on the cost of renting art (for example, by corporations) and produced high implied psychic returns, in the order of 10% to 30% per year. These high figures have been criticised for combining the cost of a valuable consultancy service, which is advising individuals on which art they ought to rent, with the enjoyment that flows from a treasured possession. In a 2013 research paper, Rachel Pownall, associate professor of finance at Maastricht University, together with Stephen Satchell and Nandini Srivastava, both members of the economics faculty at Cambridge University, have evaluated alternative approaches for measuring psychic returns to cultural assets. After taking into account the substantial transaction costs, apparent long holding periods for works of art and likely proportions of investable wealth invested in art, they estimate that psychic returns from fine art are probably in the region of a bit less than 1% to 2% per year of the cost of a painting. Among their other findings is that in France and the UK fine art may account for around 4% to 5% of investable wealth (data issues prevented the authors from considering a global approach). They find that the long periods for which works of art are generally held mean that the impact of high transaction costs in the art market (for example, commission rates at auction – see below) is less of a burden in comparison with stockmarket investing (where holding periods are much shorter) than the headline numbers suggest. Their conclusion is that an annual expense advantage to investing in equities over buying a painting of between 0.5% and 1% per year seems plausible, if both the painting and the investment in the stockmarket are held for 20–30 years.

Recent trends in prices for fine art and collectibles can be seen more clearly thanks to the publication by academics of annual price indices which trace the evolution of the prices of fine art, stamps and violins over the past 100 years. For shorter time periods there exists a multiplicity of indices for different segments of the art market (and even for individual artists) as well as for a surprisingly wide range of collectibles.

Two of the academics, Elroy Dimson, emeritus professor of finance at London Business School, and Christophe Spaenjers, associate professor of finance at HEC, a business school in Paris, have calculated that the average price increase of art, stamps and violins over the period from 1900 to 2012 beat the investment return on cash and government bonds, but noticeably underperformed the stockmarket. The three types of "emotional" assets, when measured in sterling (most of the data were originally expressed in sterling), produced average returns of between 2.4% and 2.9% per year, after inflation, compared with 1.5% per year from bonds, and 0.9% per year from cash compared with 5.2% per year from equities. Other studies have also placed the price performance of fine art over differing long time periods as being somewhere below that of equities, but better than cash.

In practice, the average collector of fine art will not have done so well, because the data take no account of the costs of buying and selling items from their collections. Transaction costs are generally higher in illiquid markets such as those for collectibles, and can easily be 25% of the price of an object offered for sale (see below). Average index returns from illiquid markets are earned by no one and they also hide fluctuations over time and of fashions within it.

An important source of detailed historical information on the prices of fine art is Gerald Reitlinger's 1960 study, *The Economics of Taste*, which, in his words, traced "the rise and fall of picture prices" after 1760. One illustration he gave was of a pair of paintings by Claude Lorrain, a 17th-century landscape artist, which were sold in 1808 for £12,600, making them, according to Reitlinger, then the most expensive paintings ever sold, the price being equivalent to roughly £900,000 in 2013 prices. The same paintings were sold together 140 years later for £5,355, equivalent to £170,000 in today's prices. Great paintings, which are bought at a high price, can represent an appalling return on money, even if held for a great length of time. If properly maintained, and if attribution is not in doubt, they are, however, not going to decline in value to zero, which is the fate of a shareholding in a company which becomes bankrupt.

Research by Michael Moses, formerly a professor at New York's Stern School of Business, and Jiangping Mei, an associate professor of finance at Stern School of Business, indicates that underperformance of the broader market by a masterpiece is not unusual. They found that indicators suggesting high quality for a work of fine art (such as the purchase price of the painting or the number of scholarly citations or the number of exhibitions featuring the work) provide no assurance that it is going to outperform the rest of the art market in the future, and it may perform considerably worse.

Most art is not a masterpiece. William Grampp, emeritus professor of economics at the University of Chicago, in his 1989 book *Pricing the Priceless: Art, artists and economics* sought to reconcile the aesthetic and the monetary value of art. He argues that there is a correlation between price and assessments of aesthetic value in fine art (presumably, he argues, the prices paid by leading art galleries reflect their judgments of artistic quality). He also asks what became of the 20,000 paintings produced each year in late 19th-century France. He points out that most art declines in value to zero when it is no longer enjoyed, and then gets discarded. Art that suffers this fate might be described as "local" art. Some fine art maintains critical appreciation from generation to generation (see below) and so keeps a significant monetary as well as aesthetic value. This is not the fate of pictures that most picture buyers buy.

Reitlinger's book has proved to be a treasure trove for researchers. It was a prime source for the art price series shown in Figure 11.1, and three of the five studies of the evolution of art prices over time that were reviewed by Grampp in 1989 used Reitlinger's data. Grampp concludes: "All except [one] give the same answer to the question: Is buying art simply to resell at a higher price likely to be profitable? The answer is no."

One of the five studies was a 1986 article, "Unnatural value or art as a floating crap game", by William Baumol, emeritus professor of economics at Princeton University. He was one of the sceptics

FIGURE 11.1 **Collectibles: Long term price indices 1900–2015**
£, after inflation, 1900 = 1.0

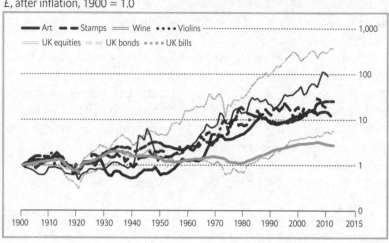

Source: Christophe Spaenjers, "The long -term returns to durable assets", in Chambers and Dimson (eds.), 2016

and argued that art prices "float more or less aimlessly and their unpredictable oscillations are apt to be exacerbated by the activities of those who treat such art objects as 'investments'". Baumol's calculations showed an average return, after inflation, of close to zero, though the other studies have given somewhat higher estimates.

This does not mean that the paintings were not worth owning, rather that a collector of paintings (or of stamps, classic cars or vintage wine) will judge a good investment differently from an institution which is only concerned with financial return. For collectors, the combination of the price change and the dividend of being able to enjoy the treasured possession provides the criteria to assess success.

Wealth, inequality and the price of art

Recent research has explored the relationship between art prices and the economy. William Goetzmann, Edwin J. Beinecke professor of finance at Yale School of Management, Luc Renneboog, professor of corporate finance at Tilburg University, and Christophe Spaenjers have shown, using UK data, that the art market has followed the fortunes of the stockmarket and is also influenced by changes in income inequality. When high-end incomes increase much faster than average incomes, art prices tend to respond strongly. This has been seen in the patterns of art market booms and stagnations over the past century. Art prices did not reach their 1914 levels, after inflation, until a strong recovery in the 1960s. The intervening long period of stagnation occurred despite personal income rising almost fourfold. It was, however, a period when income inequality declined sharply, eroding the relative buying power of the wealthiest.

The past 100 years show that a disappointing environment for the art market can persist for decades. After the 1970s, inequality (measured by the authors as the share of the top 0.1% of UK income earners in total income) increased strongly, having declined during the preceding 70 years. Since the 1960s, fine art prices have easily outpaced inflation, supported by much higher top incomes, and have climbed to levels not seen before, even though there have been significant setbacks in the overall market and marked changes of fashion within it. Figure 11.1 shows a similar pattern in the indicators for prices of stamps and violins over the past century, although their periods of weakness do not always coincide with those in the art market.

This pattern in prices for art and collectibles over 100 years is reflected in prices for luxury goods. Although millions of people reportedly collect assorted treasured items, the top end of each category of luxury goods, be it fine wine, fine art, rare stamps, classic cars or even violins, will be influenced by the incomes, wealth and perceptions of competing investment opportunities of the most affluent. The spending power of hedge fund managers, Russian oligarchs and Chinese billionaires helped to propel art prices in the years up to 2008, and the continuing demand from the wealthy in China helped the market to recover after 2009 much faster than after the bear market in the early 1990s. Investment managers as collectors of stamps, moguls from the entertainment and fashion world as collectors of classic cars, and Chinese multimillionaires as buyers of fine wine each point to similar influences on the top end of markets for collectibles as have been found in the art market.

The rise of China as a major player in the fine art market has been remarkable. London and especially New York had dominated the art

FIGURE 11.2 **Worldwide fine art auction house sales** $bn, 2002–2016

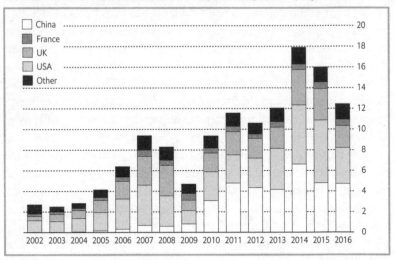

Source: www.artprice.com

auction market, at least from the early 1960s to 2008. However, from 2010 to 2016 fine art auction sales in China exceeded by revenue those in the United States in each year apart from 2015. In earlier years, Hong Kong was the principal marketplace for art in China, but according to consultancy Arts Economics, Hong Kong's share of Chinese art auction revenues in 2009–12 was less than 20%, with Beijing taking the lion's share. The change in the art auction market has also led to Chinese works of fine art overwhelmingly, by value, being sold in China, where, according to Artprice, calligraphy and traditional painting account for the bulk of sales. Nevertheless, according to Arts Economics, Chinese buyers have also represented a growing share of purchases in Western art markets.

Economics may help explain overall market trends, but it is less clear which criteria explain the financial value of the work of individual artists. The valuation of any painting ought to be an assessment of what someone else would be willing to pay for it, which will be strongly influenced by assessments of its quality. Maintenance of value is likely to be supported where critical acclaim for an artist survives from one generation to another. Several studies have looked for this. Victor

Ginsburgh and Sheila Weyers of the University of Louvain examined the critical recognition of Italian Renaissance artists over the past 450 years. They used as their benchmark the prominence given to artists in authoritative art history textbooks at different dates over this period. The measures used were the number of citations and the length of written reviews of each artist.

Ginsburgh and Weyers's analysis starts with the assessment published in 1550 by Giorgio Vasari, a notable artist and also a pioneering art historian. They compare this with six other sources spread over the years since then, ending with *The Grove Dictionary of Art*, which was published as 34 volumes in 1996 and has now been superseded by an online edition. This is widely available through public library subscriptions (particularly in the UK) and includes around 21,000 biographies, written by art experts from around the world. Ginsburgh and Weyers highlight an impressive persistence in the art establishment's apparent rating of the leading figures of Italian Renaissance painting. They show that each of the seven selected art authorities from the past 450 years appear to have chosen Giotto, Michelangelo and Raphael as among the top ten Italian Renaissance artists, with six also including Titian and five Leonardo da Vinci.

This pattern of persistent recognition of quality over five centuries of the top-ranking Italian old master painters demonstrates that some assessments of art quality can be relied on to endure. This helps to underpin the financial value of acclaimed artists from one generation to the next. It seems to be a safe bet that in 200 years a painting by Raphael will be prized and highly valued. An art gallery is unlikely to be embarrassed by owning it, but it does not mean, if it ever came to market, that it would perform well as a financial investment.

In the market for contemporary art there is no history of critical acclaim, and whether a contemporary artist's work is judged by art experts to be "strong" or "weak" is largely a matter of subjective opinion. The support of influential opinion formers and patrons has always been important in securing recognition and commercial success for artists, and this can take time even for those later acknowledged as masters. The celebrated example, which gives hope to countless yet-to-be-discovered artists, is Vincent van Gogh, who died penniless and apparently sold only one painting during his brief lifetime despite his brother being an art dealer.

Don Thompson, the author of *The $12 million Stuffed Shark: the Curious Economics of Contemporary Art and Auction Houses*, comments on the importance of brand in the market for contemporary art. Branding or, as art market people call it, "validation", can be provided by an artist being supported by a leading art dealer, or by work being offered for sale by either Sotheby's or Christie's, still the world's two dominant art auction houses, or by being exhibited at or bought by a leading modern art gallery, or by having works bought by a celebrated collector. These are the gatekeepers, the most important arbiters of perceived quality in the market for contemporary art. When a contemporary artist has been validated by several of these, he or she becomes a branded artist whose work will henceforth command a higher price. If a collector had the ability to anticipate this process by buying pre-branded, yet-to-be-discovered artists, the road to financial success in collecting contemporary art would be secured. In practice, there may be many good contemporary artists, but only a few secure financial success by becoming branded.

Over the ages there have been countless wealthy patrons, collectors and sponsors of art. Among these are some whose collections have subsequently become extremely valuable. There is little indication that a desire to accumulate wealth rather than a love of art motivated their collections, even though history might judge them to have been canny collectors. An outstanding example of this is the collection of 20th century art, including some by Pablo Picasso and Jasper Johns, amassed over the lifetimes of Victor and Sally Ganz of New York. The Ganz estate sold 114 paintings at auction in 1997, raising a total of $207 million compared with an original outlay of $764,000. William Landes, the Clifton R. Musser professor of law and economics at the University of Chicago, found that the performance of the Ganz collection easily beat investing in the US stockmarket over the same period; and although data comparisons are difficult, it seems clear that the Ganz collection outperformed the wider art market. Landes found that the financial performance of the Ganz collection was not simply attributable to the extraordinary results from one or two paintings, but showed a degree of persistence from one artist to another and across time periods of investing. He also found that paintings and prints from the Ganz collection appeared to attract a premium price because they came from the Ganz collection.

Art market indices

Art collectors wish (if only for insurance purposes) to have an estimate of the value of their most treasured works. However, various biases that seem to affect appraisal valuations of private investment, including fine art and collectibles. In recent years there has been the development of a number of competing providers of art market indices and online art valuation services. The role of the auction houses has facilitated the development of these services by providing a degree of transparency to pricing that would not be available if all transactions occurred through dealers' galleries or at art fairs. However, each of the art indices suffers from weaknesses. Some are common to the measurement of performance in any illiquid market; some are more specific to the art market; and others reflect differences in methodological approach and coverage.

Each of the leading art indices reflects transactions that occur at public auction, but not those, by their nature confidential, that occur through dealers' galleries or at art fairs. It is estimated by Clare McAndrew, founder of Arts Economics, that public auctions account for around 50% of the value of the turnover of the fine art market. However, the ready availability of price information makes auctions a goldmine for statisticians and analysts. Unlike some illiquid markets where all transactions are private and where indices of market performance need to rely on expert valuations, in the art market the index providers are able to use auction prices. As in other markets, the indices exclude the impact on financial performance of commission costs, and typically the index providers also exclude items that fail to reach their reserve price and so remain unsold (or "bought-in"). In its annual review of the global fine art market, Artprice, an art market information provider, says that 37% of items submitted for auction in 2012 outside China were bought-in, a figure broadly in line with previous experience, whereas in China, the largest marketplace for fine art in recent years, the comparable figure was 54%, much higher than indicated by recent experience.

There are three main approaches to measuring art market performance:

■ The first is simply to measure the change in the average price paid for paintings at auction. Refinement is added by breaking the indices down into the average price paid for different categories (for example, impressionist paintings) or for individual artists and by removing outliers. This is sometimes called a "naive" index, but it has some significant strengths. The weaknesses of this approach are clear – one work, even by the same artist, is qualitatively different from another and may be expected to command a very different price. However, the attractions of this approach include transparency, ease of understanding and of computation, an expectation that errors in measurement will reduce as large numbers of works are included, and importantly, that it includes all the available price information from the auction houses. Other approaches, see below, may cover a minority of the transactions at art auctions, and will be particularly weak in their coverage of paintings which have not previously sold at auction – contemporary art in particular. In practice, this approach makes use of moving averages and so will react with a lag to any market changes and can exclude the highest and lowest 10% by value of auction prices to reduce the possible distorting effect of outlying transactions.

■ The second approach attempts to take account of physical characteristics of a work of art that experience suggests influence its price. These include the name of the artist, the category of the art, the size of the painting and the name of the auction house. This is the "hedonic" approach and aims to remove non-standard influences from the movement in the art market index. The advantage of the hedonic approach over the simple average price method is that it makes use of supplementary information that appears to have been important in past auctions. It can also make use of all the price data from the auction houses.

■ The third, much loved by purists, is the "repeat sales regression" approach. This makes use of pairs of data for individual works of art, comparing a purchase price with the subsequent sales price for the same work at a later date. The strength of this method is that it uses realised returns from individual works of art and combines them into a representative series for the market as a whole. The methodology is comparable to that of the authoritative Case-Shiller series for the US housing market, where transaction information is made publicly available. There are some difficulties with applying the methodology to the art market that do not apply in the housing market to the same degree:

- The first is that the need to rely on repeat sales substantially restricts the amount of auction price data that is being used in the index.

- The second is that the auction market does not cover the whole market as it fails to capture transactions by dealers. This would not matter if price trends in the two market segments were believed to be comparable. However, there may be a survivor bias which inflates the repeat-sales indices if works by artists who were formerly fashionable are no longer accepted for sale at the leading auction houses, and instead are sold by dealers at reduced prices which are not reflected in the indices.

- The third is that the need for a pair of auction transactions (a purchase and a later sale) for an individual work before it joins the database means that it will always lag in its coverage of contemporary art.

- The fourth, the importance of which will diminish as the number of transactions measured by an index increases, is that the purity of repeat-sales analysis assumes that a painting is the same painting when it is resold. However, changes in expert opinion about a painting's authenticity or attribution will influence the price subsequently achieved at auction. This does not affect the value of other works by that artist or of the market as a whole, but it may distort the index between those transaction dates. Corresponding issues arise with real estate and the possibility of physical improvements or deterioration in a property between purchase and sale. The influence of such distortions will be diluted as the number of repeat transactions recorded by an index increases.

Price indices for other investments of passion or "collectibles"

In any market, attempts to construct price indices are constrained by the available data. A major source of price indices for a large range of collectibles is Art Market Research, a consultancy based in London, which computes prices for different categories of collectibles and then removes outlying observations. Its impressive range of items includes Colt revolvers, wrist watches, Chinese ceramics and German toy trains. Other approaches which only compare directly the prices of identical items (such as the same painting when bought and then when sold) use only a subset of the available data and will miss out on new market trends (until a record is established of purchases and later sales of particular items within the new trend).

In some markets (for example, classic cars) auctions play an important role in providing one ready source for index compilers. In other markets, auctions may have a smaller role and index compilers prefer to rely on a consistent source that is available for long periods of time. In the market for British stamps, for example, although there is an active auction market, the available long-run price information is contained in the catalogues published by Stanley Gibbons, a stamp dealer, which has been the main source of reference for collectors of British stamps. This is the source of price data used by Dimson and Spaenjers in their 2011 study "Ex Post: the investment performance of collectible stamps". These have been available around most year-ends since the late 19th century and they represent estimated selling prices of Stanley Gibbons at the time of publication for new or used stamps in "fine condition".

The attraction of this data series is that it is available, on a reasonably consistent basis, for almost all years and that the dealer provides an assurance of attribution. The weakness of the data is primarily that they reflect a dealer's valuation estimates rather than transaction prices and so are likely to lag behind market developments and be less volatile than actual prices, and that the catalogue prices are likely to be difficult to reconcile with advertised online or public auction prices. There may also be changes over time in the spread between the price at which Stanley Gibbons offers to sell and the price at which it is willing to buy. Furthermore, a catalogue encourages the unwary to interpret the dealer's offer prices for a particular item as an indication of value for a broad category of collectibles. Philatelists know that thousands, perhaps hundreds of thousands, of examples of the Penny Black, the first prepaid adhesive postage stamp in the world, have survived in some form out of the 55 million (some sources say 68 million) that were printed in the UK between 1840 and 1841. They also know that one unused Penny Black in fine condition can have a very different value from another unused Penny Black in fine condition.

Through time, stamps have sold in the market at differing

proportions of the Gibbons catalogue value. This proportion reflects, to some extent, who is actually collecting stamps. In recent years, as children have switched to other hobbies, stamps are primarily collected by wealthy individuals. As a consequence, relatively common stamps now sell at a fraction of their catalogue value while rarer stamps sell at a much higher proportion. The only way an investor can get a sense of what his collection will fetch is in situations where there are two-way prices. But these only exist for stamps that are very homogeneous in quality. One example is PRC China, where Chinese dealers regularly post buy and sell prices for many sets. Unfortunately, these are written in Chinese, limiting their informational content to the average European collector.

Stamps, coins and probably most collectibles are extremely heterogeneous and gaining and growing an understanding of their distinctive differences is central to a collector's expertise. However, making use of a wide cross-section (50 in the case of the Dimson and Spaenjers study) of catalogue prices for representative items for almost every year for over a century will greatly reduce the uncertainty that derives from the comparability of items from one period to another. A market index is not attempting to reflect the idiosyncrasies of individual items, but rather to reflect broad movements in the overall level of the market. Even in this case, there are problems which are based on the idea of survivorship bias. If we pick the best 50 stamps, based on their value in 2017, with a history of say 10 years, then we are implicitly assuming that we have bought these stamps at some past point and that they are still in existence today. To reflect investment returns, we need to take an *ex ante* approach. We may pick the 50 stamps with the highest five-year returns, and hold them for the next five years, for example. Such an approach, which is often referred to as a momentum strategy has the benefit of being forward looking and reflects what an individual could do at home, given sufficient funds.

A popular investment idea for private individuals is to buy every new issue of stamps from their particular country. For a British investor/collector, this might involve buying all the stamps, all the first day covers, all the booklets, all the yearbooks of Britain, Guernsey, Jersey, Isle of Man and even smaller Channel Islands such as Alderney and Sark. Such a strategy would certainly have cost many hundreds of pounds a year and assuming one did this from the early 1970s onwards, one could have easily spent a sum in excess of £10,000. The likely value of this £10,000 portfolio would currently be at most £4,000. We would certainly advise against such a strategy as an investment, though it may be a source of great pleasure.

Assessing changes in the level of prices in the market for classic cars introduces new challenges. In this market, a particular car which is bought and subsequently resold is only the same car in terms of its chassis number: collectors will always be working on their cars, and without maintenance they always deteriorate. Maintenance might cost between 2.5% and 5% of the value of a car each year, which can be seen as a negative dividend attached to this investment of passion. So whereas an art index or a house price index may seek data on repeat sales of the same painting or house, in the market for classic cars such information, even where it is available, is not seen as useful for constructing an index of market prices. The price level for classic cars is measured by the Historic Automobile Group International (HAGI) index, which has been constructed since 2008 by a group of finance industry car enthusiasts, with expertise in compiling stockmarket indices. The index, which includes 50 valuable car models, was estimated in mid-2013 to have a capitalisation of around $15 billion, which represents the estimated number of surviving cars multiplied by the price for the type and assumed condition of the car. The HAGI indices are based only on transactions for cars in "very good" or "highly original" condition and exclude prices strongly influenced by extraneous factors, such as celebrity former owners. The United States dominates the classic car auction market, with the UK and continental Europe in subsidiary roles. Unlike in the art market, mainland China has not emerged as a major centre for classic cars.

The prices for the HAGI indices are sourced from auctioneers (which account for around one-third of the market) and from the confidential transaction records of dealers and collectors. If there are no trades for a category of classic car during a month, the index for that category will show no change that month (which, in common with a number of other methodologies for constructing indices of collectibles, could slow the index's response to a market downturn). Although they will not collect every transaction, the index compilers are confident that

FIGURE 11.3 **Calendar-year performance of world equities and classic cars** £, 1980–2008, Dec 1980 = 100

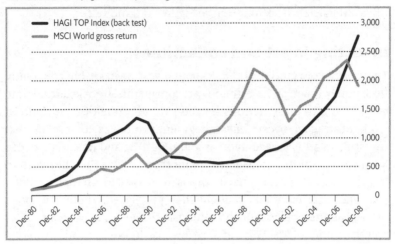

Sources: Bloomberg LP, Historic Automobile Group International (HAGI)

FIGURE 11.4 **Monthly performance of world equities and classic cars** £, Dec 2008–Aug 2017, Dec 2008 = 100

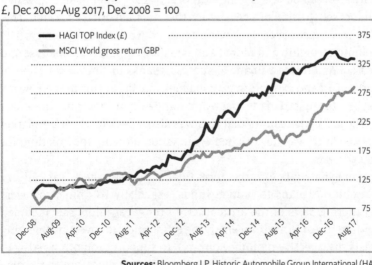

Sources: Bloomberg LP, Historic Automobile Group International (HAGI)

they are able to capture the majority of relevant transactions globally. The HAGI has supplemented the monthly series since 2008 with back-filled annual data back to 1980 (see Figures 11.3 and 11.4).

Investing in art and collectibles

There has been a great deal of talk about investing in art, but apparently little purely financial investment. Art consultants are asked from time to time to give presentations on the potential role of a portfolio of works of art in an investment strategy. But as often as not it seems that investing in art is looked upon as an interesting and imaginative idea for investors to have considered rather than an idea that they wish to implement. The one exception to this is the market for art funds, though even these are more talked about than purchased. There have been numerous attempts to launch art funds. Michael Findlay, an art dealer and the author of *The Value of Art*, says that "there is an adage among old hands in the art world that the emergence of art investment funds signals that a boom is over". He cites an early example from 1904 when a French financier and 12 friends formed a fund called, "with intentional irony", La Peau de l'Ours ("the skin of the bear") after a fable in which hunters sell the skin of a bear which they are then unable to catch. This fund was a great success, having acquired works by emerging artists including Gauguin and Monet and two then "unknowns", Matisse and Picasso. And it was a financial success, thanks to shrewd selection of works of art and extraordinary good luck in winding up after ten years, just before the start of the first world war. The new long-run price index for the art market shows that this was also a peak level for art market prices, which was not reached again, after allowing for inflation, for over 50 years.

Immediately before the 2008 financial crisis, there was a flurry of ambitious plans to launch funds, especially in China, to invest in differing parts of the art market. In the West, proposals included funds to invest in art from emerging economies, to invest in emerging artists (irrespective of home country), to support promotions so as to "brand" new artists, and to focus on relatively high turnover and also on relatively low turnover.

In 2013, there were relatively few funds operating, although the combined assets under management have been estimated at around $1 billion (which is difficult to verify). Art funds offer the prospect of making a financial investment in a diversified portfolio of works of art. In practice, the transaction charges levied by dealers and auction houses impose a difficult hurdle on relatively short-life funds to buy, hold, then sell art and give a competitive return to investors. Art funds need to get around this hurdle, and one avenue is to deal directly with buyers and sellers (who for contemporary works might be the artists). The management of funds has sought to overcome the hurdle of transaction costs by providing liquidity to art collectors who wish to sell art quickly or anonymously (or both). To this extent, investors in an art fund have been investing in and providing valuable liquidity to a business that can be compared with an art dealership. However, an attractive feature of an art fund for investors is that they may be able to borrow works of art from the fund for display in their own homes or offices.

Overall, though the development of art funds has been disappointing, there have been a few successes. A small number of private banks have flirted with the idea of launching them, but the banks' more common role is advising their wealthiest clients on the management of their art collections and, in particular, the arrangement of credit facilities secured against their art. Works of art may represent a significant part of the wealth of such investors, but they are normally better described as collections, rather than as investment portfolios.

A rare example from the past of an institutional foray into the art market was the investment portfolio created by the British Rail Pension Fund in the years following 1974. The decision to make this unusual alternative investment was a response to the financial crises of the time (especially in the UK) and led to the purchase of a portfolio comprising 2,505 individual works of art. (This total was inflated by the acquisition of several portfolios comprising modest value items.) The purchases occurred between 1974 and 1980 and the final item was sold in 2003. The fund had spent £41.1 million acquiring the works and the proceeds from the sales (net of commissions, fees and taxes, but not allowing for intervening storage and insurance costs) was £170.4 million. This represented an internal rate of return of 11.3%, or 3.7% per year after allowing for the impact of UK inflation. Set against the benchmarks that

FIGURE 11.5 **British Rail Pension Fund realised rates of return for 2,505 individual works of art acquired between 1974 and 1980**
Internal rates of return, per year after inflation

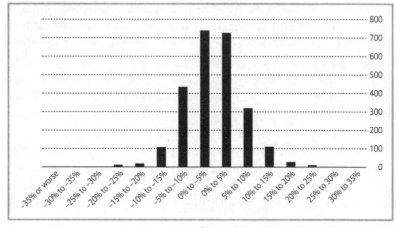

would have been established at the outset, the experience was a success. Nevertheless, it did not persuade the pension fund to continue with its experiment. This example is more relevant for potential investors than that of the Ganz collection because it does not suffer from the hindsight bias that affects that highly successful private collection. The Ganz collection is interesting because it happened to be financially successful; the British Rail portfolio is interesting because it is a single example of a well-diversified financial investment in art.

The British Rail example sheds light on the financial risk of collecting art. Figure 11.5 plots the distribution of rates of return, after allowing for UK inflation, for each of the individual items, which were originally chosen for their contribution to a diversified portfolio of works of art. The similarity between this figure and the corresponding one drawn by Baumol in his 1986 article (based on 640 purchases and then sales of paintings) is striking. Figure 11.5 shows that the performance of individual works was widely dispersed around that of the median, or middle ranking, holding, which was just −0.39% per year. Despite this, the performance of the portfolio as a whole was 3.7% per year, helped by the exceptional performance of the pension fund's holdings of impressionist paintings.

The British Rail experiment was perhaps too short term. Great collections hold works of art from generation to generation; the average holding period in the British Rail works of art collection was just 12.9 years.

Shared characteristics of fine art and other investments of passion

Investments of passion, or hobby collections, share a number of characteristics:

- The importance of "provenance", that is authentication and ownership history of any item cannot be overstated. Even the grandest art collections and galleries run the risk of having major works reassessed by experts. The implications on valuation of having an important work reassessed as "from the school of" rather than by a particular old master painter would be severe; to have a treasured work of art exposed as a forgery would be much worse. Corresponding threats confront a collection of stamps or coins: differences in qualitative assessment can seem arcane to an outsider, but can make an important difference to judgments of the quality of a collection. The expertise and passion of the collector, whether of fine art or collectibles, are directed at minimising such risk.

- The asymmetry of information that exists between market insiders and most investors is a feature that is shared with all illiquid markets. Those wishing to build a collection need to appreciate that an informational advantage almost always lies with the market professional.

- The prevalence of high transaction costs, which are normally much higher than in more liquid securities markets. At art auctions, transaction costs are dominated by the buyer and seller "premia", or commissions. For example, at one of the major auction houses, where the buyer's commission is calculated on a sliding scale, the commission payable for a purchase with a hammer price of $1.5 million could be over 20%, with 25% payable on the first $250,000. Commissions payable by the seller (or consignor) of a work are also significant, but since a price-fixing scandal in 2002, they may now be more susceptible to economic pressures. Nevertheless, it is safe to assume that the auction houses may extract 25% of the price of a high-value painting and more for smaller value items. Such transaction costs are likely to cripple most approaches to investments of passion that do not involve a patient buy-and-hold strategy.

The financial resources that could in principle be allocated to acquisitions of art are enormous relative to the size of the global art market. Deep pockets in the Middle East are funding new national galleries. More importantly, there is a traditional imbalance between the tiny size of the art market compared with total private financial wealth. Art auctions had a record turnover in 2012 according to Artprice of $12.3 billion, but investable financial wealth was estimated by the Capgemini and RBC 2013 "World Wealth Report" to have been $46.2 trillion (that is, $46.2 thousand billion), with perhaps $12 trillion available as cash or deposits.

The insignificant size of the art market, in relation to disposable wealth, means that a move by any substantial investor or group of investors to establish or extend a major art collection is likely to provide considerable support to prices. The easiest way to justify a purely financial investment in sought-after parts of the fine art market would be a belief that prices would increasingly be supported by at least some such investors for decades ahead. As Baumol implied, economics is unable to suggest any upper limit for the prices of highly prized art.

Use of expert opinion for forecasting, valuation and risk modelling

If we consider art as providing no financial dividends, then in financial terms, there are no financial fundamentals to determine the fair price. This is the indeterminacy of value alluded to by Baumol. Surprisingly, this very indeterminacy enhances the role of experts.

In relatively efficient markets, such as those of mature equity, fundamentals are of considerable importance and known future adjustments to dividends will tend automatically to be included in the current price. However, looking at art as an example, the absence of fundamentals increases the importance of experts and expert opinion is capable of influencing a current price through various mechanisms.

This may occur at the level of a category, such as Britart or at the level of an individual artist, such as Damien Hirst. A change in critical opinion today, based on a panel of experts, will lead to a change in auction realisations in the future. This predictability arises because of both lack of fundamentals and illiquidity.

A particular application of expert opinion is provided by the company ArtTactic. An important structural feature of the art auction market is the estimated price range supplied by the auction house in advance of the sale. Since 2013, the online ArtTactic Forecaster competition has gathered repeated price predictions from several hundred self-selected forecasters who choose whichever price range they expect to contain final auction prices for a selection of high-profile lots (in a multiple-choice survey). Predictions are obtained during a period starting a few days before each auction sale.

An interesting finding is that the average predictions of all forecasters, on average, tend to lie very close to the middle of the range of the auctioneer's estimates. This finding appears to be a classic example of *anchoring bias*, as discussed in Chapter 2 and this probably enhances the credibility with which the auction houses are regarded.

"Surprising" auction price outcomes are the exception rather than the rule, but they are rarely ever predicted by the average of the "crowd" forecast. Greater predictive power requires more measurement, potentially taking into account the skill levels of particular forecasters with respect to specific artists and categories of work. Nevertheless, although the average forecasts may lack significant predictive power over "surprises", the variance of opinion among forecasters is arguably more informative, with a material difference apparent between the modest range of estimates for the most liquid collectibles (such as Rolex watches) when compared with the wider ranges of expert assessments of value for relatively esoteric pieces, for example, work by younger artists who are less deeply researched and have shorter track records at auction. Since these predictions involve very short time horizons (such as a few days), they do not convey significant information about the market risk associated with a work of art over the long term. Long-term risk is challenging to assess as it involves such factors as reputation, supply-side dynamics and changing tastes. However, to some extent the ranges of expert valuations can be viewed as subjective indications of risk associated with auction sale *execution*. As collectors are well aware, even when a piece is worthy of inclusion in a sale by a top tier auction house (which might be taken for granted in the case of prominent works), there remains significant uncertainty over its actual selling price in the room on the day.

Understanding the magnitude of this price risk is, for instance, an important consideration when lending money against investment grade art as collateral (see below). An expert valuation such as an auctioneer's estimate only tells part of the story. Prediction variance presents one way of assessing this, either in estimated monetary terms, or in terms of ranking against other artists and works. This is closely related to the risk of a lot completely failing to sell at auction (effectively valued by participants at below its reserve price), an outcome which is given a careful analytical treatment by McAndrew and Thompson (2007). Taken together, estimates of no-sale probability and prediction range appear to be helpful risk metrics to enhance professional valuations.

Collectibles as collateral

The illiquidity of collectibles represents a serious issue for those who wish to collect and put substantial money into their collections. There have been a number of innovations recently to address this problem by setting up structures whereby collectors can use their collections as collateral.

Growth in the art-secured lending market is driven primarily by collectors who increasingly view their art collection as a source of capital in a low interest-rate environment. Art-secured lending can be seen as an effective way of enabling collectors to access the equity value in their artworks without having to sell their pieces, an action that could trigger a tax liability. Art lending makes it possible for collectors to redeploy their capital into new art acquisitions or attractive business opportunities, or to refinance existing loans.

The Art & Finance Report 2016 by Deloitte and ArtTactic estimates the size of the US art-secured lending market to be in the range of $15 to $18bn (based on the value of loans outstanding). The market share consists of 81% accounted for by private banks, with 11% accounted for by specialist asset based lenders and 8% by auction houses. The report estimates the US art lending market to have grown by 15 to 20% annually over the last five years.

Although art-secured lending growth is predominantly being driven by private banks, the second major source of growth comes from auction houses that have expanded or launched art lending services. According to the Art & Finance report, a potentially important source of future growth has been the expansion of non-recourse asset-backed lending from hedge funds and boutiques.

Growth in the art-secured lending market has also triggered the need for better risk management tools, and several new insurance products covering defective title, even infidelity risk and residual risk are available to potential lenders. However, banks are likely to be unwilling to digest the extra 1.5% to 2.5% in fees for these policies, and would rather rely on appraisers and experts for valuation, attribution and authenticity. Going forward, more innovation in the art and risk management sector is likely, particularly with new data tools being developed to improve the measurement of risk and performance and to translate this into language that financial institutions and investors are more familiar with.

Appendix 1
Glossary

THIS GLOSSARY DOES NOT REPEAT definitions and explanations of concepts that are provided in the main text, for example in Chapter 2 (terms relating to behavioural finance) and chapters in Part 2 (for terms relating to equity markets, credit markets, hedge funds, private equity and real estate). For references to these, please consult the index.

Active management	Investment strategies of active investment managers who are appointed in the expectation or hope that they will perform better than the market as a whole, after allowing for the extra fees paid for active management. These strategies always involve avoidable turnover (compared with a passive or market-matching strategy) and the avoidable risk of underperforming the market. See also **passive strategies**.
Annualised returns	See **geometric average returns**.
Arithmetic average returns	The simple average over time of investment returns. This is higher than the compounded or geometric average of returns. The difference is easy to illustrate. Suppose a portfolio performance in one period is -50% and in the next is +100%. The arithmetic average performance is +25% [(-50 + 100) ÷ 2]. The geometric average or compound return, however, is 100 X (0.5 X 2.0) -100 or 0%. Standard risk measures such as the standard deviation should be used in conjunction with the arithmetic average. However, the geometric or compound return describes the evolution of wealth over time.

Asset allocation	Allocation of investments among different markets. Contrast with stock selection, which is the allocation of investments within a particular market.
Base currency	Investors' home currency in which their investment objectives are expressed. Their base currency is normally, but not always, unambiguous. See Chapter 1.
Basis point (BP)	One hundredth of one per cent, or 0.01%.
Beta	A measure of the extent to which a stock might provide diluted exposure (if the measure of beta is less than 1.0) or leveraged exposure (if the measure of beta is greater than 1.0) to equity market risk. See Chapter 8 for discussion of the fundamental insights, strengths and weaknesses of the capital asset pricing model, in which the concept of "beta" plays a central role.
Bond ladder	A portfolio of high-quality bonds of successive maturities designed to provide a steady stream of investment income. See Chapter 5.
Break-even rate of inflation	This is (approximately) the difference between the redemption yield on conventional government bonds and that on inflation-linked government bonds of the same maturity. If inflation happens to equal the break-even rate, the total return on inflation-linked and conventional government bonds will be approximately identical. See Chapter 4.
Business angel	An entrepreneur who contributes finance and often business expertise to support a venture capital investment in return for a significant shareholding.
Call option	A contract that gives the right to buy a specified investment at a given time in the future for a predetermined price. See also **option** and **put option**.
Capital Asset Pricing Model (CAPM)	See **beta** and Chapter 8.
Coefficient of loss aversion	A concept from behavioural finance. The ratio of the sensitivity to losses compared with the sensitivity to gains. A commonly cited result is that the coefficient is around 2, in other words, that investors weigh losses twice as highly as they weigh gains.

Contrarian

An investor, or a strategy, that deliberately seeks to be unfashionable and to go against recent market trends. Typically, this is an adjective that is used to describe value investors; see Chapter 8.

Conventional bond

A fixed-income bond (which has a predetermined schedule of fixed-interest coupons and a fixed redemption value). The word "conventional" is used to distinguish the bond from inflation-linked or floating-rate bonds. Inflation-linked bonds have coupons and/or redemption values that are adjusted in line with inflation. Floating-rate bonds have coupons that are reset in line with a specified short-term reference rate of interest, such as the London Interbank Offered Rate (LIBOR).

Convertible bond

Usually a corporate bond that gives investors the option to convert it at some stage in the future into a given number of ordinary shares of the issuing company. Convertible bonds generally pay lower coupons than bonds issued by the same company which do not offer the option to convert into equity.

Convexity

A measure of the change in a bond's duration that is a result of a change in interest rates. Allowance for a bond's convexity enables a more accurate assessment of how its price will respond to interest rate changes than can be provided by considering only its duration. This is because the relationship between a change in interest rates and the consequent change in bond prices is generally not linear. Positive convexity is a desirable characteristic and is an attribute of conventional bonds whose duration increases as interest rates fall and decreases as interest rates rise. This is because the present value of future payments increases with lower interest rates and vice versa. Thus these bonds perform better than calculations based only on the bond's duration would suggest when interest rates change. Negative convexity is the opposite, and bonds which display this characteristic tend to underperform when interest rates fall and/or rise. Bonds which are exposed to certain types of embedded options, such as mortgage bonds, can display negative convexity. See Chapter 9.

Correlation	The degree of linear association between two variables. In other words, it is a measure of the extent to which the prices of two investments move together (but not necessarily by the same amount). The correlation coefficient, R, can vary between –1 and +1. A correlation coefficient of o suggests no relationship between the movements in the prices of the two investments. A positive correlation suggests that the prices of the two investments tend to rise or fall at the same time. A negative correlation suggests that the prices of the two investments tend to move in opposite directions at any particular time. Negative correlations are highly desirable in constructing portfolios of risky assets, because they reduce risk. However, negatively correlated attractive investments are rare.
Credit spread	The extra yield offered by a risky bond over that offered by the Treasury for a bond of the same maturity to compensate an investor for the risk that the issue might default. Extra yield may also be paid to compensate for the illiquidity of an issue.
Derivatives	Derived investment contracts, which are designed to replicate certain aspects of risk that can be obtained from direct investment in markets such as equity or fixed income.
Directional funds	A common categorisation of hedge fund strategies is to divide them between directional and non-directional strategies. Directional strategies are those whose performance is expected to be highly correlated with equity or other market risk.
Disinflation	The process of reducing the rate of inflation – that is, the rate at which prices are increasing. Disinflation should not be confused with deflation, which refers to actual declines in prices.

Duration	The average life of a bond and also a measure of a bond's sensitivity to movements in interest rates. (Slight differences in calculation are reflected in these definitions.) Duration is the weighted average time to the total of scheduled payments, where the weights are determined by the present value of each payment. Duration is shorter than the maturity of a bond, because it takes account of the earlier dates on which interest coupons are paid. The exception is a zero coupon bond, the duration of which is the same as its maturity. There are two common but similar technical definitions of duration: Macaulay duration, which is most useful in precisely matching a future stream of payments; and modified duration, which provides a measure of the sensitivity of a bond portfolio to small changes in interest rates.
Efficient frontier	On a graph which plots for different investments (and for portfolios of different investments) the expected return (y-axis) and volatility (x-axis) of those investments, the efficient frontier shows the most efficient combinations of risk and return. At any point on the frontier curve for a given level of volatility, expected return is maximised, and for a given level of expected return, volatility is minimised. See **fuzzy frontier** and Chapter 6.
ETF	Short for exchange traded fund, an investment product that gives exposure to a particular market. The ETF itself is listed on the stockmarket, and so is highly liquid and generally accessible at modest transaction prices.
Family office	The private office of a wealthy family which is entrusted with the management of the family's financial affairs.
Fat tails	See **kurtosis**.
Forward contract	Similar to a futures contract, except that it may not be standardised (though most probably it will be) and does not benefit from the transparent pricing and support of a formal exchange. As a result, forwards may not be marked to market each day. This gives rise to larger issues of counterparty risk than exist with futures contracts, which are transacted on a formal exchange.

Futures contract A standardised contract entered into on a futures exchange to buy or sell a particular investment or basket of investments at a given date in the future. The exchange guarantees payments between members of the exchange (but not their clients). In practice, profit and loss on a futures contract is calculated on a daily basis and reflected in payments of variation margin to and from the exchange's clearing house by both parties to a contract.

Fuzzy frontier An adaptation of the concept of the efficient frontier which acknowledges that, because investment relationships and investment classifications are to a degree uncertain, there is rarely one most efficient strategy that a particular investor should follow. Instead there is always a range of broadly efficient appropriate strategies. See Chapter 2.

Geometric average returns Another term for compound or annualised investment returns. For the difference between geometric or compound and arithmetic investment returns, see **arithmetic average returns**.

Hedged An indication that market risk, for example from the stockmarket or a foreign exchange market, has been neutralised using derivatives or other instruments. But see Chapter 10 for a discussion of the loose use of the term "hedging" by hedge funds.

Heuristic A simple procedure that helps find adequate though often imperfect answers to difficult questions. A shortcut.

High watermark This concept is important for the calculation of hedge fund performance fees. It refers to the preceding highest cumulative total return. Hedge fund performance fees are normally payable only if cumulative performance exceeds the preceding "high watermark". See Chapter 10.

High-yield bond A debt issue which is judged by credit-rating agencies to be at best speculative or not well secured. See also **sub-investment grade**, **investment grade** and Chapter 9.

Inflation risk premium An amount by which the break-even rate of inflation may exceed the expected rate of inflation to allow for the risk that inflation may be higher than expected. See Chapter 4.

In-the-money	A call option is said to be "in-the-money" when the market price of the underlying investment is above the "strike" price at which the option to buy that investment can be exercised. A put option is in-the-money when the market price is below the strike price at which the option can be exercised. An option can be exercised profitably only if it is in-the-money.
Investment grade	The group of credit ratings given by the principal rating agencies to debt securities whose credit rating is assessed as being at least moderate to good quality. This differentiates investment grade debt from issues which are judged to be at best speculative or not well secured. See **sub-investment grade** and Chapter 9.
Kurtosis	Also called excess kurtosis. A measure of whether a series of investment returns has more extreme results than would be suggested by the normal distribution. A distribution with more than expected extreme results is called leptokurtic. This phenomenon is more commonly referred to as "fat tails". A number of hedge fund strategies, and some stockmarket returns, demonstrate pronounced fat tails or excess kurtosis. See Chapter 8.
Large cap	One of the largest companies by stockmarket capitalisation. In the United States a common definition is that a quoted company is large cap if its market capitalisation exceeds $10 billion. See Chapter 8.
Leverage	An indication of the extent to which an investment, and thus its performance, is geared through the level of debt embedded in it.
Liquidity	An indication of the ease with which investments can be bought or sold at close to their advertised price. In illiquid markets it can be difficult to buy and sell investments.
Listed investment	An investment, typically a stock or bond, which is listed on a recognised exchange and provides regular quotations for its price. Contrast with an unlisted or private investment (such as a venture capital investment or a property investment), the price of which, except when it is bought and sold, represents appraisal valuations.

Lognormal distribution	See **normal distribution**.
Long-only strategy	A traditional investment strategy or portfolio consisting only of investments which are owned, not investments which are borrowed or sold short. See also **short position**.
Long position	An investment which is owned, as distinct from an investment which is borrowed. See also **short position**.
Mark-to-market	The process of accounting for the value of investments, and so profits and losses, at their market prices, rather than their book or historical cost.
Market risk premium	The premium return expected for investing outside the secure safe haven and incurring the risks associated with investing in volatile markets that offer systematic investment returns to investors.
Mean reversion	The belief, fundamental to the outlook of value investors, that prices in financial markets tend to overreact, oscillating between overvaluation and undervaluation. Mean reversion refers to an expectation that expensive markets can be relied upon to become cheaper and inexpensive markets can be relied upon to become priced closer to "fair value". See Chapters 4, 6 and 8.
Mental accounting	A concept from behavioural finance. The set of cognitive operations used by individuals and households to organise, evaluate and keep track of financial activities.
Mezzanine debt	Often the most junior – that is, the most risky – category of debt in a borrower's balance sheet. Typically it will be accompanied by options to convert into equity. It is best considered as sharing the risk characteristics of equity rather than debt.
Natural habitat	The natural investment home for a particular investor, such as long-dated Treasury bonds for a pension fund.
Negative convexity	See **convexity**.

Noise

Meaningless apparent market signals which make it more difficult to interpret market developments. Noise is both a cause and a reflection of uncertainty. One cause of noise is the impact on markets of the transactions of investors who lack insight or who transact for reasons other than in response to market signals (for example, investors who have an impact on markets because, for whatever reason, they need to sell). See Chapter 7.

Normal distribution

The normal and lognormal distributions are the two most commonly used statistical models in finance. A normal distribution is symmetrical, with a bell-shaped curve and one peak; a lognormal distribution is skewed to the right. Return series that are lognormally distributed lead to geometric, or logarithmic, returns that are themselves normally distributed. The popularity of the normal and lognormal distributions reflects their comparative ease of use in analysis and the evidence that they provide a plausible approximation to many market performance data series. Much effort has been invested in examining when the normal, or lognormal, distribution fails to describe how markets behave. See, for example, Chapters 4, 6 and 8.

Option

A contract that gives the purchaser the right, but not the obligation, to buy (call option) or sell (put option) a particular investment at a given price on (if a European option) or before (if an American option) the given expiry date for the contract.

Passive strategies

Market-matching investment strategies which involve minimal turnover and expense. Turnover typically occurs only to accommodate inflows or outflows of investor funds and to improve the market-matching features of the investment portfolio.

Ponzi scheme
A type of scam named after the fraudster Charles Ponzi, who in the 1920s defrauded thousands of New England residents with the promise of superlative returns on their savings by exploiting anomalies in the rates of exchange offered on international mail coupons. A Ponzi scheme is an investment fraud that offers the promise of enticing performance by diverting cash from new investors to provide the promised returns to exiting old investors. Such a scheme is doomed to fail and works only as long as new inflows at least match the demand for cash from leavers.

Prepayment risk
The risk that a bond, particularly a mortgage bond, will experience faster than scheduled repayments of principal because residential mortgage holders, particularly in the United States, can exercise the right to repay mortgages earlier than specified in a repayment schedule. This reduces the term of a mortgage bond and is most likely to happen when interest rates fall (or when mortgage providers compete aggressively for new business), giving profitable opportunities for borrowers to remortgage property at more attractive interest rates. See Chapter 9.

Price/earnings ratio
The ratio of the share price of a company to its earnings divided by the number of shares it has issued. A high price/earnings (p/e) ratio indicates that the stockmarket expects the company's earnings to grow fast, and vice versa.

Price performance
The performance of an investment that makes no allowance for its income or dividend yield. Contrast with total return, which includes the price performance and the income return.

Prime broker
A department of an investment bank which provides banking services to hedge funds.

Private investment
An unlisted or unquoted investment for which price quotations are generally not readily available.

Prospect theory
A key part of behavioural finance. It is based on experiments that indicate that people are more motivated by losses than by gains (see **coefficient of loss aversion**) and so will try hard to avoid realising losses. See Chapter 2.

Public investment
A listed or quoted investment for which prices are regularly quoted on a formal exchange at which, or close to which, transactions can be effected.

Pure discount bond	See **zero coupon bond**.
Put option	A contract that gives the right to sell a specified investment at a given time in the future for a predetermined price. See also **option** and **call option**.
Quoted investment	A public investment.
R^2	The square of the correlation coefficient. This measures the percentage of variation (that is, variance) in the price of one investment that is "explained" by a change in the price of another.
Real interest rate	The rate of interest after allowing for inflation.
Redemption yield	See **yield to maturity**.
Relative risk	Typically, the risk of an actively managed portfolio relative to that of the market or the investor's benchmark or neutral investment policy.
Risk premium	See Chapter 4.
Safe haven	An investor's minimum-risk strategy. See Chapter 4.
Sharpe ratio	A measure of risk-adjusted performance. For an investment portfolio or strategy, the Sharpe ratio is the ratio of performance in excess of the risk-free investment (generally Treasury bills) to the volatility of performance relative to the risk-free rate. Performance and volatility are generally calculated as annualised rates. Investors should be aware that illiquid investment strategies distort measurement of Sharpe ratios since the apparent volatility of those strategies will be artificially reduced by markets that rely on appraisal valuations of underlying investments. Furthermore, Sharpe ratios are only meaningful if the distribution of performance of the underlying investments approximately resembles a normal distribution. It follows that Sharpe ratios should not be used for investment strategies which resemble insurance programmes and which incorporate a marked degree of optionality. For both these reasons, Sharpe ratios shown for many hedge fund strategies are more likely to misinform investors than to inform them. See Chapter 10

Short position	Arises when investors sell an investment that they do not own. Unless the short position is established on a futures exchange, investors will need to borrow the investment to deliver it to the counterparty who bought it from them. The short seller will need to provide collateral to the stock lender when borrowing the stock (or other investment).
Skewness	A measure of the symmetry between investment returns from a market. If the returns are tilted towards the left (more negative) side of the distribution, a distribution is said to exhibit negative skewness. If returns are tilted towards the right (more positive) side of the distribution, the results are said to exhibit positive skewness.
Small cap	A smaller company by stockmarket capitalisation. In the United States a common definition is that a quoted company is small cap if its market capitalisation is less than $2 billion. See Chapter 8.
SMID	Short for small- or mid-cap companies, a group of companies that is reckoned to be either small or mid cap by value of market capitalisation. In the United States a common definition is that a quoted company is SMID if its market capitalisation is less than $6 billion. See Chapter 8.
Sovereign wealth fund (SWF)	A government-owned investment fund, typically arising from persistent balance-of-payments surpluses.
Speculative grade	A debt issue judged by credit-rating agencies to be at best speculative or not well secured. See also **high-yield bond**, **investment grade** and Chapter 9.
Standard deviation	The standard measure of the volatility of the price or performance of an investment. Common interpretations of the standard deviation derive from the normal distribution. For example, if an equity portfolio has an expected return of 7% a year and an expected volatility of 15% a year, it would be expected, approximately, to have returns of between −8% and 22% in two years out of three.
Stock selection	The allocation of investments in a portfolio within a particular market. Contrast with the allocation of investments among different markets, which is known as asset allocation.

Strategic asset allocation	Decisions, typically intended to be quite long term in nature, to manage risks and opportunities relative to an investor's ultimate payment obligations or objectives. Strategic asset allocation involves the allocation of investments between an investor's safe-haven investment and an efficient diversity of other market risks. See Chapter 5.
Structured product	An investment or investment strategy that is typically sold with some element of principal protection and/or of leverage to give accelerated exposure to the underlying market. Structured products are sold by investment banks and typically involve either some combination of zero coupon bonds, which mature with the structured product, together with call options on the relevant underlying market; or a dynamic strategy that adjusts exposure to the underlying investment and government bonds to ensure that the issuing bank will be able profitably to honour the promised capital repayment at maturity.
Sub-investment grade	A debt issue judged by credit-rating agencies to be at best speculative or not well secured. See also **high-yield bond**, **investment grade** and Chapter 9.
Systematic return	The market return that is expected to be provided for bearing well-diversified systematic risk. Often thought of in terms of equity market return, systematic return also refers to the return that should be expected for bearing any type of market risk for which market participants are willing to pay. This includes, in addition to equity market risk, credit market risk, as well as various types of insurance and other risk transfer services. Such alternative sources of systematic return are now understood to be an important potential source of hedge fund returns.
Systematic risk	The market risk that remains after diversification. Most commonly this refers to equity market risk, but it can also refer to the risk associated with a range of different sources of systematic return.
Tactical asset allocation	Decisions, typically short or medium term, to allocate more or less of an investment strategy to different markets in the hope of profiting from expected differential performance between markets.

Tobin's Q	Named after James Tobin, a Nobel Prize-winning economist from Yale University, this is the ratio of the stockmarket value of a firm to its replacement cost. If Q is less than one it would be cheaper to buy the firm's shares than to expand to replicate that firm. See Chapter 10 for its application to the US real estate market.
Total return	The total performance of an investment, combining income yield as well as price performance.
Tracking error	See **relative risk**.
Tranche	A slice, specifically of a collateralised debt obligation (CDO), that has different risk characteristics from other tranches of the same CDO. See Chapter 9.
Treasury bill	Government debt with less than one year's original maturity (typically 1–6 months).
Treasury bond	Government debt with more than one year's original maturity. In designing broad investment strategies, it is conventional to treat a government bond with a remaining maturity of less than 12 months as if it were a Treasury bill. In the United States, Treasury debts with between one and ten years' original maturity are called "notes". In this book, the expression "Treasury bond" refers to any Treasury security of more than one year's maturity.
Unhedged	An indication that market risk, for example from the stockmarket or a foreign exchange market, has not been neutralised using derivatives or other instruments.
Utility	An indication of satisfaction, often proxied by money.
Volatility	Fluctuations in the price or performance of an investment, typically measured by the annualised standard deviation of returns.
Warrant	An option to a buy a security at a particular price and subject to particular time constraints.
Yield curve	See Chapter 4.
Yield to maturity	The standard measure of the return an investor will receive from a Treasury bond if the bond is held to maturity. Yield to maturity (YTM) takes account of the interest income and any capital gain or loss on the bond over that time.

Zero coupon bond   Zero coupon bonds, also known as zeros, ZCBS, or pure discount bonds, pay no interest, only the repayment of principal at maturity. Their maturity is equal to their duration, and for long maturities they represent the most volatile of high-quality bonds. Prior to maturity, zero coupon bonds trade at a discount to face value.

Appendix 2
Sources and recommended reading

Part 1: The big picture

1 Setting the scene

There are a number of investment classics which provide a general background to the first part of this chapter (and other parts of the book). *Manias, Panics and Crashes* (6th edition, Wiley, 2011) by the late Charles Kindleberger and Robert Z. Aiber is always worth re-reading, never more so than in the light of the 2007–09 credit crunch and the scandals which it helped to uncover. The discussion in Chapter 1 on the Madoff scandal draws on extensive discussions with wealth management professionals.

Other classics that should adorn any investor's bookshelf include:

Bernstein, P.L., *Against the Gods: The Remarkable Story of Risk*, John Wiley & Sons, 1998

Carswell, J., *The South Sea Bubble*, 3rd edition, Sutton Publishing, 2001

Galbraith, J.K., *The Great Crash*, Penguin Books, 1992

Mackay, C., *Extraordinary Popular Delusions and the Madness of Crowds*, Wordsworth Editions, 1995

The introduction to risk draws on:

Bohnet,I., Greig F., Herrmann B., Zeckhauser, R., "Betrayal Aversion: Evidence from Brazil, China, Oman, Switzerland, Turkey and the United States", *American Economic Review*, Vol. 98, No. 1., March 2008

Kritzman, M.P., *The Portable Financial Analyst: What Practitioners Need to Know*, 2nd edition, John Wiley & Sons, 2003

Kritzman, M. and Rich, D., "The Mismeasurement of Risk", *Financial Analysts Journal*, May/June 2002

The discussion of risk tolerance and its relation to risk aversion and loss aversion draws on a number of different sources, including conversations with financial planners, advisers and consultants. Some particularly useful sources are:

Guillemette, M.A., Finke, M. and Gilliam, J., "Risk Tolerance Questions to Best Determine Client Portfolio Allocation Preferences", *Journal of Financial Planning*, July 2012

Kahneman, D., "The Myth of Risk Attitudes", *Journal of Portfolio Management*, Fall 2009

Roszkowski, M.J. and Davey, G., "Risk Perception and Risk Tolerance: Changes Attributable to the 2008 Economic Crisis", *Journal of Financial Service Professionals*, July 2010

2 Understand your behaviour

This chapter draws heavily on Daniel Kahneman's magisterial *Thinking Fast and Slow* (Farrar, Straus and Giroux, 2011), which provides a retrospective assessment of the progress made in recent decades (often led by Kahneman and his colleague, the late Amos Tversky) in understanding the strengths and weaknesses of how we take decisions.

Other useful sources include:

Barberis, N. and Thaler, R., "A Survey of Behavioral Finance", in Constantinides, G.M. et al. (eds), *Handbook of the Economics of Finance: Financial Markets and Asset Pricing*, Elsevier/North-Holland, 2003

Lo, A., Adaptive Markets, *Financial Evolution at the Speed of Thought*, Princeton University Press, 2017

Lo, A., "The Adaptive Markets Hypothesis", *Journal of Portfolio Management*, 30th anniversary issue, 2004

Statman, M., *What Investors Really Want: Know What Drives Investor Behavior and Make Smarter Financial Decisions*, McGraw-Hill, 2010

Thaler, R.H., *Misbehaving: The Making of Behavioural Economics*, Penguin Books, 2016

Thaler, R.H. and Sunstein, C.R., *Nudge: Improving Decisions About Health, Wealth and Happiness*, Penguin Books, 2009

3 The personal pension challenge

This chapter benefited from comments from advisers in both the United States and UK. The interface of investment and insurance with uncertainties around individual longevity and old-age care costs make financial planning both complex and fascinating.

Abraham, K. G., and Harris, B.J., "The market for longevity annuities", *Journal of Retirement*, Spring 2016

Bengen, W.P., "Determining withdrawal rates using historical data", *Journal of Financial Planning*, October 1994

Blanchett, D. "Addressing key retirement risks", *Journal of Retirement*, Fall 2014

CFA Institute, "Longevity risk and retirement income planning", 2015

CFA Institute, "Annuities and retirement income planning", 2016

Hurd, M.D., Michaud, P-C. and Rohwedder, S., *Distribution of lifetime nursing home use and out-of-pocket spending*, Rand Corporation and Network for Studies on Pension, Aging and Retirement, Tilburg University, 2017

Hurd, M. D., and Rohwedder, S., "Economic preparation for retirement", Cambridge, Ma, NBER Working Paper No. 17203, 2011

International Longevity Centre, "Understanding retirement journeys: expectations vs reality", 2015

Merton, R. C., "Thoughts for the future: theory and practice in investment management", *Financial Analysts Journal*, January/February 2003

Merton, R. C., "The crisis in retirement planning", *Harvard Business Review*, July/August 2014

Scott, J. S., "The longevity annuity: an annuity for everyone?" *Financial Analysts Journal*, January/February 2015

Scott, J. S., Sharpe, W. F. and Watson, J. G., "The 4% rule – At what price?" *Journal of Investment Management*, Vol 7. no 3. 2009

TIAA-CREF Institute, Research dialogue, no 111, "What makes annuitization more appealing?", October 2013

Waring, B. M., and Siegel, L. B., "The only spending rule article you will ever need", *Financial Analysts Journal*, January/February 2015

4 Market investment returns

Elroy Dimson and David Chambers (eds), *Financial Market History: Reflections on the past for investors today* (CFA Institute Research Foundation and Cambridge Judge Business School, 2016), provides a survey of historical risk and returns for different markets.

The section titled "Are government bonds risk-free?" draws on Carmen Reinhart and Kenneth Rogoff's *This Time is Different: Eight Centuries of Financial Folly* (Princeton University Press, 2009). Some of the historical examples of default they cite appear to have been misclassified. In the UK, instances of the government exercising its option to refinance marketable debts (gilts) to take advantage of low market interest rates in 1932 and also in the 19th century are listed as "*de jure*" defaults. The prospectus for the 1932 debt conversion indicates that this was voluntary, with an option to redeem at par. The prospectus can be found at: www.dmo.gov.uk/media/9783/announcement300632.pdf . The steps that the UK government took in the late 19th century to refinance debt were described by A.C. Miller in his 1890 article "The Conversion of English Debt", which is available from: http://qje.oxfordjournals.org .

The title for the box "A country called Europe" comes from a series of broadcasts and speeches on the prospects for European monetary union which were given in the late 1990s by Peter Jay, then the BBC's economics editor. Other important sources include the following:

The term structure of real and nominal interest rates

Buraschi, A. and Jiltsov, A., "Inflation Risk Premia and the Expectations Hypothesis", *Journal of Financial Economics*, Vol. 75, Issue 2, February 2005

Campbell, J.Y., Shiller, R.J. and Viceira, L.M., "Understanding inflation-indexed bond markets", *Brookings Papers on Economic Activity*, Spring 2009

Ilmanen, A., *Expected Returns: An Investor's Guide to Harvesting Market Rewards*, John Wiley & Sons, 2011

Ilmanen, A., *Expected Returns on Major Asset Classes*, CFA Institute 2012

Pflueger, C.E. and Viceira, L.M., "Inflation-Indexed Bonds and the Expectations Hypothesis", Harvard Business School Working Paper H-11–095, 2011

The equity risk premium

Brett, H.P., Leibowitz, M.L. and Siegel, L.B. (eds), *Rethinking the Equity Risk Premium*, CFA Institute, 2011

"Credit Suisse Global Investment Returns Sourcebook", 2017

"Credit Suisse Global Investment Returns Yearbook", 2017

Damodaran, Aswath, Equity risk premiums (ERP): Determinants, Estimation and Implications – The 2017 Edition, downloaded from SSRN.com

Dimson, E., Marsh, P. and Staunton, M., *Triumph of the Optimists: 101 Years of Global Investment Returns*, Princeton University Press, 2002

Dimson, E., Marsh, P. and Staunton, M., "Irrational Optimism", *Financial Analysts Journal*, January/February 2004

Siegel, J., *Stocks for the Long Run*, 5th edition, McGraw-Hill, 2014

Manager selection

Berk, J. B. and Green, R. C., "Mutual fund flows and performance in rational markets." *Journal of Political Economy* 112.6: 1269-1295, 2004

Hall, A.D., Satchell, S. E. and Spence, P. J. "Information ratios and the distribution of skill", mimeo University of Sydney, 2017

Louth, R., Satchell, S. and Wongwachara, W., "Is Rating Associated with Better Retail Funds' Performance in Changing Market Conditions?" *Bankers, Markets & Investors* 132 4–24, 2014

5 Advice and investment strategy

The section on advice, investment beliefs and conflicts of interest draws on discussions with advisers, investors and trustees over the years.

The provocative article underlying the discussion of model investment strategies is the late Peter L. Bernstein's 2003 article "Are Policy Portfolios Obsolete?" in the *Economics and Portfolio Strategy* newsletter. In recent years, whether market returns predictably vary from one period to another has been the subject of extensive published research. A good summary is provided by Antti Ilmanen's *Expected Returns* (2011).

The discussion of market valuations in 2017 echoes debates that will have taken place at the board of almost every investment fund. The focus in Chapter 5 is on the consequences for the valuation of all assets of very low interest rates in encouraging higher prices of other assets, including equities.

The chapter then discusses the suggestion, which arises from James Tobin's "separation theorem", that investment strategy for any investor can be reduced to an appropriate balance between just two investments: an allocation to risk-free assets and an allocation to the market portfolio of risk assets. (The market portfolio is often, as in the first part of this book, proxied by the global equity market.) Tobin set out his theorem in a 1958 article, "Liquidity preference as behaviour towards risk", in the *Review of Economic Studies* which explained how investors, with different attitudes to risk, choose to allocate monetary assets between cash and volatile assets. The separation theorem, which is also known as the "two fund money separation theorem" or the "mutual fund separation theorem", relies on strong assumptions. Thus, if the global market for risky investments is fully represented by listed equities (which it is not) and if the prices of risky investments are determined efficiently (which they are not) and if expected returns in excess of the risk-free rate are constant (which they are not), then using an investor's degree of risk aversion to select appropriate proportions of risk-free and risk assets will provide a suitable strategy for any investor.

In practice, to address the shortcomings of the highly simplified approach requires high-fee actively managed investment strategies, whereas Tobin's two-investment approach can be proxied by low-cost global equities and cash (or government bonds). The costs of the more complicated versions, which seek to address the criticisms of Tobin's simplified model, place them at a significant disadvantage to the simplicity of the low-cost two-portfolio approach. The simplified allocation between diversified equities and cash or government bonds remains a useful reference strategy for investors, and, in effect, reflects practice for many financial advisers.

6 Are you in it for the long term?

John Campbell and Tuomo Vuolteenaho's "Bad Beta, Good Beta" (American Economic Review, Vol. 94, No. 5, December 2004) is one of those occasional articles that develops a simple investment idea that then has powerful policy (as well as investor education) implications. It is the inspiration for this chapter's discussion of good and bad price declines as well as Chapter 8's discussion of apparent stockmarket anomalies. In a similar vein is Zvi Bodie's "Thoughts for the Future: Life-Cycle Investing in Theory and Practice" (Financial Analysts Journal, January/February 2003), where the different strands of traditional and behavioural finance are synthesised into designing suitable strategies for loss averse investors. And Hildy Richelson and Stan Richelson's Bonds: The Unbeaten Path to Secure Investment Growth (2nd edition, Bloomberg Press, 2011) gives a guide to the practical aspects of managing and establishing bond ladders.

Other important sources for this chapter include:

Bergstresser, D. and Cohen, R., "Changing Patterns in Household Ownership of Municipal Debt", mimeo, Brookings, 2015

Campbell, J.Y. and Viceira, L.M., *Strategic Asset Allocation: Portfolio Choice for Long-Term Investors*, Oxford University Press, 2002

Swensen, D., *Pioneering Portfolio Management: An Unconventional Approach to Institutional Investment*, 2nd edition, Free Press, 2009

PART 2: Implementing more complicated strategies

7 Setting the scene

The discussion of the costs of liquidity draws heavily on the work of Andrew Ang, for example, "Illiquid Assets" (*CFA Institute Conference Proceedings Quarterly*, Vol. 28, No. 4, 2011). and Charles Goodhart, "Illiquidity risk management" in *Financial Stability Review*, Banque de France, February 2008. During the credit crisis, it was immediately evident that illiquidity was imposing heavy costs on investors; see, for example, Laurence B. Siegel's article "Alternatives and Liquidity: Will Spending and Capital Calls Eat Your 'Modern' Portfolio?" (*Journal of Portfolio Management*, Fall 2008). There is nothing new about the dangers of illiquidity, which were amply highlighted in, for example, Dan Borge's The Book of Risk, published in 2001 (John Wiley & Sons).

Analysis of arbitrage opportunities in this chapter relies heavily on Nicholas Barberis and Richard Thaler's survey of behavioural finance (see Chapter 2 sources).

8 Equities

The treatment of the capital asset pricing model (CAPM) and the stockmarket anomalies draws on Eugene Fama and Kenneth R. French's article "The Capital Asset Pricing Model: Theory and Evidence" (*Journal of Economic Perspectives*, 2004), and John Campbell and Tuomo Vuolteenaho's article "Bad Beta, Good Beta" (see Chapter 6 sources).

The discussion of equity investing draws on papers presented and debated at seminars sponsored by Norway's Ministry of Finance and Norges Bank Investment Management, in particular papers by Campbell Harvey (2011), Andrew Ang (2011), Elroy Dimson (2011 and 2013), and Jacquelyn Humphrey and David Tan (2013).

The discussion of whether to hedge international equity investments for investors whose base currencies might have "safe-haven" status during times of crisis draws on John Campbell, Karine Serfaty-de Medeiros and Luis Viceira's article "Global Currency Hedging" (*Journal of Finance*, February 2010). A key article for the discussion of momentum strategies is Narasimhan Jegadeesh, and Sheridan Titman's "Returns to buying winners and selling losers: Implications for stockmarket efficiency," *Journal of Finance* 48, no. 1, 65–91, 1993.

9 Credit

Kay Giesecke, Francis A. Longstaff, Stephen Schaefer and Ilya Strebulaev's article "Corporate Bond Default Risk: A 150-year Perspective" (*Journal of Financial Economics*, 2011) provides the historical context for the discussion of corporate credit risk and reward in this chapter. By contrast, Kwok-Yuen Ng and Bruce Phelps, "Capturing the Credit Spread Premium" (*Financial Analysts Journal*, May/June 2011), and Anttii Ilmanen (*Expected Returns*, 2011, especially Chapter 10, The credit risk premium) explain why many investors do not manage to turn the yield premium over government bonds on offer when they buy investment grade corporate bonds into corresponding superior performance.

The discussion of debt markets and instruments draws on market contacts and on Frank Fabozzi and Steven Mann (eds), *The Handbook of Fixed Income Securities* (8th edition, McGraw-Hill, 2011).

The discussion of quantitative investment and the financial crisis draws on an article by Felix Salmon "Recipe for Disaster: The Formula That Killed Wall Street", *Wired*, February 2009 and also Cate Reavis, "The global financial crisis of 2008: the role of greed, fear and oligarchs", MIT Sloan School of Management, 2009.

10 Alternative investments

Private equity: information-based investment returns

A number of articles in recent years have sought to assess the performance, costs of illiquidity, leverage, fees and agency issues that need to be addressed before making investments in private equity funds. These include Robert S Harris, Tim Jenkinson, Steven N Kaplan, "How do private equity investments perform compared to public equity?", *Journal of Investment Management* 2016, and Andrew Ang and Morten Sorensen, "Risks, Returns, and Optimal Holdings of Private Equity" (*Quarterly Journal of Finance*, Vol. 2, No. 3, 2012) and Ludovic Phalippou and Oliver Gottschalg, "The Performance of Private Equity Funds" (*Review of Financial Studies*, No. 22, 2009). Phalippou's 2011 report for the Norwegian Government Pension Fund (Global) provides an update to earlier evidence of persistence of outperformance by some private equity managers. Preqin's 2017 Global Private Equity and Venture Capital report was another important source.

Steven Kaplan and Per Stromberg's article "Leveraged Buyouts and Private Equity" (*Journal of Economic Perspectives*, American Economic Association, Vol. 23, No. 1, Winter 2009) provides a review of how private equity firms seek to improve the performance of their investee companies. Issues in measuring risk of private equity funds are discussed in Susan Woodward, "Measuring Risk for Venture Capital and Buyout Portfolios", *Journal of Performance Measurement*, Vol. 17, No. 1, 2012.

Hedge funds

This section draws on market contacts as well as industry reviews and academic analyses. A number of articles over the past decade have highlighted weaknesses in the reporting of hedge fund risk and return, and these seem as relevant in 2017 as when the articles were first written.

Useful sources include:

Asness, C., "An Alternative Future", *Journal of Portfolio Management*, 30th Anniversary Issue, 2004

Asness, C., "An Alternative Future II", *Journal of Portfolio Management*, Vol. 31,

No. 1, Fall 2004 . Asness has updated the themes in these core articles in his "Cliff's perspectives" posts on www.aqr.com

Getmansky, M., Lo, A.W. and Makarov, I., "An Econometric Model of Serial Correlation and Illiquidity in Hedge Fund Returns", *Journal of Financial Economics*, Vol. 74, No. 3, 2004

Goltz, F. and Schroeder, D., "Hedge fund reporting survey", EDHEC Risk and Asset Management Research Centre, November 2008

Gregoriou, G. and Lhabitant, F-S., "Madoff: A Riot of Red Flags", EDHEC Risk and Asset Management Research Centre, January 2009

Hasanhodzic, J. and Lo, A.W., "Can hedge fund returns be replicated?: The linear case", *Journal of Investment Management*, Vol. 5, No. 2, 2007

Kat, H. and Palaro, H., "Hedge Fund Returns: You Can Make Them Yourself!", *Journal of Wealth Management*, No. 8, 2005

Preqin, *Global Hedge Fund Report 2017*, provided an invaluable resource on industry trends

Schneeweis, Thomas, Hossein Kazemi and Edward Szado, "Hedge fund database 'deconstruction': are hedge fund databases half full or half empty", 2013, SSRN

Real estate

This section draws on market contacts and published resources including the Journal of Portfolio Management's special real estate issues. Particularly relevant is an article by Shaun Bond, Soosung Hwang, Paul Mitchell and Stephen Satchell, "Will Private Equity and Hedge Funds Replace Real Estate in Mixed Asset Portfolios?" (*Journal of Portfolio Management*, special real estate issue, 2007) and Jim Clayton and others, "The Changing Face of Real Estate Investment Management" (*Journal of Portfolio Management*, special real estate issue, 2011). Ralph Block's *Investing in REITs: Real Estate Investment Trusts* (4th edition, Bloomberg Press, 2011) is an invaluable source on investing in REITs.

11 Art and collectibles

This chapter draws on discussions with a range of market and academic contacts. Recommended published sources include:

Baumol, W.J., "Unnatural value or art as a floating crap game", *American Economic Review*, Vol. 76, 1986

Deloitte and ArtTactic, Art & Finance Report, 5th edition, 2017

Dimson, E. and Spaenjers, C., "Ex Post: The Investment Performance of Collectible Stamps", *Journal of Financial Economics*, Vol. 100, No. 2, 2011

Dimson, E. and Spaenjers, C., "The investment performance of emotional assets", in Dempster, A. (ed.), *Risk and Uncertainty in the Art World*, Bloomsbury Press, 2014

Findlay, M., *The Value of Art*, Prestel, 2012

Goetzmann, W., Renneboog, L. and Spaenjers, C., "Art and Money", *American Economic Review*, Vol. 101, No. 3, 2011, pp. 222–6

Grampp, W.D., *Pricing the Priceless: Art, Artists, and Economics*, Basic Books, 1989

McAndrew, C. and Thompson, R. (2007), "The Collateral Value of Fine Art" *Journal of Banking and Finance* 31: 589-607.

Plattner, S., "A Most Ingenious Paradox: The Market for Contemporary Fine Art", *American Anthropologist*, Vol. 100, No. 2, 1998

Pownall, R., Satchell, S. and Srivastava, N., "The Estimation of Psychic Returns from Cultural Assets", mimeo, 2013

Reitlinger, G., *The Economics of Taste: The Rise and Fall of Picture Prices, 1760–1960*, Barrie and Rockliff, 1961

Renneboog, L. and Spaenjers, C., "Buying Beauty: On Prices and Returns in the Art Market", *Management Science*, October 2012

Satchell, S. (ed.), *Collectible Investments for the High Net Worth Investor*, Elsevier, 2009

Spaenjers, C., "The long-term returns to durable assets", in Dimson, E. and Chambers, D. (2016)

Thompson, D., *The $12 Million Stuffed Shark: The Curious Economics of Contemporary Art*, Aurum Press, 2008

Recommended reading

Acharya, S. and Dimson, E., *Endowment Asset Management*, Oxford University Press, 2007

Ang, A., *Asset Management: A Systematic Approach to Factor Investing*, Oxford University Press, forthcoming

Asness, C., Krail, R. and Liew, J., "Do Hedge Funds Hedge?", *Journal of Portfolio Management*, Fall 2001.

Athayde, G. and Flores, R., "A CAPM with Higher Moments: Theory and Econometrics", *Ensaios Economicos*, No. 317, Rio de Janeiro, 1997

Athayde, G. and Flores, R., "Incorporating skewness and kurtosis in portfolio optimisation: a multi-dimensional efficient set", in Satchell, S. and Scowcroft, A. (eds), *Advances in Portfolio Construction and Implementation*, Butterworth-Heinemann, 2003

Athayde, G. and Flores, R., "Do Higher Moments Really Matter in Portfolio Optimisation?", *Fundação Getúlio Vargas*, No. 574, 2004

Baltussen, G., "Behavioral Finance: an introduction", 2009, available at: SSRN, http://ssrn.com/abstract=1488110 or http://dx.doi.org/10.2139/ssrn.1488110

Banz, R., "The Relationship between Return and Market Value of Common Stocks", *Journal of Financial Economics*, March 1981

Bateman, H., Eckert, C., Geweke, J., Louvière, J.J., Satchell, S.E. and Thorp, S., "Investment Risk Framing and Individual Preference Consistency", UNSW Australian School of Business Research Paper No. 2010ACTL08, April 10th 2011

Benartzi, S., "Excessive extrapolation and the allocation of 401(k) accounts to company stock", *Journal of Finance*, October 2001

Benartzi, S. and Thaler, R., "Naive diversification strategies in defined contribution savings plans", *American Economic Review*, March 2001

Bilo, S., Christophers, H., Degosciu, M. and Zimmermann, H., "Risk, returns, and biases of listed private equity portfolios", WWZ Working Paper No. 1/05, 2005

Black, F., "Noise", *Journal of Finance*, July 1986

Bloomfield, R., "Traditional vs Behavioral Finance", Cornell University, Johnson School Research Paper Series #22, 2010

Bodie, Z., Kane, A. and Marcus, A.J., *Investments*, 6th international edition, McGraw-Hill, 2005

Bodie, Z., Merton, R. and Samuelson, W., "Labor Supply Flexibility and Portfolio Choice in a Life Cycle Model", NBER Working Paper 3954, 1992

Bodie, Z. and Taqqu, R., *Risk Less and Prosper: Your Guide to Safer Investing*, John Wiley & Sons, 2012

Bohnet, I., Greig, F., Herrmann, B. and Zeckhauser, R., "Betrayal Aversion: Evidence from Brazil, China, Oman, Switzerland, Turkey, and the United States", *American Economic Review*, Vol. 98, No. 1, 2008

Boyle, P.S., Loewy, D., Riess, J.A. and Weiss, R.A., "The Enviable Dilemma: Hold, Sell, or Hedge Highly Concentrated Stock?", *Journal of Wealth Management*, Fall 2004

Brealey, R.A., Myers, S.C. and Allen, F., *Principles of Corporate Finance*, 12th edition, McGraw-Hill, 2016

Brown, J.R., Mitchell, O.S., Poterba, J.M. and Warshawsky, M.J., *The Role of Annuity Markets in Financing Retirement*, MIT Press, 2001

Brunel, J.L.P., *Integrated Wealth Management: The New Direction for Portfolio Managers*, Institutional Investor Books, 2002

Brunnermeier, M. and Nagel, S., "Hedge funds and the technology bubble", *Journal of Finance*, Vol. 59, No. 5, 2004

Buiter, W.H., "James Tobin: An Appreciation of his Contribution to Economics", NBER Working Paper, 2003

Burnham, T., *Mean Markets and Lizard Brains*, John Wiley & Sons, 2005

Cai, F. and Warnock, F.E., "International Diversification at Home and Abroad", International Finance Discussion Paper 2004–793, Board of Governors of the Federal Reserve System, December 2004 (www.federalreserve.gov/pubs/ifdp/2004/793/default.htm)

Campbell, J.Y., Giglio S. and Polk C., "Hard Times", *Review of Asset Pricing Studies*, Vol. 3, No. 1, 2013

Campbell, J.Y. and Rathjens, P., *The Case for International Diversification*, Arrowstreet Capital, May 2003

Chambers, D. and Dimson, E., "IPO underpricing over the very long run", *Journal of Finance*, Vol. 64, No. 3, 2009

Chan, N., Getmansky, M., Haas, S. and Lo, A., "Systemic Risk and Hedge Funds", in Carey, M. and Stulz, R. (eds), *The Risks of Financial Institutions*, University of Chicago Press, 2007

Cole, S.E. and Cole, R.A., "How accurate are commercial real estate appraisals? Evidence from 25 years of NCREIF sales data", *Journal of Portfolio Management*, real estate issue, 2011

Constantinides, G., "Rational Asset Prices", *Journal of Finance*, August 2002

Cumming, Douglas, *The Oxford Handbook of Private Equity*, Oxford University Press, 2012

Damodaran, A., *Investment Fables*, Financial Times–Prentice Hall, 2004

Darst, D.M., *The Art of Asset Allocation*, 2nd edition, McGraw-Hill, 2008

Deacon, M., Derry, A. and Mirfendereski, D., *Inflation Indexed Securities: Bonds, Swaps and Other Derivatives*, 2nd edition, John Wiley & Sons, 2004

diBartolomeo, D., "Equity Risk, Credit Risk, Default Correlation, and Corporate Sustainability", *The Journal of Investing*, Vol. 19, No. 4, Winter 2010

diBartolomeo, D., "The Volatility of Financial Assets Behaving Badly: the example of the high yield bond market", *Northfield News*, March 2013

Dimson, E. and Jackson, A., "High Frequency Performance Monitoring", *Journal of Portfolio Management*, Fall 2001

Dimson, E., Karakas, O. and Li, X., "Active Ownership", *Review of Financial Studies*, Vol. 28, No. 12, 2015

Dimson, E. and Marsh, P., *Numis Smaller Companies Index: 2013 Annual Review*, Numis Corporation, January 2013

Dreyfuss, B., *Hedge Hogs: The Cowboy Traders Behind Wall Street's Largest Hedge Fund Disaster*, Random House, 2013

Drobney, S., *The Invisible Hands: Top Hedge Fund Traders on Bubbles, Crashes, and Real Money*, John Wiley and Sons, 2011

Dunbar, N., *Inventing Money: The Story of Long-Term Capital Management and the Legends Behind It*, John Wiley & Sons, 2000

Eichengreen, B., Hausmann, R. and Panizza, U., "The Mystery of Original Sin", in Eichengreen and Hausmann (eds), *Other People's Money: Debt Denomination and Financial Instability in Emerging Market Economies*, University of Chicago Press, 2005

Ellis, C.D., *Winning the Loser's Game*, 4th edition, McGraw-Hill, 2002

Evensky, H., Horan, S. and Robinson, T., *The New Wealth Management: The Financial Advisors Guide to Managing and Investing Client Assets* (CFA Institute Investment Series), 2011

Faff, R., Mulino, D. and Chai, D., "On the linkage between financial risk tolerance and risk aversion", *Journal of Financial Research*, Spring 2008

Fama, E. and French, K., "The Equity Premium", *Journal of Finance*, April 2002

Fawley, B.W. and Neely, C.J., "Four Stories of Quantitative Easing", *Federal Reserve Bank of St Louis Review*, January/February 2013

Fraser-Sampson, G., *Private Equity as an Asset Class*, John Wiley & Sons, 2008

Fung, W. and Hsieh, D., "Hedge Fund Benchmarks: A Risk Based Approach", *Financial Analysts Journal*, September/October 2004

Géhin, W. and Vaissié, M., *The Right Place for Alternative Betas in Hedge Fund Performance*, EDHEC, 2005

Gibson, R.C., *Asset Allocation: Balancing Financial Risk*, 2nd edition, Irwin, 1996

Ginsburgh, V., Mei, H. and Moses, M., "The Computation of Prices Indices", in Ginsburgh and Throsby, D. (eds), *Handbook of the Economics of Art and Culture*, Vol. 1, Elsevier, 2006

Ginsburgh, V. and Weyers, S., "Persistence and Fashion in Art: Italian Renaissance from Vasari to Berenson and Beyond", *Poetics*, Vol. 34, Issue 1, February 2006

Graham, B., *The Intelligent Investor*, updated by Zweig, J., Harper, 2003

Gregoriou, G., Karavas, V., Lhabitant, F.-S. and Rouah, F., *Commodity Trading Advisors, Risk, Performance Analysis and Selection*, Wiley Finance, 2004

Gregory, David, "Private Equity and Financial Stability", *Bank of England Quarterly Bulletin*, Q1, 2013

Halstead, J.M., Hedge, S. and Schmid Klein, L., "Orange County Bankruptcy: Financial Contagion in the Municipal Bond and Bank Equity Markets", *Eastern Finance Association: The Financial Review*, 39, 2004

Hammond, P.B., Leibowitz, M.L. and Siegel, L.B., *Rethinking the Equity Risk Premium*, CFA Institute, 2011

Harvey, C.R., "Allocation to Emerging Markets in a Globally Diversified Portfolio", advice to Norwegian Ministry of Finance, March 2012, sourced from http://www.regjeringen.no/pages/1934920/Harvey.pdf

Harvey, C.R., Liechty, J.C. and Liechty, M.W., "Parameter Uncertainty in Asset Allocation", December 17th 2009, available at SSRN: http://ssrn.com/

abstract=1525121 or http://dx.doi.org/10.2139/ssrn.1525121

Harvey, C.R., Liechty, J.C., Liechty, M.W. and Müller, P., "Portfolio Selection with Higher Moments", in Sury, S.M. (ed.), *Essential Readings in Applied Financial Economics*, San Diego: University Readers, 2013

Hatlapa, D., *Better Than Gold: Investing in Historic Cars*, HAGI Publishing, April 2011

Holton, G.A., "Defining Risk", *Financial Analysts Journal*, November/December 2004

Humphrey, J. and Tan, D., "Does it Really Hurt to be Responsible?", *Journal of Business Ethics*, May 2013

Ilmanen, A. and Kizer, J., "The Death of Diversification has been Greatly Exaggerated", *Journal of Portfolio Management*, Spring 2012

Kahneman, D., "Maps of Bounded Rationality", Nobel Lecture 2002, available at http://nobelprize.org/economics/laureates/2002/kahnemann-lecture. pdf

Kahneman, D. and Tversky, A., "The Psychology of Preferences", *Scientific American*, Vol. 246, 1982

Kahneman, D. and Tversky, A., "Prospect Theory: An Analysis of Decision Under Risk", *Econometrica*, 47, 1979

Kajuth, F. and Watzka, S., "Inflation expectations from index-linked bonds: Correcting for liquidity and inflation risk premia", *Quarterly Review of Economics and Finance*, Vol. 51, No. 3, June 2011

Kaplan, P.D., *Frontiers of Modern Asset Allocation*, John Wiley & Sons, 2012

Kaplan, S. and Schoar, A., "Private Equity Performance: Returns, Persistence and Capital Flows", *Journal of Finance*, August 2005

Kaplan, S.N. and Strömberg, P., "Characteristics, Contracts, and Actions: Evidence from Venture Capitalist Analyses," *Journal of Finance*, American Finance Association, Vol. 59, No. 5, October 2004

Kay, J., *The Long and the Short of it: A Guide to Finance and Investment for Normally Intelligent People Who Aren't in the Industry*, The Erasmus Press, 2009

Kay, J., *The Truth About Markets*, Penguin Books, 2004

Keynes, J.M., *Collected Writings, Vol XII, Investment and Editorial*, Macmillan, 1983

Kritzman, M.P., *Puzzles of Finance*, John Wiley & Sons, 2000

Kritzman, M.P., "The Graceful Aging of Mean Variance Optimisation", *Journal of Portfolio Management*, Winter 2011

Lack, S., *The Hedge Fund Mirage*, John Wiley & Sons, 2012

Landes, W., "The Test of Time: Does 20th Century American Art Survive?" in Ginsburgh, V. (ed.), *Contributions to Economic Analysis: The Economics of Art and Culture*, Elsevier Science, 2004

Leibowitz, M.L., Bova, A. and Brett Hammond, P., *The Endowment Model of Investing*, Wiley Finance, 2010

Lhabitant, F.-S., *Hedge Funds: Myths and Limits*, Wiley Finance, 2002

Lintner, J., "The Valuation of Risk Assets and the Selection of Risky Investments in Stock Portfolios and Capital Budgets", *Review of Economics and Statistics*, Vol. 47, No. 1, 1965

Lizieri, C., Satchell, S. and Wongwachara, W., "Unsmoothing Real Estate Returns: A Regime-Switching Approach", *Real Estate Economics*, Vol. 40, No. 2, 2012 (DOI: 10.1111/j.1540–6229.2012.00331.x)

Lo, A., *Hedge Funds: An Analytical Perspective*, Princeton University Press, 2008

Löffler, G., "Avoiding the rating bounce: why rating agencies are slow to react to new information", *Journal of Economic Behavior and Organization*, Vol. 56, No. 3, 2005

Longstaff, F., Mithal, S. and Neis, E., "Corporate Yield Spreads: Default Risk or Liquidity? New Evidence from the Credit Default Swap Market", *Journal of Finance*, October 2005

Lopes, L., "Between Hope and Fear: the Psychology of Risk", *Advances in Experimental Social Psychology*, 20, 1987

Lowenstein, R., *When Genius Failed: The Rise and Fall of Long-Term Capital Management*, Fourth Estate, 2001

Lustig, Y., *Multi-Asset Investing: A Practical Guide to Modern Portfolio Management*, Harriman House, 2013

McAndrew, C., *The Art Economy*, The Liffey Press, 2007

Malkiel, B.G., *A Random Walk Down Wall Street*, Norton, 2003

Malkiel, B.G. and Saha, A., "Hedge Funds: Risk and Return", *Financial Analysts Journal*, November/December 2005

Mandelbrot, B.B. and Hudson, R., *The (Mis)Behaviour of Markets: A Fractal View of Risk, Reward and Ruin*, Profile Books, 2004

Mehra, R. and Prescott, E., "The Equity Premium: A Puzzle", *Journal of Monetary Economics*, Vol. 15, 1985

Merton, R.C., "Thoughts on the Future: Theory and Practice in Investment Management", *Financial Analysts Journal*, January/February 2003

Merton, R.C. and Bodie, Z., "Design of Financial Systems: Towards a Synthesis of Design and Structure", *Journal of Investment Management*, Vol. 3, No. 1, 2005

Oldfield, R., *Simple But Not Easy: An Autobiographical and Biased Book About Investing*, Doddington Publishing, 2007

Perold, A., "Risk is a choice not a fate", *Journal of Portfolio Management*, Fall 2009

Peyton, M. and Lotito, F., "Real Estate: The Classic Diversifying Asset", TIAA-CREF White Paper, 2006

Phalippou, L., "An evaluation of the potential for GPFG to achieve above average returns from investments in private equity and recommendations regarding benchmarking", February 2011, sourced from: http://www.regjeringen.no/upload/fin/statens%20pensjonsfond/2011/phalippou.pdf

Poterba, J.M., "Portfolio Risk and Self-Directed Retirement Saving Programmes", *Economic Journal*, Vol. 114, No. 494, March 2004

Rabin, M., "Inference by Believers in the Law of Small Numbers", *Quarterly Journal of Economics*, Vol. 117, 2002

Ratner, R.K. and Herbst, K.C., "When good decisions have bad outcomes: The impact of affect on switching behavior", *Organizational Behavior and Human Decision Processes*, 96, 2005

Reb, J. and Connolly, T., "Decision Justifiability and Regret", manuscript, 2004

Reich, R., "Who is Us?", *Harvard Business Review*, January/February 1990

Roll, R., "Empirical TIPS", *Financial Analysts Journal*, January/February 2004

Ross, S.A., "Forensic Finance: Enron and Others", *Rivista di Politica Economica*, November/December 2002

Ryland, P., *Investment: an A–Z Guide*, Profile Books, 2009

Scholes, M., "The Future of Hedge Funds", *Journal of Financial Transformation*, Vol. 10, Capco, April 2004

Scholtes, C., "On Market-Based Measures of Inflation Expectations", *Bank of England Quarterly Bulletin*, Spring 2002

Securities and Exchange Commission, *Report on the Municipal Securities Market*, July 2012

Sharpe, W.F., "Capital Asset Prices: A Theory of Market Equilibrium under Conditions of Risk", *Journal of Finance*, September 1964

Shefrin, H., *Beyond Fear and Greed: Understanding Behavioural Finance and the Psychology of Investing*, Oxford University Press, 2002

Shefrin, H. and Statman, M., "Behavioral Portfolio Theory", *Journal of Financial and Quantitative Analysis*, June 2000

Shiller, R., "Do Stock Prices Move too Much to be Justified by Subsequent Changes in Dividends?", *American Economic Review*, June 1981

Shiller, R., "Stock Prices and Social Dynamics", *Brookings Papers on Economic Activity*, 2, 1984, pp. 457–98

Shiller, R., *Irrational Exuberance*, Princeton University Press, 2000

Shiller, R., "Bubbles, Human Judgement and Expert Opinion", *Financial Analysts Journal*, May/June 2002

Shiller, R., *The New Financial Order: Risk in the 21st Century*, Princeton University Press, 2003

Siegel, J., *The Future for Investors*, Crown Business, 2005

Sortino, F. and Satchell, S., *Managing Downside Risk in Financial Markets*, Butterworth-Heinemann, 2001

Stanyer, P. and Long, K., "Unquoted Risk: The Art of Measurement", *Professional Investor*, March 1993

Statman, M., "Behavioral Portfolios: Hope for Riches and Protection from Poverty", Pension Research Council Working Paper, 2003–9

Statman, M., "Normal Investors, Then and Now", *Financial Analysts Journal*, March/April 2005

Statman, M., "The cultures of risk tolerance", 2010, available at SSRN: http://ssrn.com/abstract=1647086 or http://dx.doi.org/10.2139/ssrn.1647086

Statman, M. and Wood, V., "Investment Temperament", manuscript, June 2004

Staub, R. and Diermeier, J., "Segmentation, Illiquidity and Returns", *Journal of Investment Management*, Vol. 1, No. 1, 2003

Stein, D.M. and Siegel, A.F., "The Diversification of Employee Stock Options", AIMR Conference Proceedings, Investment Counselling for Private Clients IV, 2002

Taleb, N.N., *Fooled by Randomness: The Hidden Role of Chance in Life and in the Markets*, Thomson Texere, 2004

Taleb, N.N., *The Black Swan: The Impact of the Highly Improbable*, Penguin Books, 2007

Temin, P. and Voth, H-J., "Riding the South Sea Bubble", *American Economic Review*, December 2004

Thaler, R.H., "Mental Accounting Matters", *Journal of Behavioral Decision Making*, Vol. 12, 1999

Thaler, R.H., "The End of Behavioral Finance", *Financial Analysts Journal*, November/December 1999

Turner, J. (ed.), *The Grove Dictionary of Art*, illustrated edition, Oxford University Press, 2003

Wilcox, J., Horvitz, J.E. and diBartolomeo, D., "Investment Management for Taxable Private Investors", CFA Institute, 2006

Zadeh, L.A., "Fuzzy Sets", *Information and Control*, Vol. 8, 1965

Zhang, L.A. and Petkova, R., "Is Value Riskier than Growth?", *Journal of Financial Economics*, Vol. 78, No. 1, 2005

Notes on sources

The publisher and authors wish to thank the following sources for the use of their website information and other copyright material:

Artprice, www.artprice.com (Figure 11.2)

Bank of England www.bankofengland.co.uk (Figures 4.2, 4.5, 4.9, 4.10, 5.5)

BarclayHedge Ltd, www.barclayhedge.com (Figures 10.5–6; Table 10.3)

Bloomberg LP (Figures 1.1–2, 5.3–4, 8.1–6, 8.8, 8.10–19, 9.3–6, 10.1–4, 10.10–11, 11.3–4; Tables 5.1–2, 6.2, 9.1, 9.4–7, 10.1–2, 10.4–5, 10.7, 10.9)

Capgemini and Merrill Lynch Wealth Management "World Wealth Report" 2003, Capgemini and RBC Wealth Management "World Wealth Report" 2013 and Capgemini "World Wealth Report" 2017 (Table 5.3)

Center for Research in Security Prices (CRSP®), The University of Chicago Booth School of Business (2013). All rights reserved. (Figures 8.1–2)

Chicago Board Options Exchange www.cboe.com (Figure 5.1)

Credit Suisse Hedge Index LLC. Copyright 2018. All rights reserved. This book (the "Work") is provided by Profile Books Limited, which takes full responsibility for providing it. Neither Credit Suisse Hedge Index LLC nor its affiliates, subsidiaries, members or parents (collectively, "Credit Suisse") have undertaken any review of this Work or any recommendations contained herein, or of the suitability of this information for anyone accessing this Work, and neither the Work nor the information contained in the Work is sponsored, endorsed or approved by Credit Suisse. The Information is provided "as is" and any use is at your entire risk. (Figures 10.4, 10.7; Tables 10.2, 10.4–5)

Deutsche Bundesbank (Figure 5.5)

Dimson, E., Marsh, P. and Staunton, M., *Triumph of the Optimists: 101 Years of Global Investment Returns*, Princeton University Press, 2002 (Tables 4.1–2, Figures 4.13–15); Dimson, E., Marsh, P. and Staunton, M., Credit Suisse Global Investment Returns Yearbook 2017 (Tables 4.1–3, Table 6.2; Figures 4.11–15)

European Central Bank www.ecb.int (Figures 4.3, 4.6)

Finametrica Pty Ltd (Figure 1.2)

Fitch Ratings Global Corporate Finance, 2016 Transition and Default Study (Figures 9.1–2; Table 9.3)

FTSE International Limited ("FTSE") © FTSE 2018. "FTSE®" is a trade mark of London Stock Exchange Group companies and is used by FTSE International Limited under licence. All rights in the FTSE indices and/or FTSE ratings vest in FTSE and/or its licensors. Neither FTSE nor its licensors accept any liability for any errors or omissions in the FTSE indices and/or FTSE ratings or underlying data. No further distribution of FTSE Data is permitted without FTSE's express written consent. (Figures 10.1, 10.10–11; Tables 10.7, 10.9)

Green Street Advisors (Figure 10.9)

Historic Automobile Group International (Figures 11.3–4)

Hurd, Michael D.; Michaud, Pierre-Carl; Rohwedder, Susann; Rand Corporation and Network for Studies on Pension, Aging and Retirement, Tilburg University, 2017 (Tables 3.3–4)

JPMorgan (Table 9.5)

MSCI, www.msci.com The MSCI data contained herein is the property of MSCI Inc. (MSCI). MSCI, its affiliates and its information providers make no warranties with respect to any such data. The MSCI data contained herein is used under license and may not be further used, distributed or disseminated without the express written consent of MSCI. (Figures 1.1–2, 8.7–19, 10.4, 10.10–11, 11.3–4; Tables 5.1–2, 6.2, 9.1, 9.5, 9.7, 10.2, 10.4–7, 10.9)

National Association of College and University Business Officers (NACUBO): NACUBO-Commonfund Study of Endowments 2012, 2106 (Table 5.3)

Railways Pension Trustee Company Ltd (Figure 11.5)

Russell Investment Group: Copyright © Russell Investments 2018. All rights reserved. Russell Investment Group is the owner of the trademarks, service marks and copyrights related to the Russell Indexes. Indexes are unmanaged and cannot be invested in directly. Returns represent past performance, are not a guarantee of future performance, and are not indicative of any specific investment. The information contained herein has been obtained from sources that we believe to be reliable, but its accuracy and completeness are not guaranteed. Russell Investment Group does not make any warranty or representation regarding the information (Figures 8.4–6)

Shiller, R., *Irrational Exuberance*, as updated, www.econ.yale.edu/~shiller/data.htm (Figure 5.2)

S&P Dow Jones Indices (Figure 10.3; Table 10.1)

Spaenjers, C., "The long-term returns to durable assets", in Dimson, E. and
    Chambers, D. (2016) (Figure 1.11)

Towers Watson "Global Pension Asset Study" 2017 (Table 5.3)

UK Office for National Statistics (Tables 3.1–2)

US National Center for Health Statistics (Tables 3.1–2)

US Treasury www.ustreas.gov (Figures 4.1, 4.4, 4.7, 4.8, 5.5; Table 5.3)

Index

Page numbers in *italics* refer specifically to figures; those in **bold** type to tables.

PublicAffairs is a publishing house founded in 1997. It is a tribute to the standards, values, and flair of three persons who have served as mentors to countless reporters, writers, editors, and book people of all kinds, including me.

I. F. STONE, proprietor of *I. F. Stone's Weekly*, combined a commitment to the First Amendment with entrepreneurial zeal and reporting skill and became one of the great independent journalists in American history. At the age of eighty, Izzy published *The Trial of Socrates*, which was a national bestseller. He wrote the book after he taught himself ancient Greek.

BENJAMIN C. BRADLEE was for nearly thirty years the charismatic editorial leader of *The Washington Post*. It was Ben who gave the *Post* the range and courage to pursue such historic issues as Watergate. He supported his reporters with a tenacity that made them fearless and it is no accident that so many became authors of influential, best-selling books.

ROBERT L. BERNSTEIN, the chief executive of Random House for more than a quarter century, guided one of the nation's premier publishing houses. Bob was personally responsible for many books of political dissent and argument that challenged tyranny around the globe. He is also the founder and longtime chair of Human Rights Watch, one of the most respected human rights organizations in the world.

•   •   •

For fifty years, the banner of Public Affairs Press was carried by its owner Morris B. Schnapper, who published Gandhi, Nasser, Toynbee, Truman, and about 1,500 other authors. In 1983, Schnapper was described by *The Washington Post* as "a redoubtable gadfly." His legacy will endure in the books to come.

Peter Osnos, *Founder*